LIVES *of*
Consequence

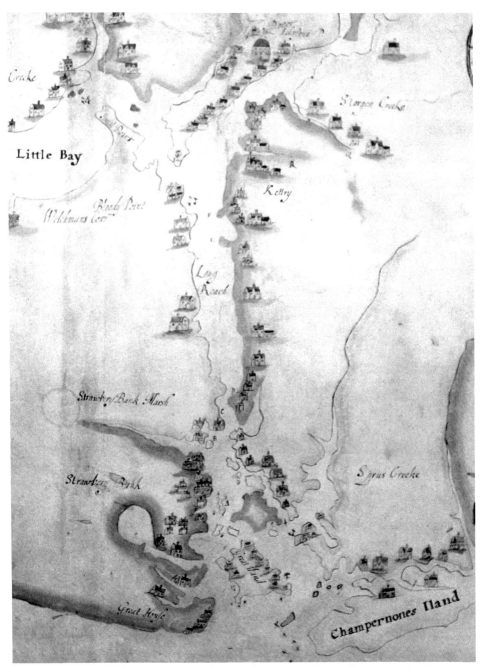

Kittery Parish along the eastern shore of the river as drawn by mapmaker John Sellers in "Piscataqua River in New England circa 1670 by J. S." Courtesy of Portsmouth Athenaeum.

LIVES *of* Consequence

Blacks in *Early Kittery & Berwick* *in the Massachusetts Province* *of Maine*

Patricia Q. Wall

PORTSMOUTH MARINE SOCIETY
for the
Black Heritage Trail of New Hampshire
and the
Portsmouth Historical Society

Portsmouth, New Hampshire
2017

Publication 37

Portsmouth Marine Society is a publication series of
Portsmouth Historical Society
PO Box 728, Portsmouth, New Hampshire 03802

www.portsmouthhistory.org

FIRST EDITION

Design: Grace Peirce
Editor: Gerald W.R. Ward

ISBN: 978-0-915819-46-1

Library of Congress Cataloging-in-Publication Data

Names: Wall, Patricia Q., author.
Title: Lives of consequence : Blacks in early Kittery & Berwick in the
    Massachusetts province of Maine / by Patricia Q. Wall.
Description: First edition. | Portsmouth, New Hampshire : Portsmouth Marine
    Society for the Black Heritage Trail of New Hampshire and the Portsmouth
    Historical Society, 2017. | Series: Publication / Portsmouth Marine
    Society ; 37 | Includes bibliographical references and index.
Identifiers: LCCN 2017026750 | ISBN 9780915819461 (alkaline paper)
Subjects: LCSH: African Americans--Maine--Kittery--History. | African
    Americans--Maine--Berwick--History. | Indians of North
    America--Maine--Kittery--History. | Indians of North
    America--Maine--Berwick--History. | Racially mixed
    people--Maine--Kittery--History. | Racially mixed
    people--Maine--Berwick--History. | Kittery (Me.)--Race relations--History.
    | Berwick (Me.)--Race relations--History. | Kittery (Me.)--Biography. |
    Berwick (Me.)--Biography.
Classification: LCC F29.K6 W35 2017 | DDC 305.8009741/95--dc23
LC record available at https://lccn.loc.gov/2017026750

Sponsors

This book is made possible by the support of our members and the following sponsors:

Stephanie T. Seacord

Peter Lamb and Faith Harrington through
Julia's Fund of the Maine Community Foundation

The David and Kathleen Rushford Murray Charitable Fund of the
New Hampshire Charitable Foundation

Eliot Historical Society
Kittery Historical & Naval Museum
Old Berwick Historical Society
Shapleigh Family Association

Portsmouth Marine Society Titles

Contents

Foreword

Based on careful research conducted over many years by Patricia Q. Wall, this book presents the first detailed look at the lives of more than four hundred Black individuals who lived in Kittery and Berwick, Maine, from the seventeenth century until about 1820. Pat has patiently combed the available public and private documents to find whatever scraps of information had been recorded about these African Americans. Because most lived their lives in the shadows of the historical record, much has been lost. As Pat reveals, however, in addition to the personal trajectories of their own lives, they also played important roles in the life of their towns. Thanks to her research, we have a much better understanding of the importance of the Black, Native American, and mixed-race populations in southern Maine, both in qualitative and quantitative terms. We congratulate Pat on her research and are proud to publish her work. As a pioneering modern social historian, she has shed light on an important but largely ignored subject.

It is our pleasure to acknowledge the contributions of several individuals who helped this project come to fruition. Essential contributions to support this publication were received from Stephanie T. Seacord; Peter Lamb and Faith Harrington through the "Julia's Fund" of the Maine Community Foundation; The David and Kathleen Rushford Murray Charitable Fund of the New Hampshire Charitable Foundation; Eliot Historical Society; Old Berwick Historical Society; Kittery Historical and Naval Museum, and the Shapleigh Family Association. We are deeply grateful for their invaluable assistance.

We are also grateful to Grace Peirce for her handsome design of this publication and for seeing it through the press, to Gerry Ward for editing the complex manuscript, and to Valerie Cunningham for contributing her eloquent preface. The trustees, members, staffs, and volunteers of our respective institutions make everything that we do possible.

We hope that you will enjoy and be enlightened by this important study that enlarges our understanding of early New England history. Its strengths—in widening the scope of historical inquiry and emphasizing the significance of inclusiveness in our understanding of the past—could not be more timely.

Kathleen Soldati
Executive Director, Portsmouth Historical Society

JerriAnne Boggis
Executive Director, Black Heritage Trail of New Hampshire

May 2017

Preface

Patricia Q. Wall has collected what she says are "scattered bits" of information about slavery in the earliest European settlements in Maine. But this is much more than a dry catalogue of names and statistics, remarkable as that alone would be. This is her passionately narrated account of the challenges encountered when attempting to research a community of Africans and their American descendants, a community of people that was ignored and then forgotten when their bodies were no longer useful to others for building personal wealth.

Lives of Consequence introduces a social scene that seems all wrong in this now quietly picturesque vacationland. Nothing today suggests that African children and adult 'servants' had been here as an involuntary workforce, held captive to provide cheap labor in the English colony. History is silent about the half-black Yankees who lived here, their status having been pre-determined at birth according to the mother's condition as free or a bond servant and, either way, the child would be valued by the dominant society according to prevailing market prices. Any surviving evidence of Black people inhabiting the coast of Maine is difficult to find, sometimes appearing, the author says, only as a "shadowy mark" on a page that testifies to a reality that was northern complicity in the antebellum trans-Atlantic economic system. She implies that even those precious "bits" of archival evidence seem to be surviving by accident, as if to spite those who prefer to forget.

The author explains that her detective work involved "little that was orderly or quick" in collecting data about the Black people and the slave holders included here. The historical record often seems to be teasing with an unexpected clue or by delivering new incomplete surprises. Regardless of how frustrating the process might have been, the researcher conveys some satisfaction in knowing that this history is becoming richer because she has invested the interest and time to notice some details that previously were simply disregarded. It is significant that a woman called 'Negro Bilhah' attended the meeting-house on a September day in 1744, a couple months after the 'Indian servant Eunice' and her infant also had recently appeared. And so much curiosity is raised about that man named Kittery who got new shoes in 1733. Before now, the existence of a man named Kittery was not known, or that he had new shoes in 1733. These are the colorful pieces that connect this human history.

Ironically, it is the documentary evidence that was recorded or that has been omitted by conscientious European Americans that reveals much about their attitudes toward the African Americans living among them. Indeed, it was the "entrepreneurial spirit" of English settlers, "those lumbermen, shipbuilders, farmers, and fishermen along the coast of early Kittery" who determined the value of each one of those Black bodies.

Chapter Ten lists more than four hundred children and adults of African descent who were recorded in business transactions, such as when they were sold off to settle the debts of a deceased slave owner, or were identified by the town as somebody's taxable property, or when the newspaper advertised a cash reward for the capture and return of an enslaved man who might be seen for the first time as an individual with a personality. Gathered together, all of these fragments indicate there is much more to the history of this place that we thought we knew so well.

"Black Will" is a name that occasionally emerges from the historical records of this region as a mysterious figure who survived enslavement and managed to prosper in this very northern place. However, when the author reveals more details of his life, William Black can be imagined as an alert child who skillfully applied his observations and talents to overcome a lifetime of challenges, a responsible family man thriving against the odds. His is a story to celebrate, not because it has a happy ending (if it does), but because it is an example of what is possible when an American has opportunity and self-determination.

Many stories remain to be discovered—the unnamed infant daughter of Cicaro and Phyllis, and that 108-year-old who was called Molly Miles; documentation of those African descendants who migrated across town lines and into neighboring states, adding depth to conversations on issues of race. Some among us will be inspired to continue the quest and build upon this foundation of historical documentation. Unknown descendants now living under other suns will make their ancestral pilgrimage to Maine, bringing treasured family stories and fragile memorabilia to confirm the lives now acknowledged within these pages. This collection will demonstrate that, while some stories are not finished, Black history is American history worth knowing and exploring.

By consistently respecting the humanity of both the named and the nameless, the author of this book is a drum major for social justice and a hero!

Valerie R. Cunningham, Trustee *emeritus*
Black Heritage Trail of New Hampshire

Introduction

The presence and role of enslaved Blacks—Africans and people of mixed African, Native American, and white heritage—in the Parish of Kittery is an essential chapter in the history of the Massachusetts Province of Maine that has long been hidden and overlooked. Discovering that missing chapter, at least what little remains of it, was the intent of this project. And, in doing so, to push aside the barrier word "slave" to try to *see* the men, women, and children to whom that inhuman label applied, in order to discover their circumstances and actions so that we can better understand their impact on the early development of this region.

One soon learns, however, that attempting such a history is to create a tattered garment plagued with holes. Records are hidden and scarce, their contents meager, often consisting only of a scattered bit or two. Even worse, the documents are frequently enigmatic as to exactly who, what, when, and where are being referenced. Questions accumulate, but nearly all of their answers are yet to be found. Even discovering such records often occurs more by happenstance than by intent. During nearly five years of research, it often felt as if some long-ago Black New Englander was tapping on my shoulder and whispering, "You need to look over there," or "Don't give up. Just keep turning pages and leafing through those piles of documents and you'll find my people."

The idea for this project occurred in the fall of 2009 while I was sitting in the First Congregational Church of Kittery Point, Maine. Looking up at the empty spaces where the side galleries used to be, I started wondering about the long-ago Black people who had been segregated there. Who were they? What sort of life did they lead? What were their circumstances? And, were there really only "just a few slaves" in early Kittery as history books have always insisted? With the up-coming three-hundredth anniversary of that building in 2014, I decided to stop musing and try to find some answers, perhaps to contribute an article to a proposed church history.

However, a preliminary inquiry into probate records for slave own-ers—a logical starting point—indicated a serious difficulty. So many of the references cited owners as being "of Kittery," but did not specify in which part of the original elongated parish they lived, at least not until after 1713, the year when Berwick broke away to become a town. However, that only eliminated part of the difficulty. There was still no clear designation in the records as to where in the remaining parish—upper (now Eliot), middle (Spruce Creek), or lower (Kittery Point)—a specific, cited owner lived. Furthermore, quite often an enslaved man, woman, or child was willed to owners' heirs in a different part of the parish. Ambitious as it was, I decided to expand the project to include the entire Kittery Parish boundary as it was established in the 1630s. Since Berwick continued its close relationship with Kittery—through familial, business, and public connections—I proceeded to collect its relevant data after 1713. Those expansions made all the difference. Had an attempt been made to study Kittery Point separately from the rest of the parish, the fuller truth about slavery's existence in this region might still be hidden.

So, as tattered and wanting as this history is, the following chap-ters are presented with the hope that their content will prompt others to continue the search. The ultimate goal, where possible, is to fill in empty spaces and bring about a greater public recognition of the exis-tence and essential nature of Blacks' lives in this region of early New England.

LIVES *of* Consequence

Chapter One

Setting the Scene

By the year 1660, the Parish of Kittery had become a town but it was still little more than a series of rough breaks in the vast forested wilderness, an eighteen-mile-long chain of tiny, rustic settlements hugging the northeasterly shore of the Piscataqua River. From the beginning of British settlement about thirty years before, life revolved around two major resources: timber and fish—especially timber.

On a regular basis, thousands of sawn boards from a dozen or so water-powered mills, untold numbers of clapboards, house shingles, and barrel staves, as well as great quantities of salt-dried codfish, were being shipped to ports along the Atlantic seaboard, to Caribbean island plantations, and to England. In trade, ships returned not only with a wide assortment of scarce and resalable British goods and Caribbean-produced molasses and sugar, they also began bringing a different sort of commodity: small numbers of enslaved Africans. Whether they were first brought on speculation or preordered by local farmers, tradesmen, mill owners, or shipbuilders is unrecorded.

Today, at least in most parts of the civilized world, the very idea of slavery is abhorrent, inhuman, never to be justified. However, the seventeenth-century men and women of New England lived in a very different and sometimes brutish world. Like most colonials, Kittery men saw nothing wrong or illegal in acquiring enslaved Africans. If questioned, they would have simply said it was just a matter of business, an answer to a great shortage of European laborers, and also maybe a good investment. After all, they would add, what was purchased was property and one day might be sold at a profit. One man might also have also pointed out that slavery was nothing new, that it was as old as Biblical times and had existed long before then.

However, in ancient times, slavery was not based on race. Up until the mid-1400s, for example, white or Caucasian people from the Black Sea area had been the main source of slaves for European-owned sugar plantations on Mediterranean islands. However, in 1453, when the Turks captured Constantinople, they cut off that supply of labor and the Europeans began looking to Africa for cheap slave workers. Then, in 1492, came the discovery of the western hemisphere. After that, Portugal, Spain, and other European countries became feverish in their desire to lay claim to and exploit its vast resources. Western Africa eventually became the primary source of slave labor to enable colonial development of America's northern and southern continents. Like a sea ripple that would one day become a tsunami, ships began transporting thousands of captive African men, women, and young children across the Atlantic.[1]

Strategy

The first significant settlement in what would become Kittery was still about a half dozen years in the future when the Colony of Massachusetts Bay was founded in 1630. From the beginning, Colony leaders and investors, here and in England, fretted over getting enough labor to speed up development and realize some return on their huge investments. Efforts to encourage, even coerce, more English settlers to cross the Atlantic were not going well. In the meantime, colonial leaders were attempting to use native people (so-called Indians) captured in warfare as slave labor. Some of the captive men, women, and children were retained to serve in Massachusetts while a great many others were sent into bondage in various parts of New England. Such practices largely failed to solve the labor shortage because most native people eventually refused slavery's yoke and departed their master's household. However, it was during that time of government-directed re-locations of captured natives that a solution of a different sort occurred, one that would mark the beginning of a momentous change in New England's economic, cultural, and political life.

In July 1637, at Governor John Winthrop's orders, the ship *Desire* under command of William Pierce of Salem, Massachusetts, transported seventeen captured natives—fifteen boys and two women—to the Caribbean and sold them at Providence Island. On its return to Massachusetts, seven months later, that ship's cargo for sale included "cotton, tobacco and Negroes."[2]

Whether such an exchange of one group of captives for another was intentional or not, the die was cast. The African slave trade had begun in New England. A few years later, in 1641, the Massachusetts Bay Colony established legal guidelines for slavery in its new Code of Laws entitled "The Body of Liberties." In law it is often the exceptions that are most telling. Article 91 of the Code reads:

Liberties of Foreigners and Strangers
There shall never be any bond slavery, villeinage or captivity among us unless it be lawful captives taken in just wars and such strangers as willingly sell themselves *or are sold to us* [emphasis added].[3]

No doubt, word of this article of the Code soon spread throughout New England and beyond. Barely a year later, Maine's new deputy provincial governor, Thomas Gorges, was pondering ways to get more laborers and speed development along the region's southern coast. Writing to his superior and royally appointed claimant to Maine, Sir Fernando Gorges, he stated, " . . . if their bodies could tolerate the cold of the country, they [the Africans] would be excellent."[4]

Putting the matter even more bluntly, Emanuel Downing, the brother-in-law of Governor Winthrop, wrote, "I do not see how we can thrive until we get into a stock of slaves sufficient to do all our business . . . and you know very well how we can maintain 20 Moors [Africans] cheaper than one English servant." Downing also pointed out what was becoming obvious. The majority of English settlers, the so-called servant class, were not (or would not long be) content working for others. With growing business opportunities and land so plentiful, many were eager to strike out on their own and reap the benefits. Of course, such entrepreneurial spirit was exactly what was driving those lumbermen, shipbuilders, farmers, and fishermen along the shores of early Kittery.[5]

First Impressions

We can only guess at what the first few captive Africans thought and experienced in the mid-1600s as the ship transporting them entered the mouth of the Piscataqua River. Arriving there, either directly from West Africa or from a Caribbean island plantation in the West Indies, those men and women or young boys and girls would have been brought up on deck from the ship's dark hold to be made ready for sale. If the weather was not too cold, buckets of seawater would have been tossed over them to reduce the stench from the filthy conditions under which they had been forced to live during the long sea voyage. Old, soiled clothing would have been replaced with some sort of fresh garment—a simple shirt and pants for males, a long shift for females. In all probability they were a very small group, so they might have been allowed to remain on deck afterward. Secured with a rope or chain to prevent their escaping overboard, they were then left alone to stare out at their new surroundings.

On both sides of the river they were confronted with dark, dense forests of tall, massive trees covering much of the shoreline. To early European explorers and settlers, such forests had been a welcome sight, a promise of great wealth in harvested timber. To the Africans, however, those forests may have seemed forbidding, fortress-like, perhaps ratcheting up, one more notch, their ongoing fear of what lay ahead.

As the ship moved closer to the Maine shore they would have seen some tidal inlets and marshland and a few fishermen's huts with outdoor wooden racks for drying salted cod and other fish. Then, coming into view, was the small settlement of Kittery Point at the mouth of a large creek. There, at the tip of the land, was a scattering of rustic wood-framed houses on small farm lots. Nearby, as Massachusetts' Puritan laws required, stood a modest wooden structure, the First Parish Church, commonly known as the meetinghouse.

At the shorefront were a couple of shipyards and small buildings for craftsmen and tradesmen. Though some lumbering business was ongoing at or near the Point, the main focus was the developing maritime trade and supplying the needs of ships anchoring just off shore. Until wharves were built later on further up river at New Hampshire's Strawbery Banke settlement (present-day Portsmouth), Kittery Point's broad, deep-water harbor was a preferred anchorage for large ships. Arriving people and cargo were often transferred to shallow-draft gundalows, rafts, or canoes. Boatmen then waited for the Piscataqua's swift in-coming tide to carry them to locations up river. Until late in the eighteenth century, travel by water was much preferred over the onshore narrow, rough, and discontinuous footpaths through the wilderness.

A few of the captives were probably put ashore at Kittery Point while others would have continued to locations on up river. Their drifting or paddled craft gave them plenty of time to study the passing scene on both shores—stretches of wilderness, disrupted now and then by evidence of human activity. And, most of those sites contained little more than a small cottage or two in conjunction with fishing, a tanning operation, the building of boats or sometimes a modest-sized ship. Upon reaching the much larger settlement of Strawbery Banke on the New Hampshire side of the river, a few of the enslaved may have been left there to be sold locally or to men crossing from the Kittery shore.

At any rate, those enslaved who continued the river journey would eventually witness the real drivers of this region's early economy: water-powered mills. Entering one of Maine's tributaries to the Piscataqua such as Sturgeon Creek, Great Works River, or Salmon Falls River, the newcomers likely stared fearfully at the sight of great wooden mill wheels in action. Strange sounds emanating from attached sheds also likely increased their apprehension: the loud, steady swoosh-bang from a vertical saw blade tearing its way through great timbers or the incessant pounding of a corn-stamping mill or the duller grinding noise from a grist mill. Most mill operations were located in Upper Kittery (today's town of Eliot) and in what would eventually become the town of Berwick.[6]

But, no matter where they landed, the Africans' greatest anxiety was undoubtedly focused on the white people waiting on shore. Such fear would have been highest among people coming here directly from Africa. What most of them knew of Europeans was based on rumors and the brutal treatment they had endured before and during a horrific Atlantic crossing.

Doubtless, those from the West Indies also felt fear, but probably less so than the others. This group was referred to as "seasoned," women and men who had been part of an island's slave population for a number of years or had been born into it. New England buyers much preferred them, especially those whose enslavement had brought them into close contact with white families and had learned English ways and language.

There is no knowing how soon apprehension began diminishing among the newly arrived people once they were brought ashore and sold, mostly by ones, sometimes twos, and then led away. But, considering that Puritan New Englanders intended a paternalistic attitude toward their slaves, their anxiety may have eased in a relatively short time. That is, of course, if Fate did not place someone in the hands of an abusive or cruel owner.

Settling in on their first day they were given food, probably the same as whatever was available for the white family and, quite likely, seated with them at the same table. Depending on their gender and skills, the enslaved were put to work in the house and/or on the farm or in an owner's workshop or other site of business. At that time, there would have been little hierarchy in division of work. Black and white often worked side by side at the same tasks. When night came, the Blacks bedded down on the floor, not far from the owner and his family. Since most of this region's seventeenth-century houses were small, one- or two-room structures, it was not uncommon to have adults plus a half dozen or more children and maybe even an overnight paying traveler, all sharing such limited space. Through the years, as houses grew larger, most of the enslaved probably continued living close to the family in an attic or cellar. However, a few owners in this area eventually built an attached shed or a separate small cabin for them.[7]

All this might suggest that slavery here was going to be less tragic for Blacks compared to what many thousands of others were experiencing on southern and Caribbean slave plantations. In terms of the amount of physical brutality and death, that was undoubtedly true. Documented incidents of killing or the maiming of slaves in New England are rare. In Kittery, except for two cases involving a killing and severe abuse, records are silent on such matters.

Other forms of abuse (psychological as well as physical) of the enslaved must have occurred in local households, but how often is unknown. Still, it should be remembered that in Puritan-governed Massachusetts, there was strong belief in severe punishment for even minor offenses. Court-ordered, bareback lashings of offenders were common public spectacles, regardless of race or gender. Further, in this era, men were given complete legal control over their households and everyone in it. Civil authorities rarely intervened, short of murder. The institution of slavery in New England was different in some respects from that in other parts of the British colonies, but in the end, certainly no less inhuman and tragic.

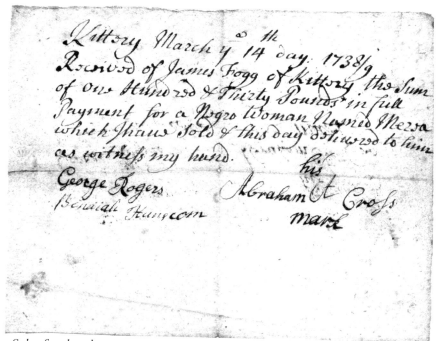

Sale of enslaved woman, Mezsa. Courtesy of the Maine Historical Society.

1. James Oliver Horton and Lois E. Horton, *Slavery and the Making of America* (New York: Oxford University Press, 2005), 13.

2. George H. Moore, *Notes on the History of Slavery in Massachusetts* (New York: D. Appleton & Co., 1866), 4–6.

3. Moore, *Notes*, 12.

4. Robert E. Moody, ed., *The Letters of Thomas Gorges, Deputy Governor of the Province of Maine 1640–1643* (Portland, Me.: Maine Historical Society, 1978), 55.

5. As quoted in Moore, *Notes*, 10.

6. Richard M. Candee, "Merchants and Millwrights," *Old-Time New England* 60, no. 4 (Apr.-June 1970): 4–18.

7. Lorenzo Johnson Greene, *The Negro in Colonial New England* (New York: Columbia University Press, 1942; reprint, New York: Atheneum, 1969), 222. Samuel G. Drake, ed., *Early History of New England . . . By Increase Mather* (Boston: for the Editor, 1864), 150. For cabins, see Martha Lord, Ebenezer Moore, and Maj. Nicholas Shapleigh in Appendix Two.

Chapter Two

Finding Substance

Late December 1754—On deck, the six young Black girls huddled together against a bitterly cold sea wind. They watched as a rope ladder unrolled down the ship's bulging side and then stop to swing just short of a heaving rowboat. Giving a nod of reassurance to her companions, the first girl lifted a leg over the side and secured her bare foot on the ladder's first rung. Of one thing she was certain. The waiting boatman below, like always, had strict instructions to see that she and the other girls got safely ashore. They were a cargo too valuable to lose.

This marked the third time these enslaved girls had been shipped between Boston and the small village of Kittery Point; the third time they would be hustled unceremoniously from the wharf and secured behind locked doors to await their sale or disbursement otherwise.

A telling of the past is most satisfying when its records lend themselves to a full story with rich detail. It comes alive with fact-based statements of who, what, where, and when. Sentences are unencumbered with cautious qualifiers such as likely, possibly, may have been, no doubt was, and so forth. There is little reason to engage in speculation or envisioning.

Not so this history. This telling, or attempt at telling, of Blacks' presence and enslavement in Kittery and its spin-off town of Berwick, is based on a small quantity of records, most with scant substance—brief jots, often only one relevant word or two here and there. Making sense of it all and creating a narrative frequently resembles a patchwork quilt stitched together with qualifiers.

However, documentation for the somewhat dramatized scene above is a rare exception. Based on three letters by Nathaniel Sparhawk, a merchant and slave trader, it is the only record found in which a contemporary Kittery person discusses the arrival of the enslaved and also provides substantial insight into the nature of their bondage as applicable to this region.

On November 29, 1754, Sparhawk, then in Boston, sent the first of the letters regarding those six girls to his business manager at Kittery Point, Thomas Cutts. Issuing instructions, he wrote, "I am obliged to send back all the New Negro girls . . . they must have Cloaths & shoes . . . more shirts & shifts . . . see that they have a good fire and good room & an old sail to lay upon & the ruggs to cover them. Be sure that they don't suffer . . . see them 2 or 3 times a day." (Those "ruggs" were coarse woolen coverlets sent along with the girls.)

Sparhawk went on to say that their food was to be provided by Juba, an enslaved cook in his sumptuous mansion which stood on the hill above the waterfront and next door to the Kittery Point meetinghouse. From that letter and two subsequent ones it seems clear he intended to sell the girls either locally or elsewhere. In the meantime he suggested that Cutts try, with Mrs. Sparhawk's approval, placing some of them with local families on terms of their work for food and lodging. If that failed, a Mrs. Greenough was to see to their care.[1]

Among the few other documents which mention an arriving Black person was recorded on December 7, 1663, when William Ellingham, mill owner and tavern keeper of Sturgeon Creek, Kittery, purchased "one Negro boy Mingoe and a sorrel horse for three score pounds" (£60) from his father-in-law, Thomas Booth of York. In 1676, a Boston merchant informed Major Nicholas Shapleigh of Kittery that the Major's newly purchased Negro man, Coffe, was in custody and waiting to be shipped from the Island of Barbados. Then, late in 1719, William Pepperrell of Kittery Point received word that a consignment of "rum and five Negro slaves" was on the way to him from Africa. However, when the ship arrived at his wharf, he was informed that four of the slaves had died at sea. The survivor, a woman branded with a "Y" on her breast, was very ill. Pepperrell paid the bill of fifty shillings for her and then summoned a local doctor, but such effort came too late. The woman died a few weeks later and her death, as well as that of the other Africans, was blamed on the ship captain's failure to provide adequate clothing for the wintry sea voyage.[2]

The only other source found concerning Africans arriving here is a newspaper item in *The Boston Post Boy* in 1752:

Kittery, June 14th

This day arrived the *Betsy*, Samuel Lanphere commander, from the coast of Guinea, with a quantity of very likely Boys and Girls of the blackest sort: All persons who incline to be purchasers may apply to me the subscriber, where they shall be dealt with on reasonable terms.

Alexander Raitt

According to the Portsmouth Naval Office Register, the *Betsy*, owned by Raitt in partnership with Charles Chauncy of Kittery, had arrived carrying a cargo of thirty-nine Negroes. How many in the group were sold to slave buyers on this side of the river or in Portsmouth is unrecorded. However, those enslaved young people destined for Kittery were likely brought ashore in the same location as the six girls mentioned previously. Though Alexander Raitt lived in Kittery's Second Parish (now Eliot), he owned property near Sparhawk's waterfront warehouse at Kittery Point (located at the bottom of today's Lawrence Lane). Furthermore, the Capt. Lanphere mentioned in the advertisement lived just down the road from there with wife, Joanna (Deering).[3]

So far, it remains to be discovered exactly when the first enslaved Blacks were brought to Kittery or Berwick. Except for the above examples, other Blacks are noted in the records only after the fact, after they had been held by an owner for some unspecified period. A typical case is the 1674 estate inventory for Robert Cutts, a wealthy shipbuilder whose establishment was located on Kittery's Crooked Lane (site of today's Gate Two at Portsmouth Naval Shipyard). Among the eight

Negro slaves mentioned are two "ould and decreped men." It is not known when Cutts may have acquired them. Perhaps when he moved to Kittery ca.1648 from the West Indies he brought their younger, sturdier selves with him to help establish his shipbuilding enterprise.[4]

Adding to the puzzlement are two records of enslaved persons in early Kittery whose race is not stated. Nicholas Frost's 1663 inventory simply lists "a servant boy 7 and ¾ years at £40." In 1667, the estate for Humphrey Chadbourne, long-time mill owner in Kittery's upper parish (later Berwick), listed "five servant men and mades [maids] at £40." It has been suggested that the price indicates they were indentured Europeans, but one cannot be certain. The term "servant" was also a common euphemism when referring to an enslaved African.[5]

It remains unlikely that we will ever know the full extent of slavery in this region, neither its beginning nor its gradual ending after 1783. In fact, before Massachusetts imposed a duty or customs fee of £4 per head on imported Negro slaves in 1706, a man could have bought, utilized, sold, or given away any number of his slaves without any required recordkeeping. Only if he died before that date or some other circumstance brought him into public notice during ownership would we ever know there had been enslaved men, women, or children in his household or business.

After 1706 and during the rest of the era of slavery in Massachusetts, various measures, but not a general sales tax, were taken by the Colony to create greater public accounting of importation and ownership of slaves. Success of such measures remains questionable for the Colony in general. As for Kittery, no official records regarding slave imports have been found even though the town did have its own customs or Naval Office from the above date until British officials moved it to York, Maine, in 1740. Even in that town, whatever records of slave imports were kept are now missing.[6]

Other early Massachusetts accountings of slaves, such as several census and property tax records, are inconclusive because of variations in collection requirements and methods of data collection. For example, census takers and tax assessors were instructed to count only a limited age group of slaves: the able-bodied, ages sixteen and above in some years and sixteen to forty-five in other years. Making things more confusing, in 1754 census takers were instructed to count slaves; in 1765 they were to count Blacks, a number of whom were or could have been free.[7]

Nevertheless, ever so brief notations in wills, estate inventories, court and church records, and a few other sources do indicate significant numbers of slaves in the Kittery/Berwick region from the early period until about 1783. Regrettably, while those records reveal much about slave owners, they contain almost nothing of substance concerning the enslaved—what kind of life they led, how passing events affected them, or what sorts of abilities and knowledge they brought to improve owners' financial and family life and the general economic development of this region.

Still, it is that "almost nothing" in the records, those intriguing small mentions, scattered bits upon bare bones, that when set within the larger framework of daily life and events, bring the past alive, bring us closer to an important group of Kittery people so long ignored.

---

1. Henry S. Burrage, "Colonel Nathaniel Sparhawk of Kittery," in Maine Historical Society, *Proceedings of the Maine Historical Society, Second Series* (Portland, 1899), 9: 240–44.

2. York County Deeds (YCD), Alfred, Me., 1:159. 12: 215. William Blake Trask et al., *Suffolk Deeds*, 14 vols. (Boston, Mass.: Rockwell & Churchill Press, 1880–1965), 5:336. Bryon Fairchild, *Messrs. William Pepperrell: Merchants of the Piscataqua* (Ithaca, N.Y.: Cornell University Press for the American Historical Society, 1954), 118. "1719 Bill of Lading," MS35, Maine Historical Society.

3. *Boston Post Boy*, June 29, 1752. John Knowlton, comp., "British Shipping Records, Portsmouth, New Hampshire, 1694–1775" (microfilm printout with indexes, 2014, Portsmouth Athenaeum, Portsmouth, N.H.), Group 1: 33. YCD 29: 262. Everett S. Stackpole, *Old Kittery and Her Families* (Lewiston, Me.: Press of Lewiston Journal, 1903), 341.

4. Stackpole, *Old Kittery*, 333. Neal W. Allen, *Province and Court Records* (Portland, Me.: Maine Historical Society, 1975). 2: 292, 341, 360, 364.

5. Allen, *Province and Court Records*, 2:383. John T. Hull, ed., *York Deeds* (Portland, Me.: Thurston & Co., 1887). 2: fol. 31.

6. Ellis Ames et al., *Acts and Resolves, Public and Private, of the Province of the Massachusetts Bay*, 21 vols. (Boston: Wright & Potter, Printers to the State, 1869–1922), 1: 578, 579; 2: 527.

7. Joseph H. Benton. *Early Census Making in Massachusetts* (Boston: C. E. Goodspeed, 1905), 72–73.

Chapter Three

Significance and Impact

Insignificant. Of no lasting impact . . .

Such impressions regarding slavery in Maine have long been conveyed in history books. In the Kittery/Berwick area, they echo the often repeated notion that slavery here involved just a few wealthy men with just a few slaves. The results of this project certainly point in the opposite direction as to numbers and also question that "wealth" factor. They also suggest that if similar intense research were to be carried out in other early southern Maine coastal towns, it might further reveal the prevailing misunderstanding about slavery's prevalence and impact.

Data for the Kittery/Berwick area refutes that notion of "just a few." Undoubtedly, we will never know slavery's full extent here, beyond the sum of that data: the presence of 500 or more Blacks, most of whom were enslaved, plus the identity of 186 slave owners and 57 other white persons possibly involved in slave owning. However, that regrettable institution's impact certainly had greater weight than previously reported. To recognize that, we just need to look with keener insight. What follows is an effort to take such a look and perhaps get a bit nearer to historical accuracy. In no way, however, is any part of this chapter intended to excuse or justify slavery.

By the turn of the eighteenth century, people—Black as well as white—had made considerable progress in building up the various small settlements along this Piscataqua River edge of Maine's vast wilderness. Working together, often shoulder to shoulder in the fields, at the hearthside and on the shorefront, all played a role in that progress. Whatever misfortune assailed them, such as storms that washed away mills, disease that devastated whole families, or terrifying Indian raids and massacres, was confronted and dealt with by whomever was at hand, regardless of the color of their skin or condition of servitude. However, enslaved Blacks were denied any stake, beyond personal survival, in those shoulder-to-the-wheel economic efforts.

In about 1712, this area contained an estimated 800 people in about 180 households. In 22 to possibly 37 of those households, there were (or had been) a total of 43 to 64 enslaved Africans. Such cautious estimates are the best that can be offered, given the peculiar nature of the records. Nevertheless, while numbers of Africans were relatively small at that time, their presence was undoubtedly having an impact on families as well as town wide.[1]

In those earliest years, it is unknown who may have taken notice of the changes, subtle and otherwise, that slave labor was making in this area's early rustic households and settlements. Perhaps it was the neighbors, the non-slave-owners, who were quickest to recognize it, to notice changes in some households' activities and routine. When such neighbors gathered for news and gossip at the public house, the mill, the blacksmith's shop, or at the noon break between Sabbath Day services at the meetinghouse, they likely discussed their observations.

Most noticeable would have been change in a male slave-owner's daily routine. He was no longer totally responsible for a supply of wood to keep the hearth fires going, for tending crops and farm animals, clearing more acreage and surrounding it with stone walls. Neighbors might have begun seeing him sitting by a window more often, even late at night, writing or reading. Or, folks might have noticed (or heard about) his more frequent absences from home in order to initiate new business or expand a market for his craft. His name and opinions may have become more prominent in connection with developing town and colony government.

His acquisition of a slave had brought him not only a permanent and controlled source of labor, but a change in his most important asset: time. And, the value of that asset cannot be underrated, especially in those early settlement years. The chance to free up more of one's time, to re-direct its use—that was what enabled men of even little means to prosper, to progress from a primarily household or domestic economy to a market or business economy. Further, such progress by individuals would eventually lead, in one way or another, to progress for an entire community and also for its governance. Quite a few male slave owners listed in this project eventually became prominent in local and/or Massachusetts colonial government.

Acquiring a slave would change a male owner's life and perspective in other ways. He was adding to his property holdings, in effect giving himself more financial options. If need be, he could sell his human property or even mortgage it or loan out the labor of an enslaved man or woman in exchange for goods or money, even use Black labor as a way to pay his or her bills at the local general store.[2] If an owner had a craft or skill—potter, weaver, shoemaker, tanner, blacksmith, shipbuilder, house carpenter, etc.—he had the opportunity to train his male slave to that work and thereby increase not only his output, but the potential sale price of his slave as well. Of course, there were times, perhaps many times, when an arriving African already had such a craft or skill, and might have even been purchased specifically because of that. Eighteenth-century newspaper advertisements commonly cite a wide variety of skills of Black men and women for sale.[3]

Another factor involved in owning a slave was the possibility of an increase in such property. Though the early enslaved population in this locale was widely scattered in small numbers and their social life relatively limited, the inevitable mating and eventual childbirth did happen. However, the fact that owners had no particular reason or government requirement to keep account of slaves' newborns is the main reason why there is barely a trace of them in Kittery or Berwick records. Aside from a couple of infant baptisms, only one document has been found regarding an actual slave birth. And, that only came about because town authorities were concerned over a breaking of the law against race mixing.

In 1737, Grace Foye, a Kittery Point midwife, testified before town selectmen saying that "on July 9, I delivered a Negro woman named Libby belonging to Timothy Gerrish, Esq., of a female white child born of her body named Celinda and further say that I have at sundry times before delivered the same Negro woman of six other black children . . . ."[4]

Foye's testimony regarding that latter group of children clearly shows the problem of estimating total Black population in this area at any given date. Among white women, birth rates were commonly high—six, eight, ten, or more children. Undoubtedly, the same was true for Black women in general. Furthermore, had Libby's baby not been seen as white we likely would never even know of Celinda's existence or of her mother and the six other enslaved children, or, for that matter, the full extent of Timothy Gerrish's slave-owning. The only other relevant record for him is a 1756 estate inventory listing three Negro men, but no females. Incidentally, there would have been no question as to Gerrish retaining ownership of Libby's baby regardless of who was its father. Under commonly accepted tradition, although not stipulated in Massachusetts law, a female slave's children were the property of her owner.[5]

As to a slave-owner's wife in the earliest settlement years and how her life might have been changed by the acquisition of a Black servant, such change was probably marginal in most cases. Under all but total legal control of her husband and in what often appears as a continual state of childbearing, plus shouldering an enormous burden of labor-intensive household work, she was little more than a slave herself. If the newcomer Black was an enslaved young child or a male, that probably only added to her work load, adding another mouth to feed, more clothing to be attended to, and so forth.

Of course, if the slave was a female teenager or adult, that gave the white woman some relief in her daily labors and child caring. In the absence of any letters or diaries, one can only speculate as to what sort of relationships may have eventually developed between white and Black women in this area's rural setting. Still, the presence of a female servant must have made a significant, at times even crucial, difference in the quality of life and well-being of a wife, her children, and household.

One example of this occurred in 1719 when an unnamed enslaved woman assisted Elizabeth Skillings of Kittery through her husband, Josiah's, long illness and death. Then, seven months later, she helped her through an epidemic that led to the death of three of Elizabeth's five children. Mercifully, that outbreak spared the Black woman's children—a boy aged four and an eighteen-month-old baby. As so often is the case in historical records, the second shoe failed to drop. We are left to wonder what happened to that unnamed woman after so much tragedy and loss in the Skillings household. Did Mrs. Skillings show her gratitude in some way, perhaps even offering to eventually free her slaves? Or did she, once her husband's estate was settled, simply sell her inherited Black property, together or singly, in order to collect its £65 value as listed in the inventory?[6]

In regard to the wealth factor said to be associated with, even a requirement for, slave owning here, there is much uncertainty. Available financial data on most Kittery and Berwick slave owners prior to the 1740s (wills, estate inventories, a couple of tax lists) only reveal their situation *after* they had been slave owners for an unknown period of time. Though some owners appear to have become prosperous or moderately so by the date of such records, little is known about their actual financial circumstances when they first acquired a slave years or even decades before. Given the relatively humble status of this area's population from the beginning and on up into the 1750s, their struggles "up from poverty," as described in Everett S. Stackpole's *Old Kittery and Her Families*, one wonders how much it was financial risk-taking rather than discretionary spending that was involved in the initial purchase of a slave.[7]

Research in other parts of New England has shown that a man could acquire a slave on various terms: through barter, on credit, or by payments in goods, labor, or cash over time. A local example of credit purchase is that of Samuel Plaisted of Berwick who, upon his death in 1731, still owed £70 to Hugh Hall "for a Negro."[8]

Slavery's impact on this area in general does involve educated guessing. However, it is not difficult to see the probability of social impact, recognize a training ground in racism for generations of white children, and envision ongoing public disquiet as whites exercised control over Blacks. Communities undoubtedly functioned under a certain degree of stress as they made sure to relegate Blacks to meet-inghouse galleries and generally keep them on the margins of public life during slavery's era and long afterward.

Economic impact is just as difficult to discern, other than the previously suggested ripple effect from slave ownership in the early set-tlement. So far, no seventeenth- or eighteenth-century town treasurers' records for Kittery and Berwick have been found, but without a tax imposed on purchases, sales, or gifts of property, treasurers' accounts would likely offer little of relevance. Property tax records, what few survive, are unhelpful. Some do list owners and numbers of qualifying slaves that they held (ages sixteen to forty-five), but give no evaluation for them as separate from total property value. Other than during the peak of slavery here in the late 1760s, tax revenues from that "human property" must have been barely noticeable.

By 1771, there were more than fifty, but perhaps fewer than one hundred, enslaved Blacks laboring from Kittery Point to the far reaches of the original Berwick. Even making such an estimation is difficult because so many Blacks were always unaccounted for, as with unknown numbers of women (poll taxes only counted males), slaves over age forty or forty-five, and doubtless many dozens of children.[9]

A Daunting Problem

Some explanation is needed regarding the estimates of slave population in 1712 given at the beginning of this chapter. The major challenge to this project was trying to quantify the enslaved population for any date or period of time. Given the nature of existing records, their sometimes puzzling content and the circumstances of their occurrence, the best one can do is develop cautious estimates.

Nearly all slaveholding records or references found for this project only mention the enslaved *after* they have been in place for some unknown period of time and rarely is their age mentioned. In addition, at the date of such a record, we simply do not know how many other enslaved people were then in the town who would not be accounted for until some later time in a will, estate inventory, a sale, and so forth—or never accounted for at all. Nor, in most cases, is there a record of what happened afterward—if or for how long a listed enslaved Black remained among the town's population.

Other issues further compound the problem of quantification, such as duplications of slave names. As examples, from one document to the next, often one cannot be certain which Phyllis or which Caesar is being referred to. Further, in some wills, an owner may name a slave, but when that owner dies many years later and the estate inventory merely lists "a Negro girl" or "a mulatto man," there is no certainty that she or he is the same person referred to in the will. Generic group references in documents such as "all my Negroes" or "the rest of my Negroes" serve to further block our knowledge of slavery's extent. As to property tax records, they also present problems as to possible duplication. They only record numbers of slaves, not identity. The list of Blacks in Chapter Ten contains numerous unnamed and generically listed persons, some of whom could be duplicates, but there is no way to know.

Keeping all that in mind, the method of presenting estimates on the 1712 enslaved population does edge us closer to actuality. Until now, slavery's presence has always been stated relevant to Maine's total population, an estimate of somewhere between 1 and 2 percent at any given time. However, if slavery's presence is viewed in terms of numbers per household, there could be a marked difference. After all, the real impact of the labor, skills, and knowledge of hundreds of enslaved Blacks was not on the general population. It was on households and businesses. Viewed in that way, at least for this area, percentages are higher and significance more evident.

For the year 1712, those cautious estimates on page 16 suggest that as much as 30 percent of the total 180 households in the region had (or had had) enslaved Blacks. Household count for that year is particularly accurate because it was taken at the break-off point for the new town of Berwick. From then on there are only a couple of years when it is possible to attempt such a statistical view. If one combines the report in the 1754 Massachusetts Census of a total of 57 "slaves" for this area (Kittery 35, Berwick 22) and an estimated total house count of about 500, the percentage of slave-owners appears to have been about 11 percent. However, a glance at the compiled data for this research (Appendix One) suggests that percentage may be low. Estimates for 1764, based on that year's census, are made more difficult due to a word change on the census form: Blacks were counted instead of slaves. Still, with so few apparently free here by then, the percentage of slave owners could have been close to 20 percent—a total of 510 households and 106 Blacks "ages 16 and above." The above compilation again suggests a higher percentage but the complexity of the data complexity defies proof. Also blocking a more accurate view of slavery's presence are, as mentioned previously, the "Unaccounted-for," the always disquieting specter of untold numbers of enslaved and laboring small Black children and teenagers under sixteen missing from census, tax, and most other records.[10]

There can be no doubt that the presence of enslaved Blacks had significance and impact in numerous ways on Kittery and Berwick and its families over the years, just as it did elsewhere in the Massachusetts Province of Maine. Regardless of the lack of an exact number and full documentation, common sense speaks to that.

––––––––––––

1. Everett S. Stackpole, *Old Kittery and Her Families* (Lewiston, Me.: Press of Lewistown Journal Co., 1903), 177. See also Appendix One.

2. For examples of such mortgages, see Francis Hooke and Charles Frost, 3rd, in Appendix Two.

3. Lorenzo Johnson Greene, *The Negro in Colonial America* (New York: Columbia University Press, 1942; reprint, New York: Atheneum, 1969), 11. Joanne Pope Melish, *Disowning Slavery: Gradual Emancipation and "Race" in New England, 1780-1860* (Ithaca, N.Y.: Cornell University Press, 1998), 8, 18. Regarding use of slave labor to pay bills, see Chapter 9. For African traditions and culture, see James Oliver Horton and Lois E. Horton, *Slavery and the Making of America* (New York: Oxford University Press, 2005), 41–42.

4. Kittery Town Records, Kittery, Me., Town Clerk's Office, book 2: 135–36.

5. Ibid. See also John E. Frost, *Maine Probate Abstracts, 1687–1800*, 2 vols. (Camden, Me.: Picton Press, 1991), 438; Greene, *Negro in Colonial America*, 126.

6. York County Probate Court Records (YCPCR), Alfred, Me., docket 17158.

7. Stackpole, *Old Kittery*, 14, 213. Re continuing impoverishment, see Memorial of Kittery Committee to Massachusetts Council, 1751, in *Collections of Maine Historical Society, First Series*, 4:199–205.

8. Greene, *Negro in Colonial America*, 6. YCPCR 5: 28, 29.

9. Bettye H. Pruitt, ed., *The Massachusetts Tax Evaluation of 1771* (Boston: G. K. Hall, 1978), 736, 748.

10. For the census of 1754, see Joshua U. Benton, *Early Census Making in Massachusetts, 1643–1765* (Boston: C. E. Goodspeed, 1905), 17. For property owners in 1712, see Stackpole, *Old Kittery*, 149–51. The numbers of property owners for other years are derived partly from the Kittery Petition of 1751, *Collections of Maine Historical Society*, 4:199–205, and an estimated number of houses probably then in Berwick. See also Evarts B. Greene and Virginia D. Harrington, *American Population Before the Federal Census of 1790* (New York: Columbia University Press, 1932), 29–30.

Chapter Four

Climate of Denial

July 1674—At Robert Cutts's house and shipyard on Kittery's Crooked Lane, there are five enslaved Black adults, three men and two women, who are no doubt fearful for themselves and the future of three little children. Whatever family connections there are among them, those may soon be broken. Mr. Cutts has died and his "human property," some or all, may be sold or relocated. Husbands might be separated from wives and their children scattered to new owners.

April 1683— Now that the estate of deceased Nicholas Shapleigh in upper Kittery has been inventoried, all but one of his enslaved Blacks—two men, one woman, and a small child—are likely dreading what lies ahead for them. The other Black, a man named Will, is a bit less apprehensive, at least for the time being. A while ago he was given, or perhaps he negotiated for, a little cabin and the use of three acres of Shapleigh land to farm for himself. And, according to an estate agreement, he is to remain with the widow Alice Shapleigh as long as she lives. Also included in the estate are two indentured Irish boys, but they have little to fear. Unlike the Blacks, they are not slaves for life. No matter what, they will be free in two years when their term of service ends.

December 16, 1685—At Kittery Point, Frances Hooke has decided to put most of his property—houses, lands, two shallops, ten cows, and "one Negro boy Tom"—at risk in a mortgage from Henry Dearing of Boston. Term of repayment is one year. Tom and a Black girl named Hannah had recently been shipped here from a Barbados plantation as part of an inheritance to Mrs. Hooke. Likely, neither of the enslaved youngsters is aware they might be parted forever if Hooke defaults on the mortgage.[1]

Although just a small sample of early cases, such fleshing-out from history's meager bits reveals slavery's stark nature, as it continued to spread throughout Kittery's small settlements. Although denial of enslaved Blacks' humanity and their treatment as mere chattel to be bought and sold was common everywhere in the Americas, in Puritan New England *denial* had other personally invasive and detrimental aspects. Many enslaved Blacks were brought to or raised in a social climate that worked in various ways to deny them of their African-ness.

As to what eventually happened to the enslaved men, women, and children in the above scenes, all but three of them disappear from the record. For the vanished, Fate allowed only a momentary middle to their story, but no beginning and no ending. Unfortunately, that is the situation for most all of close to five hundred Black persons, enslaved, free, or status unknown, cited in this book.

History does allow Hannah to re-emerge, briefly, twenty-one years later along with a two-year-old mulatto boy who may have been her child. Both are listed in Widow Mary Hooke's 1706 estate inventory which valued Hannah at £25, the child at £2. As to Tom, he seems to have been given to Henry Dearing in some sort of mortgage settlement in April of 1686. There is, however, more to the story of Francis Hooke's ownership of human beings. In 1683, Maine's Provincial Court allowed him to "dispose of [Mary Crucy] to his best advantage" after she was convicted of stealing from him. (Having a surname at that time suggests she was white and indentured.) Later, in Hooke's 1695 will, he ordered that "after my wife dies . . . my boy Samuel . . . be disposed of to a religious family." Hooke had no children of record, so it is most likely that he was ordering "disposal" of a one-word-named Black slave. Whose child Samuel was is an interesting question, but apparently he was no longer on the scene when Mrs. Hooke died.[2]

Will, later known as Black Will or William Black, is the other person in the above scenes to re-emerge in historical records, so much so that he has become the most well-known Black person in early Maine (see Chapter 5).

In those opening scenarios, denial of Blacks' humanity and any right to personal and family relationships is all too evident. Men, women, and children were treated simply as assets to be sold or re-distributed regardless of their relationships with other Blacks in a household or even of whatever close relationship may have developed over time between an owner and the enslaved. In the end, the bottom line, the monetary value of an enslaved human "property," most often took precedence.[3]

Such inhumanity is clearly seen in estate inventories. Though occasionally the inventory taker would list a slave or slaves (almost never by name) as a separate line item, most often they were denied even that small distinction. They were simply listed on the same line with farm animals. And, more often than not, the animals rated first place on that line. Truly, it is jarring to encounter line items listing a cow or two, some sheep and then a Negro boy or woman followed by a value for the entire lot. In one inventory even an inanimate hunting trophy rated first place. "Item—a pair of moose horns and a Negro man—£8."[4]

As further degradation, nearly all Blacks in this location were denied recognition of that most personal possession, their parental-bestowed names. For some, that loss may have occurred elsewhere before they came to Kittery or Berwick. Still, by assigning only a one-word name such as Will, Caesar, Hannah, Bess, Pompey, Cato, or Phyllis, slave owners were rejecting their African roots and, in effect, rendering them as anonymous. According to the records, except for three cases, no other known enslaved Blacks had surnames.

Compounding that name disconnect was the duplication of names for different Blacks in different households, even within the same Kittery or Berwick neighborhood. Often it is impossible to know which of nine Dinahs, twelve Phyllises, seven Ceasars, nine Pompeys, or other such multiples is being mentioned from one document to the next. And, were there really that many distinct individuals by those names in this locale? Or, were some such named persons merely re-sold a number of times or otherwise duplicated in records? One can only wonder.

In local documents we do find a few enslaved Blacks with non-English names such as Cugis, Mingo, Cumbo, Juba, Mezsa, Quam, Quash, and Sambo. At least one, Mezsa, is Spanish in origin. Others are either clearly African or an anglicized version of one. It is heartening to know that at least a few enslaved persons had the small satisfaction of hearing a daily reminder of their homeland or family origins from the lips of their slave owner and other townspeople.

There is also that large group of people of color whose slave or other name remains unrecorded. More than 43 percent of the enslaved included in this project are merely designated in records as "Negro, mulatto or black." Those persons were likely assigned some sort of one-word name at the time, but the historical record has denied them even that small bit of recognition. Such naming or no-naming practice has left obfuscation in its wake. Not only does it deny us knowing the proper identity of hundreds of Blacks, it is one of the main blocks to any reliable statistical analysis. Existing records also present a quagmire of uncertainties as to who, when, and where.

Another component of "denial" in early New England was de-Africanizing, an intentional effort to re-make Black "servants for life" to suit the needs and cultural mold of slave owners. Such re-making could go far beyond training and education for the work to be done. Puritans believed that Divine Providence had placed what they considered as heathen Africans in their care so they might "rescue" their souls and convert them to Christianity. Of course, success of such conversion and de-Africanizing would have depended, among other things, on the Black's age and past experience, whether they were New England born and or lived in relative isolation from the influence of foreign-born Blacks.[5]

As to the age factor, it is apparent from slave sale advertisements and other documents that many New Englanders preferred to begin such a process with young teenagers or small children. Though data is lacking on ages of all but a couple of arriving Blacks in this area, such preference was probably often the case. In this area, however, isolation or semi-isolation might have been a particularly significant factor in the progress of de-Africanizing.[6]

Unlike neighboring Portsmouth, New Hampshire, Kittery was slow to develop a central town. Well into the middle of the eighteenth century, while its cross-river neighbor grew into a bustling commercial seaport with a sizable population of enslaved Blacks, Kittery continued as a collection of four or five small rural settlements along the shores of the Piscataqua River. They were separated from one another either by a sizable waterway, long stretches of swamps and/or forested wilderness, or by miles of developing farmlands. Though there was some clustering of houses near the center of a settlement, many other houses were scattered at some distance from one another over the countryside. Berwick, once separated, also remained a series of small, mostly rural farming communities—south, middle, and north—during much of the era of slavery.

In such a setting, with the enslaved Black population widely scattered, mostly by ones in households, there would have been fewer opportunities to socialize with other Blacks and find some reassuring commonality that could serve as a buffer against cultural changes being imposed by their slave owners and the white community. True, at times, even when opportunities occurred, there may have been a language barrier to overcome because slaves were brought from different countries on the West African continent and its off-shore islands.

Without any records of enslaved Blacks' daily lives in Kittery or Berwick, one can only speculate on the rate of de-Africanizing or how much of their native spiritual ways and traditions were eventually laid aside and not passed along to their children. Still, much of the practical aspects of their African-derived culture—alternatives in cooking methods and recipes, ancient knowledge of medicines, and of agriculture and animal husbandry, plus a variety of traditional skills in basketmaking, leather and metal crafts, and others—must have been in evidence here, just as they were throughout parts of New England and elsewhere in colonial America.

In all probability, though, the rate of non-practical cultural fading away was higher in a rural setting than in New England's urban centers. In Portsmouth, for example, where the household and business-related enslaved population was generally more centralized, there was more opportunity for socialization and for continuance of at least some African ways and traditions. In fact, as in Boston and some other New England towns, Portsmouth Blacks had developed their own social community by the mid-eighteenth century with a court of leaders based on African traditions. At some time, they began holding an annual public parade and feasting to celebrate election of a king. Later, during Revolutionary years, their concerns became political as they tried to effect legislation to bring an end to slavery. It is likely that some enslaved Blacks from Kittery and Berwick occasionally crossed the Piscataqua to join in those festivities, but how many might have done so and how early in time is unknown.[7]

Over the years, though, the colonial Black population in this southern Maine locale would have become much like that most elsewhere in rural New England. Except for a few physical features, most people of African ancestry would have appeared little different from people of European ancestry in the working population as to dress and manner as well as in the wide variety of their abilities. However, slave owners and those who benefitted from the economic and social impact of slave labor never intended, despite their efforts at re-culturing and religious conversion, that Blacks would become fully assimilated into the dominant white society. Waiting in the wings at slavery's end would be another cruel phase of "denial"— growing racism and an unjust and detrimental re-writing of history.[8]

No word haunts the subject of slavery in New England more, even to the present day, than the word *denial*. Thanks to a number of nineteenth-century white and biased historians, a myth was created that slavery was only a Southern occurrence. Their revised histories, many of them New England town or regional ones, either omitted slavery's existence entirely or treated it as merely incidental, as if the presence of an enslaved Black here or there was more a source of belittling stories to amuse readers than of any real significance to community life and history. Such histories, some of the first to chronicle America's past, were published near the time of the Abolition Movement and the Civil War or shortly thereafter. Despite the efforts of other more enlightened nineteenth-century historians—Black as well as white—to buck the tide of misinformation, the myth prevailed, denial persisted.

Since that time, numerous twentieth- and twenty-first century historians and writers have thoroughly refuted and shredded that myth. But yet it lingers in many parts of America and elsewhere. Today, most all school book publishers and far too many elementary school curricula in the United States continue to avoid the truth about New England's involvement in slavery. Many institutions of higher education, especially those for public school teachers, are evidently also following that same erroneous and detrimental path.[9]

---

1. For each scene, see applicable data for named Blacks in Chapter Ten, and for slave owners in Appendix Two.

2. See Francis Hook, Appendix Two.

3. Lorenzo Johnson Greene, *The Negro in Colonial America* (New York: Columbia University Press, 1942; reprint, New York: Atheneum, 1969), 211.

4. John E. Frost, *Maine Probate Abstracts, 1687–1800*, 2 vols. (Camden, Me.: Picton Press, 1991), 1:619.

5. Greene, *Negro in Colonial America*, 61–62.

6. Ibid., 33. See also William D. Pierson, *Black Yankees: The Development of an African American Subculture in Eighteenth Century New England* (Amherst: University of Massachusetts Press, 1988), 5.

7. Mark J. Sammons and Valerie Cunningham, *Black Portsmouth: Three Centuries of African-American History* (Durham, N.H.: University Press of New England, 2004), 52–53.

8. Pierson, *Black Yankees*, 7–38.

9. Joanne Pope Melish, *Disowning Slavery: Gradual Emancipation and "Race" in New England, 1780–1860* (Ithaca, N.Y.: Cornell University Press, 1998), xiii–xv.

— Chapter Five —

Into the Spotlight

As far as published histories show, Kittery's enslaved Blacks remain in the background, out of public notice until 1690. However, there is a possibility that date might be pushed back a decade or so. By late summer of 1675, settlements along the New England frontier were suffering from periodic Indian raids as part of what became known as King Philip's War, the first of a series of such conflicts lasting until a treaty settlement in 1725. Toward the end of October 1675, Captain Charles Frost was being pursued through the woods in upper Kittery by a party of hostile Indians. As he got closer to his house "he shouted out to three boys there as if the house were well garrisoned [by militiamen] and the Indians were alarmed and did not venture within gunshot." At that time, Frost had no sons, just three very young daughters. However, Frost's will, made fifteen years later, shows that he owned "Negro man Tony and two Negro boys, Esquire and Prince." Though there is no proof, one cannot help wondering if they might have been the "three boys" who somehow aided in saving lives that day—on both sides of the conflict.[1]

Every entry in the long list of Black persons in this research fires the imagination with a possible story, but only a very few have enough on record for a coherent telling. For most of the rest, they have mere one-liners—their sale or pass-along in an estate, a notice as a runaway in an advertisement, a baptism or listed as serving in the military. Sometimes a person is accorded several more bits, but only enough to raise tantalizing but unanswerable questions. Most intriguing, for example, are two brief notations in a 1720 Kittery Point account book concerning an unnamed mulatto woman who purchased three quarts of rum at William Pepperrell's wharf-side general store. She turned over two deer skins in partial payment and a short time later settled the account with three raccoon skins. What a flood of questions comes forth! Was she the hunter and preserver of the skins or some man's go-between? Was she part Indian, part African, part white? Free or enslaved? What clues might there be in that sale of rum? Given the law against selling liquor to Negroes and slaves, did that mean she was a special friend of the store clerk who decided to ignore the law? Undoubtedly, we will never be able to shine a full spotlight on that woman's history or on that of hundreds of other intriguing Black people in early Kittery and Berwick records.[2]

The Brightest Star – Black Will

One man, however, can now be brought into the full spotlight: William Black, more commonly referred to as Black Will. (His son with the same name also shares that spotlight, but that is getting ahead of the story.) It is through Will Sr., that we first begin really *seeing* into this era of history. We get to know a Black person in action, confronting his enslavement and eventually gaining his freedom.

Black Will's story opens in Upper Kittery in 1682 when he was among five enslaved Blacks—three men, one woman, and "one little Neager"—listed in the estate inventory of Nicholas Shapleigh. Shortly thereafter, Shapleigh's heir, nephew John Shapleigh, made a property agreement with Nicholas's wife, Alice, and included the loan of Black Will for her lifetime. By 1685, however, it was apparent that Will had already begun striking out on his own, farming and doing odd jobs for other people in the area. A deed agreement that year between John and Alice Shapleigh cited "land her Negro lives on [is to be] reserved to his [the] sd Negro's use being about three acres."[3]

Evidence of Will's further enterprise shows up that same year in the list of expenses paid out by Mrs. James Chadbourne for her husband's funeral. Black Will was paid £1.10, but for what is not recorded. It is tempting to suppose it was for making the coffin, but another man was paid for that. Perhaps Will might have taken up gravedigging as a side-line or he was hired to cart barrels of rum or quantities of foods commonly prepared for those occasions. Such evidence, the only bit found so far, merely hints at his determination to thrive and how, in time, he would manage to accumulate a significant amount of money. If, along the way, Will had to share any of his earnings with John or Alice Shapleigh, a common practice among slave owners in New England, that adds even more weight to the significance of his eventual financial accomplishment.[4]

All seems to have gone well from then until 1690 when a white girl, Alice Hanscom, crossed Will's path. Circumstances of their meeting are unknown but, some months later, unmarried Alice was obviously pregnant, and she was accused of fornication and bastardy and brought before a Kittery magistrate named Francis Hooke. When asked to name the father, she blamed a white man, John Metherill, and shortly thereafter he agreed to marry her. Later, when she gave birth to a mulatto baby boy, the scandal really escalated. Another inquiry was held at the home of John Shapleigh where once again magistrate Hooke asked Alice to name the father of her child. It appears that Shapleigh already suspected the answer. When Alice said that it was "William," Hook asked, "Which William?" Before Alice could reply, however, John Shapleigh said, "It is our Black Will she means."

Oddly enough, none of this part of Black Will's life would have seen the light of history had it not been for Alice Hanscom Metherill's much later sexual misbehavior. Not until 1695 in conjunction with an entirely different court case involving Alice, but not Black Will, was the 1690 incident revealed for court record.

At the October 1695 session of York County Court, Alice was brought in on charges of bastardy, this time with John Thompson of Kittery as the father of her baby. Among various witnesses called to testify as to Alice's long-standing bad reputation was a Kittery constable, Richard Eliot. He supplied the details of what occurred back in March 1690 at Black Will and Alice's hearing before Francis Hooke. The constable told the court that a warrant had been issued at that time for Alice's arrest, but a sudden outbreak of brutal and destructive Indian attacks in Berwick and at Salmon Falls on March 18 prevented him from carrying out his duties. Apparently, nothing further was ever done and there is no mention of the Will/Alice affair in court records in 1690.

As to Will's child, who was eventually named William Black, Jr., he would have been considered free at birth because his mother was free. There is some uncertainty as to who cared for him in the beginning, his mother or Mrs. Francis Hooke. The 1695 court case revealed that the child was then in the care of Mrs. Hooke; perhaps Alice Hanscom placed him there in desperation. In October of that year she and her children were destitute and being supported by the Town of Kittery.[5]

It is unknown how much access Black Will had to his growing son or how soon they came to live together, as they eventually did. But whatever public scandal was occurring regarding him during those years, it apparently did not affect Will's work opportunities in the town. He continued to prosper and managed to save enough money to purchase a sizable piece of property, an occurrence quite rare, if not unique, for an enslaved Black man in Maine at that time. On Wednesday, December 5, 1696, he paid £25 in cash to James Gowen for one hundred acres of land in upper Kittery just south of Charles Frost's property and eventually built a house there.[6]

Another dramatic, long-awaited change in Black Will's life occurred on Sunday, February 13, 1701, when John Shapleigh signed the following document:

> These may certify whom it may concern that I John Shapleigh of Kittery do release and forever set free one Negro man commonly called Black Will which was formerly Maj. Nicholas Shapleighs and now in my Possession. I do by these presents release and forever set free from me, my heirs, executors, administrators and from all persons whatsoever laying any Lawful claim to or right to him.[7]

A story is often related, without documentation, that Will's freedom came about because John and/or his wife were suddenly moved by anti-slavery sentiment, but that appears most unlikely. John was still a slave owner when he died four years later and his estate inventory listed the Negro man Sampson at a value of £35. Much more likely, it was Black Will who convinced John to free him. In New England households it was common for enslaved people to negotiate with owners for time off and other privileges and needs. Black Will, evidently a strong-willed, self-motivated man, must have pursued the matter, probably over several years, until he finally achieved his freedom.[8]

Another of Will's remarkable achievements a few years later was securing the freedom of an enslaved man, Tony, being held by Charles Frost, Jr. Perhaps the two Black men were related in some way or just longtime friends who had always lived near one another, or maybe they had even arrived together many years before to await purchase by Shapleigh and Frost. Tony had been listed in the will of Frost's father, Charles Sr., in 1691 and was possibly on the scene of that previously mentioned 1675 Indian raid. He was passed along to Charles Jr., in 1697 after Indians finally succeeded in killing Frost Sr. As Black Will soon discovered, however, securing Tony's freedom would not be a simple and risk-free matter.

Until 1703, an owner could dismiss or free any of his slaves whenever he wished with no restrictions. If a slave was unable to work, became lame or too old (they called it superannuated), he or she could be turned out to fend for themselves. If afterward they became indigent or had problems, the slave owner assumed the town would handle that. However, by 1703, Massachusetts towns had balked at the rising cost of such cases and a law was passed requiring slave owners to post a bond of £50 with the town before freeing a slave. Further, if the former slave should become ill or indigent, he or she was to be cared for by their previous owner.[9]

Charles Frost, Jr., considered the wealthiest man in Maine by that time, was unwilling to post such a bond. So, in order to free Tony, Frost required Black Will to assume permanent legal responsibility for Tony, financially and otherwise, by way of a conditional mortgage to Frost on all of Will's property. As of November 13, 1708, upon Will's signing of the agreement, Frost removed Tony from his list of a half-dozen slaves. He also removed himself, his "heirs, Executors, Administrators, and Assigns" from any future responsibility for Tony, a man who had been forced to serve the Frost family without pay for thirty years or more. Further insight into Will's generous and thoughtful nature is revealed by the fact that sometime after that date, he provided Tony (later, Anthony Freeman) with two acres of land on which to build a house with the proviso that Tony would eventually pay him for that property. No record of the amount has been found.[10] From then on, there are just a couple of hints of Black Will's progress. Several tax records show his property evaluation about average with most of the town. In 1714, three-quarters of town residents paid 5 shillings or less. Will paid 4 shillings. Back in 1704, he appears to have suffered property loss along with the rest of the town due to various Indian attacks. On the list was a William Blacket applying for a tax rebate of 10 shillings, a bit more than most other residents. (Such alternate spelling for Black was sometimes used by Blacks.)[11]

Will's further life and that of his son, Will Jr., should have played out in the same manner as most other farmers in the area. The land he owned, though bordered somewhat by swamps, contained some of Kittery's most fertile soil. Unfortunately, however, the law and racism would disrupt their lives and threaten their livelihood a number of times.

Like elsewhere in New England, this town's Puritan-run government kept close watch for people's misdeeds, minor as well as major. Ministers and church deacons regularly inquired into parishioners' private and public behavior and publicly exposed "sinners" at Sabbathday services. Many times, the unrepentant were brought before the county court on charges of swearing and blaspheming, drunkenness, non-attendance at church, fornication, and bastardy. To gather information on the latter charge, an official sometimes appointed several "discreet persons" to snoop and report back. Since Massachusetts law forbade sexual relations as well as marriage between Blacks and whites, no doubt the officials and their "persons" were keeping close watch on town Blacks, especially those who were free.[12]

In January of 1712, Black Will was wrongly accused of fathering a child with a white single woman, Elizabeth Brooks. (Records do not indicate which Black Will, the father or the twenty-two-year-old son.) At any rate, when the case came to trial it was determined that "no Evidence appearing sufficient to convict him, he is acquitted." However, he had to pay court fees of £1.6. No further documentation has been found regarding Elizabeth's baby or any connection between Elizabeth and Will after the 1712 case. However, she may have continued to associate in some manner with Black men. Five years later, when Elizabeth was again involved in a case of fornication and bastardy, she had been living for some time with a married white man, Thomas Reed, of Kittery. He testified that until the baby was born (and seen as white) he was afraid it had been fathered by a Negro.[13]

Scandal again descended on the Will Black family in 1715, this time involving Will Jr. He was called into court on charges connected with Elizabeth Turbit, a white girl, and her baby. In this case, however, young Will and Elizabeth (now living in their house in Berwick) were either already married or in the process of getting married. On November 22, 1714, they had gone before Constable Joseph Abbott to record the following: "This may satisfie [to whom] it may consarne [*sic*] that william blaik [*sic*] and Elizabeth Torbit are lately published." This officially certified their intent to marry, a common step before final nuptials. Considering Massachusetts law, however, the constable's willingness to make such a record seems odd. Perhaps Will's skin coloring was light enough that Abbott took no special notice. In the meantime, while awaiting an official marriage, the couple began living together.

Then, seven months later on July 12, 1715, Will Jr. was brought before Justice of the Peace Charles Frost for being "vehemently suspected to be the father of a child begotten on the body of Elizabeth Turbit of Berwick . . . ." During the hearing that day, Valentine Scates and Samuel Allen testified that mulatto Black Will, Jr., and Elizabeth Turbit "has for some time past dwelt together both at one house and they the Deponents know of know [*sic*] other person or persons that dwells in the house with them and having frequent occasion to be at the house [we] have seen them in bed together . . . ."

A further hearing was scheduled and the court ordered Will to post bond, but he lacked the money and was sent to York jail. Two days later, his father and a friend, Adryan Fry, each put up a £20 surety bond on their properties and young Will was released.

The following spring, Elizabeth Turbit was brought to court, found guilty of bastardy and given the usual sentence of a choice between a public whipping on her naked back or to pay a substantial fine. Her choice is unknown, even if she even had one, financially. As for Will Jr., he failed or was unable to show up for that court session and, having thus forfeited bond, the judge ordered the sheriff to find Will Jr., and collect court costs of £2.6.10 payable in money, goods, or chattel, or put him in jail until such was paid.

Once again, historical records leave us with more questions than answers, but it appears that Will Jr.'s legal problems were somehow resolved and the young couple were able to get on with their lives. Also, there must have been some settlement regarding the bond originally posted by Will Sr., and his friend as there is no evidence their property was ever seized.[14]

How different all these cases likely would have been had Black Will, Sr., and his son been white. Court records on their transgressions, alleged and otherwise, would have been much shorter, maybe a sentence or two such as those which dot page after page of records regarding white persons who were charged with fornication and bastardy. Cases involving Black/white sexual relationships are rarely found in York County Court records. Other than the ones discussed above, only one more has been found for this area. In January 1710, Joanna Barnes (possibly the widow of Henry Barnes at Spruce Creek) was accused of having a bastard child by an unidentified Negro man. Resolution of her case is unknown.[15]

The final notice in records concerning Black Will, Sr., comes with his undated last will and testament which was probated in 1727. That thoughtful document, written when he was very ill, might suggest a scene in which he was surrounded by his wife, Sarah, and his sons, Joshua and Will Jr., and perhaps his long-time friend, Tony, whom he had rescued from slavery so long ago. Regardless of that friendship, though, Will made it clear in his will that Tony was in debt for the allotted two acres of land.

All that aside, it was his grandchildren whom Will Sr., was most concerned about. Instead of giving property outright to his sons, the will directed that the land be divided in half and "managed" by each son until their eldest sons came of age. Will Jr., was to manage the half containing the house and orchard, but both he and Joshua were charged with lifetime care of Sarah and required to bear equal share in cost of her burial.[16]

Black Will's estate inventory and other probate records are missing, so we are denied knowing the level of his financial accomplishments and those details which often speak so poignantly of a man's skills and personal interests. Still, considering the scarcity of records on the vast majority of Kittery's early colonial residents, white as well as Black, it is remarkable that such a nearly complete story can be related— and that it be of a man who was the founder of Maine's first Black community. The content and extent of this community by the mid eighteenth century is difficult to determine. Beyond the growing families of Black Will, Sr.'s descendants and those of Anthony Freeman, it is quite likely that some other local people of color, newly free or living independently, would seek and find at least temporary welcome at Will's one hundred acres. It is possible, although not documented, that some others may have been allowed to live as squatters on the margins of adjoining white-owned property, perhaps in exchange for labor or other means of barter.

Like his father, Black Will, Jr., was an enterprising man and would also one day play a leading role in Maine's earliest Black heritage. In his early twenties, Will Jr., purchased twenty-five acres of what was likely virgin timber land in Berwick along a mast way (now Blackberry Hill Road) and then sold them shortly afterward. Later he acquired thirty other acres in that area and ten more near his father's farm in upper Kittery. In 1722, he apparently attempted to gain leverage by getting a one-year short-term mortgage of £30 on all but ten of those acres. Unfortunately, he failed to meet the deadline and mortgage-holders, William Leighton and John Furbish, were soon divvying up bits of that property between them.[17]

Will's story after that time is unclear in records, but it appears that perhaps not long after his father died he decided to move his family to the wilderness of eastern Maine on what would later become Bailey's Island. They remained there until 1745 when deed-holder, the Reverend Timothy Bailey, forced them off the land. Tracing their whereabouts for a while afterward is difficult, but Will was in North Yarmouth in 1745 when he obtained a £30 mortgage on his remaining ten acres in Kittery from Simon Frost. This time, luck was with him and in two years Frost agreed to cancel the debt for payment just £2 shy of the total. At some point Will finally settled his family on Orr's Island and eventually was joined by other free Blacks coming to settle nearby. Today, William Black, Jr., is recognized as the founder of Maine's second oldest Black community and his presence there is permanently noted on navigation charts. The passageway between Bailey's Island and Orr's Island is marked "Will's Gut."[18]

Memories of Sarah

Berwick Church records show that on Sunday, November 7, 1742, "Sarah the servant of Lt. Samuel Lord owned covenant and baptized. Amy her child baptized." In the 1764 will of Mrs. Samuel Lord (Martha) she states that:

> I give to my maid servant Sarah three of my kitchen chairs, a pine chest, a small iron pot and kettle, also one bed and bedding . . . also my common and daily or everyday wearing apparel together with my old black gown & black hood and apron for mourning [wear]. It is also my will and pleasure that at my decease she be discharged from slavery and become a free woman to be at her own dispose if she sees fit to accept it.[19]

This is the sum total of Sarah's documented life. The rest of her story comes to us through the filter of time, hearsay, and changing social perspective. In 1897, a Berwick historian, William F. Lord, a fourth-generation descendant of Sarah's owner, Samuel Lord, wrote "Black Sara," a somewhat romanticized sketch of her life as a servant in several Lord family households. He never uses the words 'slave' or 'slavery' and he takes an apologist's approach typical of his time, but here and there, racism is evident. Though Lord provides no sources for his information, it is likely that much of the basic information is accurate.[20]

According to the author, Sarah was born in the Berwick area in 1720 and purchased at age four by Samuel Lord for a pair of oxen. She "married early in life the servant of a neighboring farmer" and then, shortly after their child, Amy, was born in 1742, her husband accidentally drowned in the Piscataqua River. Six months later during some sort of epidemic, baby Amy died. Sarah was sent to work in the newly established household of one of the Lord's sons. One wonders if this change in Sarah's location was merely expedient or prompted by something else. Her recent loss of both husband and child no doubt affected her deeply. Perhaps, Samuel Lord, Sr., sought to lift her spirits by loaning her to a family with young children.

How long Sarah remained in that location is unknown, but when she was twenty-four she began working in the household of John Owen Sullivan, a neighbor of the senior Lords. Perhaps her labor was just a neighborly loan on the part of the Lords or maybe even a lease arrangement. Lord makes it seem as if Sarah had some choice in the matter. He writes of her frequently "visiting" there to care for the children while Sullivan and wife Margery were tending to the farm. Of her time there, he writes: "For many years she fondled in her sable arms those children who, in her lifetime became illustrious in the Commonwealth." Lord is referring to her care of John and James, later General John Sullivan and Judge James Sullivan, Governor of Massachusetts.

We gain more insight into Sarah's abilities when the author writes about the Lord family's mill operations. In addition to her household work, she attended to the needs of customers at the grist mill when the mill owners were away caring for their farms or "engaged in river driving"—moving rafts of logs to lumber mills. From Lord's description, it is apparent she saw to the entire grist-mill operation, from lowering levers to engage the grinding wheels to filling the sacks and hauling them about. "The corn was usually brought to the mill on horseback," Lord wrote, "and, if by a woman or child, Sara would throw the sack of meal upon the horse's back with the ease of Hercules."

From then on in this often lyrical sketch it is difficult to sort out probable fact from fiction. Lord writes of Sarah attending church with her master and her being "an ardent and consistent member" of the South Parish Church and then, in 1755, of the new North Parish Church at Blackberry Hill. Sarah was present at the ordination for its first pastor, John Morse. She "took an active part in the vocal exercises with her associates in the Negro seats and her strong clear voice blending with the lighter, but no less melodious voices of Candis, Marie and Phyllis, thrilled the congregation." (No Blacks are listed as members in that church's eighteenth-century records. Many by the name of Sarah are listed, but always with a surname which Samuel Lord's enslaved Sarah likely would not have had.) Lord mentions "there were free seats for the colored servants kept by a large number of the parishioners" at the North Parish Church. Such seats in the gallery were actually paid for by the slave owners as part of annual church pew rents or fees.

Moving on, the writer attempts to bring Sarah into the foreground of on-going events but only alludes to her involvement in the making of clothing for militiamen in the 1745 Louisburg Expedition and later on for Lord family sons going off to fight in the Revolution. Throughout this entire article, there is never any reference to other enslaved Blacks in the Samuel Lord, Sr., household, but records reveal at least four others were there along with Sarah in the 1760s: Cato, Enos, Amy Hall, and her brother Amos Hall. Source of the surname for the last two Black persons is unknown.[21]

William Lord's description of Sarah's death and funeral reads like an oft-told Lord family story, here and there romanticized and perhaps embellished through the years. Still, since it occurred just twenty-six years before author Lord was born, it probably came to his later hearing pretty much intact. He does not mention the year Sarah died, but research now shows that it was 1793 when she was age seventy-three. And, though she was free well before that date (Mrs. Lord died in 1776), it is evident Sarah was still a servant to the Lord family.[22]

Setting the scene as a "beautiful October night when the harvest moon was round and clear over Mt. Agamenticus," Lord describes that sad occurrence at his grandparents' house. "A few of the neighbors had gathered at the homestead to finish husking the corn, Sara had remained up late to put in order the room where the work had been done. The family arose unusually late the next morning and noticed there was no fire kindled on the hearth, no preparations for the morning meal. They went to Sarah's room. There had been no struggle; everything was peaceful, calm, and still. Sara was dead. The messenger in the night had released *"the white soul from its dark casket"* (emphasis added).

With much sentiment, the author describes the aftermath when neighboring women gathered at "the homestead" to offer aid and sympathy. A Mrs. Sullivan "boisterously extolled [Sara's] virtues saying, 'the like of her will never be seen again." Mr. Hansen of Somersworth, New Hampshire, came to make the coffin and Parson Andrew Merriam, Sarah's "beloved pastor for twenty-five years," was notified.

Lord then describes her funeral "attended by nearly every colored person and most of the members of the parish" and that, after her coffin was carried by four men to the cemetery, "the colored people remained until the grave was covered and the undressed stones were set." Those two small, round stones (likely head and foot markers) can still be seen today near the edge of the cemetery, but at considerable distance from the very prominent and formally engraved headstones of the Lord family. Probably in more recent times, the name Sarah was crudely chiseled on one of the stones.

One short paragraph in the conclusion of William Lord's sketch strikes at the truth, not only of how Sarah is remembered by the Lord family, but of the valuable role she and countless other enslaved Blacks played in early New England households. Lord wrote, "Sara was an important acquisition to the new settlement for she was strong and energetic, of great endurance, had common sense and a kind and sympathetic heart, and she was versed in all the home remedies for the sick and watched at their bedside with patience and sympathy." If a proper marker were to be placed beside Sarah's burial stones and the words "an" and "acquisition" were removed from the previous quotation, that tribute would serve as a most fitting epitaph.[23]

Cicaro and Phillis of Kittery

If their story were also to be told by a nineteenth-century apologist, he would show a young Black couple and their newborn daughter in 1765, happily settled in a small rent-free cabin near the shore of a quiet cove at Kittery Point. Cicaro would be described as a faithful 'servant' whose wealthy, benevolent 'mistress,' Lady Mary Pepperrell, provided for all his needs. In like manner, Phillis would be introduced, but as a 'servant' to a benevolent 'master,' Nathaniel Sparhawk, wealthy son-in-law of Cicaro's mistress. Then the writer would likely spend pages extolling the prominence of the master and mistress, their anteced-ents and the elegance of their two mansions—one across from the Kittery Point meetinghouse and the other just east of that church. Toward the close of the piece, there would be mention that the mis-tress granted Cicaro his freedom but, because he was so dedicated to her, he remained in her service until her death. As for Phillis, the writer might not bother to pursue the matter of whether or not she was ever set free. Instead, there would be a kind of happily-ever-after ending saying the Black couple had become so fond of the late mistress' family, they continued into old age caring for her widowed daughter.

While that version is basically true for Cicaro and Phillis, it cer-tainly hides a stark reality and also much significant detail. True, they were a couple and perhaps officially married when documentation on them first appears in the following oddly worded church record: "January 8, 1764, Negro servt. Phillis Col. Sparhawk owned covenant. March 24, 1764, Negro servt. Lady Pepperrell Cicaro baptized." A year later on July 7 the parish minister recorded, "Baptized privately a daughter of Cicaro and Phillis servants of Lady Pepperrell and Col. Sparhawk."[24]

How long Cicaro had been in the household of Lady Pepperrell, widow of Sir William Pepperrell, Baronet, prior to 1764 is not known. Most likely he came from the 1759 estate of Sir William when his will allowed widow Mary to "choose any four of my Negroes." No list of her choices has been found. Those selected, however, would have soon been put to work preparing for her move into her newly built mansion just across from the Kittery Point meetinghouse.[25]

As for Phillis' origins, she could simply have been purchased at some point by Nathaniel Sparhawk. Or, she might have been part of his wife Elizabeth Pepperrell's wedding dowry in 1742. If that were the case, Phillis might have arrived at the Sparhawk mansion as a small child, one probably still struggling to break in her new pair of shoes.

"Please to make ye Negro Phillis one pr [size] 3 shoes and charge by acct. to William Pepperrell." That order was sent sometime in the early 1740s to Kittery shoemaker, James Kerswell, by Pepperrell's son, Andrew. Since baby shoe size was zero, that order suggests a little girl about age three or four.[26]

As usual, there are only stray bits and passing mentions to flesh out the rest of this story. Cicaro and Phillis were able to remain a life-long couple and they did have some sort of house or small cabin at the head of a tiny cove on Kittery Point. As for their daughter, no further record of her has been found. That phrase "privately baptized" (unusual in Kittery church records) might suggest a baby who was ill or perhaps near death at the time.[27]

In the fall of 1775, Cicaro's routine was disrupted, at least for a short while, by the on-coming American Revolution. Rebel forces on both sides of the Piscataqua River were scurrying to get better fortifications in place to protect Portsmouth Harbor from possible British invaders. High on the list for improvements was the old Kittery Point earthworks commonly called The Battery (now Fort McClary). As of November 5, Cicaro was serving in a local militia unit assigned to that task and, though it is uncertain, his being there may have been by his own choice as a newly free man. According to Lady Pepperrell's 1779 will she had freed all her slaves sometime before that year.[28]

Her will also made special provisions for each one. "Whereas I have since liberated all my slaves, I ratify the same, viz. Cicaro, Zilphah and Dick and whereas Dick has since died leaving two children, I give 20s [shillings] to each and to Cicaro and Zilphah a good cow, 2 sheep and 6 pounds sterling each." It is unknown if Cicaro was aware of those provisions, but he remained with Lady Pepperrell as a paid servant until her death in 1789. His legacy was paid to him in January 1790 along with wages due of £5.8. By then, he was apparently working alongside

Phillis at the nearby mansion of Lady Pepperrell's widowed daughter, Elizabeth Sparhawk, who was struggling with severe depression.[29]

A continuation of their story was found merely by chance in a short, tiny-print footnote in the appendix of a biography on Mrs. Sparhawk's son-in-law, William Jarvis of Boston. It revealed that shortly after Lady Mary Pepperrell died in 1789, the ailing Mrs. Sparhawk, along with Cicaro and Phillis, left Kittery Point and moved into the Jarvis household. That footnote also shows a typical example of nineteenth-century romanticizing of slavery and its aftermath.

> Two faithful old family servants, Cicaro and Phillis, unwilling to be separated from their loved mistress, followed her to Boston and remained with her and Mrs. Jarvis until their death. Their greatest happiness was expatiating on the various incidents and former grandeur of the Pepperrell family. Aunt Phillis had taken care of Mrs. Jarvis when a baby.[30]

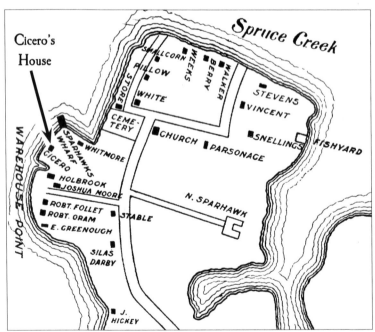

Cicaro & Phillis' house at Kittery Point, 1775. From Everett S. Stackpole, Old Kittery and Her Families (*Lewiston, Me.: Press of Lewiston Journal Co., 1903).*

Despite what seems indicated, Cicaro and Phillis did not die in Boston. They were back in their small cabin at Kittery Point in time for the first U.S. Census in 1790. It is unknown for how long afterward Cicaro enjoyed their waterfront view but, when the census taker came in 1810, Phillis was head of the household and had assumed the surname Pepperrell. As the years went by, Phyllis became so well known in the community that people began referring to the cove where she lived (at the bottom of present day Lawrence Lane) as "Phyllis Notch," a quiet anchorage still known to present-day sailors and boaters.[31]

Caesar Sankey—"Servant," Quaker, Farmer, Soldier

Caesar was quite young, perhaps only a few years old in 1757, when his owner, Andrew Neal, 3rd, of Kittery died. And, it is clear from Neal's will that he was concerned for the boy's future. Whether such concern was personal or just a matter of preserving "property" is unknown. Caesar, valued at £30, was given to Neal's unmarried, twenty-one-year-old son, James, with the proviso that the boy must also serve James' mother and younger brother, Andrew. Furthermore, Andrew Senior's will charged James with the full care of his mother and, if James failed in that capacity, Mrs. Neal "shall or may" take Caesar away from him. Oddly, the will also said that if Andrew Neal, Jr. (then aged fifteen) "settled in Berwick, Caesar shall serve him two years and [be returned] as well clothed as he was when he took him," It is unknown if such a sojourn ever occurred.[32]

Caesar grew to manhood in a household and a community that was a bit different from elsewhere in the area. The Neals, located close to the border between Kittery and Berwick, were members of the Society of Friends (Quakers), as were quite a few other neighboring families. At least four (possibly more) of those Quaker families had enslaved Blacks. Without a meetinghouse of their own until 1769, the members either traveled across the river to the Society of Friends in Dover, New Hampshire, or held meetings in their Kittery homes. Some of those meetings had been held in the Neal household since 1721.

In Caesar's time, he probably stood at the back of the room with other Blacks or maybe he shared an isolated 'Negro bench' with elderly Hannah and Sampson owned by Nicholas Shapleigh. Likely, Joe and Tobey would have been there with owner, John Morrell, and perhaps also Dillo, an enslaved woman in the senior Neal family. Toney and another Black man (name unrecorded) owned by Samuel Johnson, might also have been brought to meeting. If the Johnson group was present that meant the roads were clear for travel. They lived ten miles away at Spruce Creek. Caesar appears to be the only Black in this locale to openly adopt Quakerism and be recognized as either an official member or perhaps given some designation that was sometimes reserved for Black members.[33]

Readers may be surprised to learn that some Quakers were slave-owners. True, their founder, George Fox, was eventually opposed to slavery and led an unsuccessful fight against it in England in the mid seventeenth century. But in colonial America, many Quakers viewed slave-owning in the same way as did the Puritans—simply a matter of business, of having a controlled source of labor and a means to building wealth. Of course, both religious groups rationalized their behavior by saying they were rescuing the souls of Africans. Quakers did often speak out against harsh treatment of slaves and the only record of apparent mistreatment by a Quaker in this region involved Samuel Johnson of Kittery and his enslaved man, Toney.

By 1773, Caesar's life had begun to change. James Neal was preparing to free him—undoubtedly because of a Quaker ruling that year forbidding members to own slaves. According to Neal, he had begun allowing Caesar to work for other people—"laboring for himself." However, the wages from that labor were paid to Neal. Then, sometime in early 1774, he freed Caesar and made arrangements to apply those accumulated wages for Caesar's use "in purchasing a piece of land with house in Berwick on Oak Hill for which a deed is taken in his name."[34]

Saturday, April 16, 1774, was undoubtedly a joyous day for Caesar who had now adopted the surname Sankey. For the price of £16.10 paid to David Allen, he now had a house and thirty-six acres. Quite likely, he was already planning to seek the hand of Sarah Sharp whom he may have first met when the Kittery Quakers attended meetings with the Dover Society of Friends. On November 23, 1774, Caesar and Sarah were married and also formalized their membership in the Society. Unlike the Puritans' business-like civil marriages, this Quaker couple's wedding was a religious celebration.[35]

In January 1776, they celebrated the birth of their son, Simon, but their joy was tempered by the urgencies of an on-coming war with Great Britain. In late winter Caesar enlisted as a private in a New Hampshire militia company heading for defense of New York. As a result he and Sarah soon lost the emotional and spiritual support of the Dover Society of Friends. In 1777, its members voted to officially "disown" the young couple.

Caesar continued in military service until 1781, and sometime after 1802 he and his family left Kittery for New Hampshire. As to his property, there is no trace of it in York County records under Caesar or Caesar Sankey. Despite James Neal saying it would be so, Caesar did not sign or make his mark on the original deed. Only Neal signed it, thus in effect making it his property.

It appears Caesar and his family lived in several places, including Portsmouth, before finally settling in Pomfret, Vermont. In 1830, he applied for and received a pension for his service during the Revolution. He stated his age as seventy-four, but he may not have known his exact birth date—a circumstance not uncommon as a result of slavery's disruption in Black family life. It seems doubtful he was a newborn back in 1757 when James Neal's will issued all those instructions. To date, Caesar's final resting place has not been found.[36]

Molly and Her Table

Molly Miles of Kittery Point and Eliot, Maine, was a unique and remarkable woman, in her own time, as well as in the annals of southern Maine's early Black history. In her long lifespan of almost 108 years, she endured slavery's inhumanity, witnessed its rise in the 1760s and its gradual ending here after 1783, and she undoubtedly experienced the oppressive racism which followed. Interestingly enough, Molly Miles got to tell her *own* story, at least a small bit of it, for the record, apparently the only survivor of slavery to do so in this region of Maine.

However, were it not for a small, round, eighteenth-century maple table (see p. 55) and a message written on its underside, her story would not have come to light on these pages. Four years into research for this project the only bit of data found for a Black woman with the surname Miles was a Mary Miles of Kittery who married Richard Black in 1757. Then in spring 2013, I received an e-mail inquiring for information about an eighteenth-century enslaved woman, Molly Miles, and reference to an existing table given to her by Sir William Pepperrell. Since Molly was often a substitute name for Mary, I thought there might be a connection. Further research, however, left Mary by the wayside for the moment and, instead, brought Molly front and center.[37]

Molly Miles began revealing her story in 1826 when she was interviewed by a Kittery Point resident, Andrew Gerrish, as he sought to know more about the famous Pepperrell family. Molly told him that she was born in the household of Col. William Pepperrell on May 9, 1718, and then was brought up in the family of his son, William Pepperrell, Jr. In Gerrish's published account of that interview, he mentioned only two of Molly's reminiscences about the Pepperrells. She told him of youngsters making fun of the elder Col. William's paunch by taking a pair of his breeches and pulling them over a large barrel and, she said, "it would meet around and button." Molly also related a horrifying incident when Lady Mary Pepperrell's brother, Samuel Hurst, was accidentally buried alive. When the family tomb was opened a few weeks after his interment for a different person's burial, they were shocked to discover that Samuel had broken open his coffin and made his way to the closed door before dying. Molly said Lady Pepperrell was very upset and the incident "was hushed up as much as possible in the family."

Whatever else Molly may have told Andrew Gerrish on that occasion is lost to us. In his brief write-up, he made note of Molly's advanced age of 107 years and said "she was very intelligent, and her memory was apparently unimpaired . . . [she] walked with a firm step, and perfectly erect, had not a winkle in her face, and could read the smallest print without spectacles in 1825."[38]

As is the case for nearly all persons of color in this Kittery/Berwick history, the greater part of Molly's life remains without record. Notice of her stated 1718 baptism does not appear in Kittery or Kittery Point parish books. Nothing regarding her has been found in available Pepperrell family records and there is only silence as to her parental connections. It is possible that Molly was the Mary Miles of Kittery who married Richard Black in 1757. And, it is also possible she was the Mary Miles listed in the 1790 U. S. Census as Head of Household containing five "Other Free Persons," i.e. Blacks. Further, Molly's surname, Miles, might link her in some manner to one of the Miles families that had been living along Spruce Creek near the Kittery Point meetinghouse since the 1640s, at least some of whom are on record in the early eighteenth century as Black and mulatto. But such connections remain unproven.[39]

The Molly of this story did have a daughter, Hannah (birthdate unknown), as deduced from a Portsmouth newspaper item in 1822: "Black woman (mother of the late Hannah Bradley) whose birthdate is recorded in the parish books in Kittery, May 1718, is in her 104th year." A year after that notice, thanks to an alert reporter, we gain an expanded view of Molly's abilities and attitude in a mere twenty-six words.[40]

On Tuesday, October 14, 1823, *The New Hampshire Gazette* printed the following notice: "We are informed that a few days since, Molly Miles, a colored woman, 104 years of age, walked to Kennebunk [Maine], a distance of about 30 miles." It was a small print item, really just a column-filler at the bottom of page three. But, within a few days, this notice was picked up by other newspapers in Maine, Massachusetts, Connecticut, and New Jersey.[41]

Molly's last years were spent at the Alms House which had opened in Eliot, Maine, in 1823. Keeping her company there were a dozen or so other residents, two of whom had also weathered the century mark. Nonetheless, Molly apparently continued her enjoyment of long, strenuous walks on this area's rough and dusty country roads until near the end of life. She died on Wednesday, March 7, 1827, and her obituary appeared in the *Portsmouth Journal of Literature & Politics* the following Saturday.

> [Died] At the Alms House in Eliot, Me, on Wednesday last, Molly Miles, aged 107 years 10 months; she was born at Kittery Point in May 1719: she dates her age from the fact that a Meeting House at the Point was burnt by lightening the year she was born; she retained the faculties of her mind to the last, walking perfectly erect, with a firm step, and had not a wrinkle on her face, and could distinctly see to read her Bible without glasses; she walked to Kittery Point a year ago last summer, a distance of twelve miles in one day, and then did not complain much of fatigue.[42]

Remarkably, her passing rated far more space than the one-liner obituaries so common for most everyone else, white or Black. And, as occurred before, a number of more distant newspapers also carried at least parts of the notice as it appeared in the *Portsmouth Journal*. Mollie Miles's burial site is unknown. It may have been somewhere near the Alms House in Eliot, but there is no record to confirm that.[43]

Molly's Table

"This table came from / Sir William Pepperell / He gave it to his slave / Molly Miles / Uncle Tom Payne / cut it down 6" / Grandfather Foye / got it from / Mollie Miles." This message, handwritten on the underside of the top of Molly's small maple table, was placed there by a Foye descendant probably many years or perhaps decades after Molly died. The grandfather was William Foye of Haley Road, Kittery Point, and the down-sizing of the table was possibly done around 1848 when his daughter, Sarah, and her husband, Thomas Payne, were gathering furniture for their new Kittery Point cottage at what is now 65 Pepperrell Road. According to Foye family lore, the table was given that reduction so it would fit into a corner of one of the low-ceiling bedrooms. (By a strange, if not haunting, coincidence, I owned and lived in that Payne house before and during the research and writing of this history.) The Reverend Alan Cutter of Baton Rouge, Louisiana, the twenty-first-century owner of the table and a Foye descendant, recently gave the table

Table ("Molly's Table"), Seacoast New Hampshire, area, ca. 1750 with later alterations. Maple; two replaced legs, oak. H. 27 in., Diam. 27 in. Portsmouth Historical Society; Gift of Alan and Anne Cutter (2017.2). Photo, Ralph Morang.

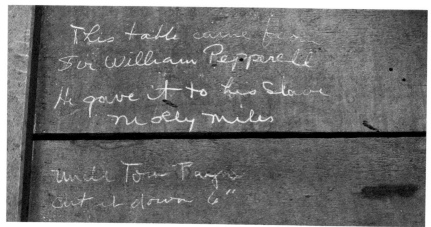

Notation found on the underside of Molly's table. Photo, Ralph Morang.

to the Portsmouth Historical Society. It retains much of its original appearance—minus those six inches, of course. It now measures 26½ inches in height and 27 inches in diameter.[44]

One intriguing, but likely never answered, question will always linger regarding this table. How might it have come into the Foye family's possession and when? Was it simply a matter of being bought from Molly at some point when she was living with her family in Kittery Point or later on when the elderly woman was preparing to move into the Alms House? Perhaps Molly gave Foyes the table out of gratitude or even as payment for something. As mentioned in an earlier chapter in this work, a Sarah Foye of Kittery Point was a busy midwife in the mid-1700s and perhaps she or a trained Foye daughter aided Molly in childbirth.

As always, there is hope that what information is presented here about Molly Miles, William Black, Cicaro and Phillis, Sara Lord and, Caesar Sankey—as well as concerning the great number of early people of color in Chapter Ten—will prompt further research by their descendants and/or other historians.

---

1. Everett S. Stackpole, *Old Kittery and Her Families* (Lewiston, Me.: Press of Lewistown Journal Co., 1903), 161.

2. Pepperrell Papers (MSO28), box 1, folder 8, Portsmouth Athenaeum, Portsmouth, N.H.

3. John T. Hull, ed. *York Deeds* (Portland, Me.: Thurston & Co., 1887), 3: 126; 4: 43, 52, 88.

4. York County Probate Court Records, Alfred, Me. (hereafter YCPCR), docket 2642.

5. Maine Historical Society, *Province and Court Records of Maine*, 6 vols. (Portland: Maine Historical Society, 1928–75), 4: 48, 49, 64-66; 5: x, lvii (hereafter *PCRM*). Some writers have confused two unrelated court cases and incorrectly identified a child, Jonathan, as son of Black Will, Sr.

6. Hull, *York Deeds*, 6: 43.

7. Hull, *York Deeds*, 6: 88.

8. John E. Frost, *Maine Probate Abstracts, 1687–1800,* 2 vols. (Camden, Me.: Picton Press, 1991), 1: 52.

9. Lorenzo Johnson Greene, *The Negro in Colonial America* (New York: Columbia University Press, 1942; reprint, New York: Atheneum, 1969), 138–39. See also Ellis Ames et al., *Commonwealth of Massachusetts Acts and Resolves, Public and Private, of the Massachusetts Bay*, 5 vols. (Boston: Wright and Potter, 1869–96), 1: 520.

10. Hull, *York Deeds*, 7: 113–14. William M. Sargent, comp., *Maine Wills, 1640–1760* (Portland, Me.: Brown Thurston & Co., 1887), 290.

11. *PCRM* 5: 39, 40: 4: 19. Stackpole, *Old Kittery*, 175–76.

12. *PCRM* 5: liii.

13. *PCRM* 5: 126, 201. The name of 1712 Brooks' child is unknown and no record has been found linking Brooks to Black Will's second son, Joshua.

14. *PCRM* 5: 48, 49, 64–66, 126, 169, 171.

15. *PCRM* 4: 389, 123.

16. Sargent, *Maine Wills,* 290–91.

17. Hull, *York Deeds*, 11: 107; 16:8; 12: part 1: 14.

18. Hull, *York Deeds*, 11: 107; 16: 8; 12: part 1:14.

19. H. H. Price and Gerald E. Talbot, *Maine's Visible Black History: The First Chronicle of Its People* (Gardiner, Me.: Tilbury House, 2006), 2, 13. York County Deeds, Alfred, Me. (hereafter YCD), 31: 163.

20. William F. Lord, "Black Sara" (unpublished memoir, 1897), Collections, Old Berwick Historical Society, Berwick, Me. Joseph C. Anderson, *Records of the First and Second Church of Berwick, Maine.* (Camden, Me.: Maine Genealogical Society, 1999), 58. YCPCR, docket 12221.

21. Lord, "Black Sara."

22. Sarah's death date is based on the fact that the Reverend Andrew Merriam became pastor at North Parish Church in 1768 and he was her "beloved pastor" for twenty-five years prior to her death.

23. There has been reference to a Caesar in connection with Sarah, even to a probably modern-day chiseling of that name on one of Sarah's burial

stones, but there is no evidence of any such person connected with her. Lord never mentions Caesar or any name for Sarah's husband.

24. "First Parish Church Records, Kittery Point, Maine 1715–1797," *New England Historical and Genealogical Register* 152 (1997): 448–49.

25. Sargent, *Maine Wills*, 845.

26. Pepperrell Papers, MS093, item 14, Portsmouth Athenaeum, Portsmouth, N.H.

27. Stackpole, *Old Kittery*, 48–49.

28. Oliver P. Remick, *A Record of the Services of the Commissioned Officers and Enlisted Men of Kittery and Eliot, Maine, Who Served Their Country on Land and Sea in the American Revolution, from 1775 to 1783* (Boston: Alfred Mudge & Son, 1901), 72. (Militia unit commanded by Lady Pepperrell's neighbor, Robert Follett.) William Bell Clark, ed., *Naval Documents of the American Revolution*, vol. 2 (Washington, D.C.: U.S. Government Printing Office, 1966), 832.

29. John E. Frost, *Maine Probate Abstracts, 1687–1800*, 2 vols. (Camden, Me.: Picton Press, 1991), 959.

30. Mary Pepperrell Sparhawk, *Life and Times of the Hon. William Jarvis* (New York: Hurd & Houghton, 1869), 428–29.

31. Stackpole, *Old Kittery*, 48–49.

32. Sargent, *Maine Wills*, 814–16. Frost, *Maine Probate Abstracts*, 483.

33. *Maine History & Genealogical Recorder* (1884) 7: 208; Stackpole, *Old Kittery*, 205, 20. See also Appendix Two. H. J. Cadbury, "Negro Members of the Society of Friends," *Journal of Negro History* 21 (1936): 97. "Minutes of the Dover [Quaker] Meeting," ii, 139, Dover Public Library, Dover, N. H. The deed was not signed or marked by Caesar; instead, James Neal signed it. There is no Caesar Sankey in the index to YCD.

34. YCD, 76: 23. "Minutes of the Dover Meeting," 139.

35. "Minutes of the Dover Meeting," 123

36. Glenn Knoblock, *Strong and Brave Fellows: New Hampshire's Black Soldiers and Sailors in the American Revolution* (Jefferson, N.C.: McFarland & Co., 2003), 164–65.

37. Joseph C. Anderson II and Lois Ware Thurston, eds., *Vital Records of Kittery, Maine, to the Year 1892,* Maine Genealogical Society Special Publication no. 8 (Camden, Me.: Picton Press, 1991), 125

38. "Notes and Queries," *New England Historical and Genealogical Register* 36 (1882): 193–94.

39. *1790 Census of Maine, Annotated Edition,* Maine Genealogical Society Special Publication 20 (Camden: Picton Press, 1995), 60. York County Court of Common Pleas and General Sessions (hereafter YCCCP), box 24: 19. See also Stackpole, *Old Kittery,* 52, 141,191.

40. *Portsmouth Journal of Literature & Politics,* Nov. 20, 1822, and Oct. 23, 1823. *New Hampshire Gazette,* Oct. 14, 1823.

41. *Newburyport Herald,* Oct. 21, 1823. *Hartford Times,* Oct. 21, 1823. *Sentinel & Witness* (Middletown, Conn.), Oct. 22, 1823. *Trenton Federalist,* Oct. 21, 1823. *The Washington* Whig (Bridgeton, N.J.), Dec. 6, 1823.

42. *Portsmouth Journal of Politics & Literature,* Mar. 10, 1827.

43. *New Hampshire Gazette,* Mar. 12, 1827; *New Bedford Mercury,* Mar. 16, 1827; *New Hampshire Patriot & State Gazette,* Mar. 19, 1827; *Weekly Eastern Argus* (Portland, Me.), Mar. 20, 1827; *Hallowell Gazette* (Me.), Mar. 28, 1827.

44. The Reverend Alan Cutter provided extensive written details on the table's descent from Sarah Foye Payne to various Foye family relatives; see the object file, Portsmouth Historical Society. See also Gerald W. R. Ward, with Hollis Brodrick and Lainey McCartney, *Four Centuries of Furniture in Portsmouth, with the New Hampshire Furniture Masters,* Portsmouth Marine Society no. 38 (Portsmouth, N.H.: Portsmouth Marine Society, 2017), cat no. 23.

CHAPTER SIX

A Matter of Control

Along with the myth of slavery being uncommon in New England there often goes the notion that enslaved Blacks here were passive, that because of generally better living conditions and reportedly less harsh treatment than in southern regions, they bore slavery's yoke without much struggle. But such was definitely not the case. Evidence abounds throughout New England of Blacks' resistance, of their escaping or confronting owners for a means to freedom or finding ways to lessen slavery's restrictions on them and their family members.[1]

Ran-away from his Master, William Pepperrell, Esqr. at Kittery, in the Province of Maine, a Negro man-slave named Peter, age about 20, speaks good English, of a pretty brown complexion, middle stature, has on a mixt gray home-spun coat, white home-spun jacket and breeches, French fall [faille] shoes, sad coloured stockings or a mixt worsted pair and Black hat. Whoever shall take up said Negro and bring or convey him either to his master or to Andrew Belcher, Esqr. of Boston shall be well rewarded.
— *The Boston News-Letter*, December 10, 1705

Ran-away from Ichabod Goodwin of Berwick, a Negro man named Pompey, a short thick-set fellow, had on when he went away a homespun double breasted light colour'd jacket, plain pewter buttons: one of his ears is cut . . . . Four pounds reward.
— *The Boston Post Boy*, January 25, 1748

Ran away from me the subscriber, a Negro man named Newport, about 34 years of age, five feet five inches high; had on a brown homespun round tail jacket, tow shirt, tow long trowsers, a felt hat, speaks good English, had a pair of moose skin breeches and is scar'd in his temples, which was done in Guinea . . . five dollars reward and all necessary charges paid by Tilly Higgins [of Berwick].

     —*The Freeman's Journal*, August 2, 1776

How many slaves in this area may have chosen self-manumission is unknown. Likely, there were more than the eight found in newspaper advertisements—the above named men and also Pomp, held by Dennis Fernald, Adam held by Benjamin Fernald, Cato held by William Wentworth, an unnamed man held by Samuel Johnson, and another Cato held by William Haley. Today, we might not even know of those intrepid Kittery Blacks if the owners had remained anonymous as was often the custom when placing advertisements for runaways. In that case, responders or informants were merely told to leave word at the printer's office.[2]

Advertisement in Essex Gazette, *June 1772, Salem, Massachusetts. Courtesy of American Antiquarian Society.*

Except for Peter and Pompey, the records are silent as to what happened to the others later on. Perhaps Fate was kind and allowed those men to avoid recapture and the brutal punishment that could follow. Slave owners also had the option of selling troublesome Blacks or shipping them away to the greater harshness of slavery on a southern or Caribbean island plantation. The possibility of that fate no doubt deterred many of New England's enslaved people.

Peter managed to get as far as Charlestown, South Carolina, before being caught by authorities. In April 1706, he and another enslaved person, "an Indian," were shipped back to Pepperrell. Whatever their treatment afterward was remains unrecorded. Also missing is any mention of how Charlestown authorities happened to spot Peter. Doubtless they knew of Pepperrell's quite descriptive advertisement and just maybe it was those fancy silk-covered shoes that gave Peter away. More likely, though, they discovered him because he lacked the official pass required for slaves to move about unaccompanied in public.[3]

Eight years later the record picks up Peter's story and, though in much poorer condition than in 1705, he had again made a bid for his freedom, but this time from a different slave owner. In May 1714, Joseph Tuck of Beverly, Massachusetts, sought return of his runaway Negro man-servant named Peter "who formerly belonged to William Pepperrell." The newspaper advertisement gave more clues as to Peter's subsequent life. From it we learn that not only did Pepperrell soon sell him to someone in the Boston area, Peter was re-sold three times in the next eight years to different owners: a Mr. Boremen, tanner of Cambridge, Mr. Merecock of Boston, and Mr. Hubbard of Middleton. Peter's strong will may have labelled him as "trouble," but he must have had a special skill or ability that made him quite resalable despite that.

Tuck's description of Peter is revealing, not only of what slavery had done to the now twenty-nine-year-old Black man, but of his courage in risking escape once more. He is "a slim fellow, not very tall, goes a little lame, lost his fore-upper teeth, has on a close-bodied coat and pale copper-coloured jacket, coat and jacket tarr'd [torn] in some places, white worsted stockings, leather breeches and French fall shoes, the heels goes much back." The outcome for Peter after 1714 is unknown. Perhaps freedom was finally his for the keeping, and he soon found the wherewithal to replace those run-down fancy shoes with something sturdy and less conspicuous.[4]

As for previously mentioned Pompey, he was still on his own a year and a half later when Goodwin again advertised for "Pomp" and stated, "It is said he has changed his clothes since he ran away." Unfortunately, Pompey was soon re-captured, but that did not deter him. On July 19, 1750, he again escaped and four days later the following appeared in *The Boston Post-Boy*[5]:

> RAN-away the 19th of *July*, from *Ichabod Goodwin of Berwick*, in the County of *York*, a Negro Man named *Pompey*, about 40 Years of Age, a fhort well-fet Fellow, fpeaks good Englifh, he had on a pair of Pot-hooks when he went away, a pair of Trowfers, a homefpun Jacket, and a check'd woolen Shirt, and has one of his Ears cut. Likewife a tall flim young Fellow named *William Najon*, of light Complection and light Hair: Whoever takes up faid Servants and delivers them to their Mafter, or fecures them fo that they may be had again, fhall have *Ten Pounds* Old Tenor Reward, with all reasonable Charges paid by   *Ichabod Goodwin.*
>
> *N. B.* All Mafters of Veffels are hereby forewarned carrying them off, as they may expect to anfwer at their Peril.

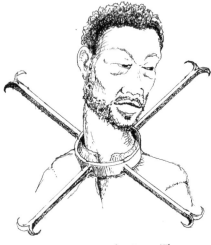

Pot-hooks. Drawing by Steve Thompson.

That notice not only paints a clearer picture of Pompey and the circumstances of slavery in this region, it reveals something quite dreadful—a brutality rarely mentioned in connection with New England's enslaved. Pompey "had on a pair of Pot-hooks when he went away." In addition to bearing a cruel ear-mark, a cutting or notching more commonly used to identify cattle, Pompey had also been fitted with a painful iron slave's collar, one with long, hooked prongs that hampered normal movement and even made lying down just about impossible. Such a device was placed on slaves prone to running away. And, Goodwin, being a blacksmith, likely was the person who made that collar and saw to its placement.

What is particularly intriguing about Goodwin's advertisement is the casual mention of pot-hooks. Not only was it assumed that readers would know what that device looked like, it suggests that use of it may not have been as uncommon as believed in New England.

Negotiating for Control

Although no first-hand accounts of slaves' daily life in Kittery or Berwick have been found, various other records show, or suggest, efforts by some to gain a bit of control over their personal life while having to remain in place. Living in such close contact with owner families sometimes made it possible to negotiate special privileges—time off to visit nearby friends or loved ones, earn a bit of money of one's own by farming a separate small patch of the slave owner's land and selling the produce, and/or by doing odd jobs for neighbors. A wise owner would have soon realized that, short of freeing his slave, it was in his own best interest to allow some accommodations while keeping his household or business in working order. Black Will's story is a prime example of gradually loosening slavery's bounds before finally gaining one's freedom.

Standing up for oneself, seeking privileges and a bit more self-determination sometimes carried the risk of slave owner displeasure. In a household where the owner or his wife, or both, were short-tempered, even the mildest form of resistance or self-assertion—a slave's quiet comment, a ventured opinion—could result in a slap, a punch, or worse. Considering Puritans' stern disciplinary beliefs and practices as applied to family and the general public, severe punishment of slaves may have been more common in New England than what little is documented. Hereabouts, records are silent on that matter until 1694 when an enslaved Black woman, Rachel, was beaten to death. And even that record, as it now exists, reveals nothing about what actually happened.

On January 1, 1695, a Kittery grand jury brought the following indictment before the York County Court: "We present Nathaniel Keen for suspicion of Murdering a Negro woman as appears in several evidences." Such determination was based on "eleven evidences" (number of witnesses testifying) and inspection of Rachel's body. Such an indictment no doubt caused a sensation far and wide. Though killing of a slave was rare in New England, colonial law at that time was murky regarding its criminality. Nine years earlier, the government in England had issued a directive that it should be made a capital offense, punishable by death, but there was no follow-through on making such a law—at least in Massachusetts—and the issue remained unclear for an extended period of time.[6]

Keen was arrested and jailed for two weeks before being released on bail. Then at trial the following May, for some unknown reason, the Grand Jurors presented a reduced indictment. Instead of murder, Keen was tried and convicted merely for "cruelty to his Negro woman by cruel beating and hard usage." His sentence: a fine of £5. The judge, however, delayed Keen's paying of that "until further order of this court." More immediately, he was ordered to pay court costs of £5.10.0 or be jailed until he did so. Regarding the stated punishment for Keen's crime, that other £5 fine, no "further court order" has been found requiring him to pay it.[7]

Commonly, the existing files of the York County Courts are replete with accounts of case proceedings and much very detailed testimony. In this case, however, all papers regarding testimony of the eleven witnesses summoned by the constable and also most of the proceedings during Keen's trial disappeared from court files long before any historian could take note. There remains only a tantalizing mystery as to who saw what and who became suspicious and reported Rachel's death to authorities. Nor can we know what or who influenced Grand Jurors to change their minds on that later indictment.

However, hints concerning the background of Rachel's killing are revealed in a series of other court cases involving Keen as well as his wife, Sarah. It appears all too evident that Rachel endured her enslavement at the hands of owners infamous for their hot tempers, vindictiveness, and occasional acts of violence against their neighbors and others. In one thoroughly detailed case, Nathaniel Keen went after a neighbor's child with a stick and then assaulted and nearly strangled the mother when she came to rescue her child. During another incident, Keen and his wife took up a handspike and an axe to threaten a local official.[8]

Today, Keen's property has been obliterated by the Kittery Traffic Circle and nearby Town Hall. All that remains is his family's tiny, out-of-sight, and neglected burial ground containing a few markers—none of which bears the name Rachel.

Violence Compounded

Another case of owner violence against his slave had a different outcome. The slave retaliated against the owner in a strange and horrifying way. That occurrence is the only known example in Kittery or Berwick of a slave committing crime against his owner. It also is the only record of suicide being mentioned as a way out of slavery.

During the night of July 15, 1755, near the head of Spruce Creek, enslaved Toney killed five-year-old Mary, daughter of his owner, Samuel Johnson, by throwing the child down a well. Toney then walked to the next town, York, and turned himself over to the county sheriff. He gave a long, convoluted confession of his crime, saying his master's repeated beating had driven him to murder as a way to get himself killed. He was held in jail until his trial and conviction a year later. On Thursday, July 29, 1756, Toney was hanged before the public in York Village. (Probably just outside of present-day Old York Gaol.)

"Do not spare [murderers] upon any pretense if they be clearly proven such." Judicial doctrine of the times offered no alternative but the gallows. Toney's confession apparently was the only evidence considered. If a defense attorney presented arguments during the trial or before sentencing, no record of that remains. In modern times, an astute lawyer would have offered a plea of insanity and pointed out mitigating circumstances, perhaps enough to at least change the sentence to life in prison. There likely would have been testimony and evidence revealing slave-owner Johnson's well-known hot temper and combativeness, perhaps getting into details of an earlier court case involving his alleged beating of a neighbor, Mary King. Perhaps local Justices of the Peace, William Pepperrell and Robert Cutts could have been called to testify as to Johnson's belligerent behavior in their court in 1748. Upon Johnson being fined at that time for "public swearing and profane language" and ordered to post bond for his future good behavior, he told the justices "he'd be damned if he did."[9]

Something else might have been brought to such a court's attention. Six years before Toney was "driven to murder," Johnson advertised for the return of an unnamed runaway Negro man, a fact which might have made jurors wonder about Johnson's treatment of his slaves. If by chance, that runaway was Toney and he had suffered severe beating upon re-capture, that could add weight to Toney's claims in his confession and also to a lawyer's plea against a death penalty.[10]

Aside from speculating on what might have been, there is really little of solid record on this case, other than a one-page jury determination of the sentence and the judge's order that it be carried out. Even Toney's original confession is missing from the archives. All that remains of it are second-hand sources—several contemporary newspaper reports of the incident with edited or paraphrased references to parts of the confession. Reports carried such things as Toney saying he was driven to desperation, if not insanity, by Johnson's brutal beating, so much so, that he wanted to find a way to die. Another reported that Toney said he first considered suicide, but realizing that was a sin, he thought by killing someone else he would be brought to the gallows. Further, Toney reportedly said he first considered killing Johnson but "doubting whether he was fit [spiritually] for so sudden an end, he altered his design and pitched upon the poor innocent child because it had fewer sins to answer for and that would be a less evil to destroy such a one as any other."[11]

The Isolation Factor

As mentioned previously, one hardship which many rural New England enslaved Blacks endured, that most Southern or Caribbean ones did not, was isolation or limited contact with other Blacks. Although it is difficult to know exactly how much that hampered those New Englanders' efforts to gain some control over their personal lives or find a less hazardous way to freedom, there seems little doubt that it did in this Maine area.

Though full details are lacking, it appears that many enslaved Blacks existed as the only "servant" in white households which were often distant, sometimes far distant, from one another. Travel to visit other Blacks (if an owner permitted more likely for men than for women) could be difficult, even dangerous, prior to about 1730 or so. Roadways were little more than rough paths over difficult terrain and possible attack by marauding Indians was still a fact of life. Maine's long, snowy winters and spring mud season only compounded the problem.

Such isolation must have been quite stressful. Much would have depended on factors such as the age, an individual's emotional stamina, whether they were recent arrivals or native-born New Englanders and, of course, on the attitude of his or her slave owner. But no matter how benign an owner may have been, it is likely that the weight of slavery, its hopelessness and alienation, whites' occasional verbal reminders of 'otherness' and inferior status, would have pressed downward.

For some, a lessening of isolation came when another enslaved Black was added to a household. Such was the case in households of the Cutts, Shapleigh, Frost, and a couple of other slave owners before 1700. After that time, only about a quarter of the 186 slave owners so far identified in this research had more than one enslaved Black (rarely more than two) in their household at a time.[12]

Of course, the presence of a white indentured servant could also ease a Black's isolation and provide some companionship, at least until the white's term of service was ended. Records of the indentured in this locale, however, are far more scarce than that for enslaved Blacks. Beyond the three or four found in this research, there is no way to estimate their number.[13]

It should be mentioned, however, that there were some occasions prior to 1725 when local Blacks, both enslaved and the very few free by then, did gather together in small numbers. During the period of

various Indian wars between 1674 and the Peace of 1725, white settlers had built fortified houses or garrisons at various locations. When
an alarm sounded, they and their servants would take shelter at an
assigned garrison. Some of those were large enough to shelter four or
five families. One built in Berwick by Ichabod Plaisted in 1700 had
8 fireplaces and could accommodate 74 people or 14 families. One
can well imagine the range of human drama and interaction in such
crowded conditions while they all waited out the danger, perhaps for
many days at a time.[14]

A more dependable source of relief from an enslaved Black's isolation came when owners began bringing her or him to the meetinghouse on Sabbath day, if circumstances and a given owner's religious
inclinations made that possible. Though Puritan law required such
attendance (and even threatened a fine if owners left their servants at
home), weather and illness in the family could cancel attendance. Also,
if an owner was one of the many persons cited in parish and court
records for frequent non-attendance, the isolated slave had to forego
even those few hours of comforting social contact.

How soon enslaved Blacks began attending church in this area is
unknown. Ministers' records prior to 1714 are missing and, up until
the late 1720s, slave owners may have had some reluctance about their
attending. Leading Massachusetts ministers such as John Eliot and
Cotton Mather had long been urging the Christianization of slaves,
but many New Englanders believed that might not be in owners' best
interest. They worried that it might make slaves unmanageable or that
baptism might mean automatic emancipation due to certain biblical
teachings. Finally in 1729, Puritan leaders appealed to British author-
ity in England for clarification and the reply assured them that baptism
did not result in emancipation.[15]

Coffee, a.k.a. Cuff, owned by Elisha Plaisted of Berwick, appears
to have been the first local Black to formally join the church. In April
1722, he accepted church doctrine by the traditional owning of the covenant and was baptized. For some odd reason, he repeated this process
twenty-two years later, but his relationship with the church became a
bit rocky. In 1744, he was accused of fornication (an accusation quite

often found in church and court records, regardless of race) and he was suspended from communion. Two years later, however, Cuff repented and the entire congregation "voted in favor of his restoration."[16]

Next came Richard "Blisk or Black, Negro" who joined the Kittery Point Church on October 27, 1728. Possibly free, he was living on a small piece of land near the Battery (now Fort McClary) which he purchased at some time from William Pepperrell. Within a decade or so, the number of Blacks establishing a church relationship either through baptism and/or owning the covenant began to increase. Caesar, his wife, Dinah, Richard's wife, Dinah, and Pompey had done so by 1740. Their status as free or enslaved is unknown.

During the next ten years, thirty-three more enslaved Blacks added their names to church records. This rapid increase was no doubt the result of the Great Awakening in New England, a time when fiery sermons by traveling preachers such as George Whitefield and Jonathan Edwards stirred Congregationalists into a frenzy of spiritual renewal. In the fall of 1740, Whitefield journeyed between Portsmouth and York and may have paused to preach from the high pulpit at Kittery Point Church.[17]

After that time, however, the number of additional Blacks joining the church or being baptized dropped off radically. During the rest of slavery's era, only nine others are found in records. Still, such a small number of officially church-connected Blacks would not have meant that segregated benches or galleries were nearly empty. Black population apparently continued to be substantial in every parish location—at the Point, in upper Kittery, and at Berwick. Aside from government-required attendance, those meetinghouses must have provided the one consistent, sanity-saving opportunity—especially for the more isolated Black women—to strengthen emotional fortitude through contact with other Blacks.

Marriage and Family

In trying to loosen slavery's restrictions, gain a sense of control over some part of one's life in slavery, finding a mate and having a family likely brought that goal closer, at least for a time. Acquiring a mate could provide opportunity to negotiate with one's owner for more living space, perhaps even a separate cabin and additional furnishings, clothing, and other amenities. That is, if one's intended mate lived in or was allowed to be brought to the same household. Otherwise, the man or woman had to negotiate for visitation time. With perhaps one or two exceptions, there is nothing in the records to indicate which enslaved couples lived together or apart. There were very few publicly noted marriages among the known enslaved. Only two are on record before 1750 and just eight others occurred before 1783. Records, mostly in the latter part of the century, show twenty-two other married Black couples, but determining their free or slave status at the time is not possible.[18]

Officially performed marriages or those carried out with African traditions did not mean that slave owners were bound to respect such marital ties when it came to a future sale or re-distribution of property. In the eyes of Massachusetts authorities, slaves' marriages were little more than useless ceremonies and not accorded the same legal standing as white marriages.[19]

Uncertainty haunted the life of an enslaved Black person, especially so for married or otherwise established couples. The possibility of owner-forced separation was dreadful enough, but even the thought of having one or more of their children sold or given away was unbearable. The latter occurrence could also happen to a couple in which the man was legally free and his wife was not. As mentioned here previously, the slave or free status of a child traditionally followed that of the mother.[20]

However, at least one Kittery Point enslaved man found a solution to safeguard his future children's status (see Underwood deed of sale on next page).

Since one of the very few rights granted to Blacks by Massachusetts was that of owning property, Sambo could now be certain that Phillis (who most likely became his wife) as well as any future children would always be with him no matter what his owner, the Reverend Stevens, wanted to do. And, while there is no record of such, if Sambo also publically declared Phillis free, that would have further assured her

Underwood deed of sale. November 9, 1778. Source: York County, Maine, Probate Records, 13:1.

security and that of their offspring. Curiosity always begs for more, but there was little else of reliable record found concerning Sambo. In 1790, according to the U. S. Census, he and his family of four were still living with or near the Reverend Benjamin Stevens at Kittery Point, but what happened to them after Stevens died a year later is unknown.[21]

---

1. Lorenzo Johnson Greene, *The Negro in Colonial America* (New York: Columbia University Press, 1942; reprint, New York: Atheneum, 1969), 144–66.

2. J. L. M. Willis, ed., *Old Eliot: A Monthly Magazine of the History and Biography of the Upper Parish of Kittery, Now Eliot* (Eliot, Me.: Augustin Caldwell, 1897–[1909]), 1: 144 (original document not found). See Appendix Two. See also *New Hampshire Gazette,* June 1, 1764; *Boston Weekly Post Boy,* May 18, 1749.

3. *Boston Weekly News-Letter,* Apr. 22, 1706.

4. *Boston News-Letter*, Mar. 14, 1714.

5. *Boston Post Boy,* July 20, 1750.

6. Greene, *Negro in Colonial America,* 233–34. Greene spells the enslaved person's name as "Cane."

7. Ibid., 234.

8. Neal W. Allen, *Province and Court Records of Maine* (Portland: Maine Historical Society, 1958), 4:34–35, 372. Neal W. Allen, "Nathaniel Kene of Spruce Creek: A Portrait from the Court Records," *Old-Time New England* 53, no. 4 (April-June 1963): 92–94. Greene, *Negro in Colonial America*, 234.

9. York County Court of Common Pleas, Collections of the Maine State Archives, Augusta, Me., 66: 2; 10: 451–52. Allen, *Province and Court Records of Maine*, 1:216.

10. See Samuel Johnson, Appendix Two.

11. For Tony's indictment, see Massachusetts Superior Court of Judicature (Boston), vol. 1755–56: 250. For his death warrant, see Suffolk County Court Files, 859: 27–28. *Boston Evening-Post*, Aug. 11, 1755, and June 28, 1756. Daniel A. Hearn, *Legal Executions in New England, 1623–1960* (Jefferson, N.C.: McFarland & Co., 1999), 143–44.

12. See Appendix Two.

13. Ibid.; see Chadbourne, Hook, and Shapleigh.

14. Everett S. Stackpole, *Old Kittery and Her Families* (Lewiston, Me.: Press of Lewistown Journal Co., 1903), 177.

15. Greene, *Negro in Colonial America*, 260.

16. Joseph C. Anderson, ed., *Records of the First and Second Churches of Berwick, Maine*, Maine Genealogical Society Special Publication 33 (Rockland, Me.: Picton Press, 1999), 57, 59.

17. "First Parish Church Records of Kittery," *New England Historical and Genealogical Society Journal* 152 (1998): 232. York County Deeds, Alfred, Me., 48: 211, 212. "First Parish Church Records," 46, 357. See also list of Baptisms, Appendix Three B. Reverend L. Tyerman, *The Life of the Reverend George Whitefield, BA of Pembroke College, Oxford* (New York: Anson D. F. Randolph & Co., 1877), 416.

18. Re marriages, see Appendix Three B.

19. George Washington Williams, *History of the Negro Race in America, 1619–1880* (1883; reprint, New York: Arno Press, 1968), 191–93.

20. Greene, *Negro in Colonial America*, 211.

21. John E. Frost, *Maine Probate Abstracts, 1687–1800,* 2 vols. (Camden, Me.: Picton Press, 1991), vi, 727. U.S. Census 1790, Maine. Sambo is

mentioned without documentation in Eliza Buckminster Lee's *Memoirs of the Reverend Joseph Buckminster and His Son, Joseph Stevens Buckminster* (Boston: William Crosby & H. P. Nichols, 1849), 54. (Clergy owning slaves was quite common throughout New England. For this Maine area, see J. Newmarch, J. Rogers, A. Spring, and J. Wise in Appendix Two.)

Chapter Seven

False Dawn

By the late 1760s, nearly a decade before the American colonies declared open rebellion against Britain's autocratic rule, a new hopefulness was beginning to spread among enslaved Blacks throughout Massachusetts. Public opposition to the slave trade and slavery was gradually coming to the forefront. Such hope among the enslaved was no doubt enhanced by an awareness of a gradual increase in the number of free Blacks in this area, men as well as a few women.

On Sabbath Days, when gathered in those Blacks-only galleries at the various meetinghouses, the enslaved would have been well aware of the free Blacks seated among them. At times, such awareness and the longing it could engender must have proved a distraction as the enslaved tried to concentrate on those hour-long prayers followed by the minister's two- or three-hour sermon.

Such distractedness was likely more common at the meetinghouse in Kittery's upper section and at Kittery Point than it was in Berwick. By the 1760s, those sections not only had substantial populations of the enslaved, they also had a large number of independently living Blacks, some free and others possibly so. It is probable that most of the upper Kittery group were settled on or near those one hundred acres purchased in 1697 by Black Will, Sr. Among them were two generations of his descendants and their families as well as those of Will's friend, Anthony Freeman. Over time, other Black men and their families such as Lambo Marsh and persons with surnames Patch, Wittam, and Hanscom also joined this enclave of farmers, sheep herders, spinners, and weavers.[1]

Given the scarcity of exacting records, it is impossible in many cases to say who was legally free and who still remained under slavery's yoke. For some, in the end, it all came down to the status of one's mother. Also, for quite a number of persons living independently, it is unknown if they had been in this area for a long time, perhaps once enslaved, or were newcomers at some point.[2]

At Kittery Point Parish, however, legally free Blacks were much in evidence by mid-century. Some, such as Tobey, Scipio, and George had been set free in the will of William Pepperrell, Sr. Here, too, were Henry and Bridgit Miles, and Thomas Hercules and his wife, Mary. Those two families of color lived close to what is now Spruce Creek Bridge. About a half-mile away was probably free Richard Black and his family. Living nearby may have been a free woman named Clear and her elderly mother, Bess. Both had once been enslaved by the Elliott and Gerrish families. Even so, by the mid-1760s, this First or Lower Parish, like Kittery's Middle Parish, still had a considerable population of enslaved Blacks.[3]

Anti-Slavery Movement

Aside from an enslaved person's musings about the free status of others during those long Sabbath Day services, a greater distraction would probably have been the latest news concerning a possible end to slavery. And, such news would not have been slow in coming to their notice.

Life constantly placed enslaved Blacks in the path of the latest news and rumors, making them silent witness to owners' conversations and arguments, presenting opportunities to read cast-aside newspapers and pamphlets, or glance at owners' letters and journals left unattended. Those who accompanied owners on weekly, sometimes daily, ferry rides to Portsmouth and on frequent trips to Newburyport, Salem, Boston, and elsewhere, brought home treasure troves of news. Of course, one major occasion for local Blacks' to share such news and discuss it among themselves was during the noontime break between Sabbath Day services.

By the spring of 1767, encouraging news was arriving from many directions. In Newburyport, mulatto woman Jenny Slew had finally won her four-year-long court battle for freedom from owner John Whipple, Jr., of Ipswich. She was also awarded "four pounds money and [court] costs." But even more exciting news was emanating from Boston. On March 13, a bill to end slavery and the slave trade had been introduced into the Massachusetts House of Representatives.

Pressure for that came from Boston and several other towns, but apparently not from either Berwick or Kittery. Boston wanted a law to "prohibit importation and the purchase of slaves for the future." The town of Worcester instructed its representative to the House to "use his influence to obtain a law to put an end to that unchristian and impolitic practice of making slaves of the human species" and to use his vote to block potential new members to "His Majesty's Council who will use their influence against such a law."[4]

Also, about that time, there were rumors that some Massachusetts towns were considering the freeing of all their slaves and then indemnifying their owners "from any expense . . . that might arise [afterward] by reason of [Blacks'] age, infirmities, or ability to support themselves." Such rumors were likely little more than that, especially considering towns' long-standing policy of avoiding any expense involving freed slaves. But, the effect of such rumors must have been stunning to all concerned.[5]

One can well imagine the excitement at those Sabbath Day noontime gatherings in Kittery and Berwick as Black young people and their elders—perhaps optimists versus skeptics—would have worked over such glimmers of real hope. Passing around jugs of cider and munching on fat chunks of meat pies, young men and women may have expressed belief that freedom was near at hand, while some older, longer-suffering Blacks might have shaken their heads in doubt. Perhaps one of the skeptics might have tried to put a damper on such excitement by pointing out an ominous occurrence over in Portsmouth in the last few years: that small numbers of Blacks had been shipped away to southern colonies and other distant ports. And, just maybe that would increase because slave owners were trying to sell out before slavery became illegal. Optimists, however, might have quickly pounced on that damper as simply more evidence of a change in the law coming soon.[6]

Over the next eight or so years, however, Fate seemed to toy with the enslaved in Massachusetts, at times raising hopes high, at others letting it fade away. That proposed bill in 1767 went nowhere. In fact, by the time initial news of it would have reached this area, it was already failing. Within a few days after it was introduced to the House of Representatives in early March, then passed around and debated, a majority of legislators backed away. It was simply ordered "that the matter subside"—i.e., do nothing and let it go away.[7]

In the meantime, hope of freedom was being kept alive by more newspaper articles and several pamphlets by Massachusetts clergy and other prominent men decrying such inhuman practice and pointing out its great hypocrisy at a time when colonials were likening Britain's oppressive tactics to slavery. In 1771, Blacks may have been encouraged by a couple of other bills before the Massachusetts Legislature calling for an end to the slave trade. It is unknown if their content included any measures to end the practice of slavery, but like that earlier bill, those also failed to be enacted.[8]

By 1773, however, hope was again on the rise and even reaching new heights. In this area those young optimists must have delighted in extolling the latest developments. By then, a few more Blacks elsewhere in the colony had won their freedom through the courts, and controversy over the slave trade, as well as slavery itself, was escalating in Massachusetts and elsewhere in New England. What no doubt raised hopes of even the most skeptical Blacks was special news from Boston early in January of that year. A group of enslaved Black men from there, along with others from a few surrounding towns, had begun a very public campaign for freedom.

On January 6, they sent a petition to the governor and his council describing their inhuman conditions and appealing for an end to their enslavement. That adroitly written petition was quickly published as a pamphlet. Soon, the group launched another and more widespread public appeal. On April 20, they sent copies of a printed petition to each House of Representative member from towns throughout Massachusetts, lobbying for their support. In their petition to the legislature they pointed out that "The divine spirit of freedom [now] seems to fire every human breast on this continent . . . " and they went on to say, "we cannot expect but that your [House] will again take our deplorable case into serious consideration and give us that simple relief which, as men, we have a natural right to."[9]

If a copy of that petition ever reached the House representatives for Kittery or Berwick, there is no mention of it or anything relating to the topic in either town's records. However, what happened elsewhere a month later seems more than just coincidental, it seems directly connected with that enterprising petition. In mid-May 1773, the towns of Salem, Medford, Leicester, Barnstable, and possibly others, instructed their representatives to act on the matter of the slave trade. And, on June 25, a petition from the Boston Black men was read before the House and a committee was appointed to consider its contents.[10]

Along with such heartening news that summer also came word New England Quakers had decided at their yearly June meeting to disown members who continued to hold slaves. Evidence of that change was soon apparent in this locale when Cesar Sankey gained his freedom from owner Andrew Neal. Other local slave-owning Quakers may have followed suit, but records of that have yet to be found.[11]

Even in 1774, at least for a while, Black optimists must have held sway over counterpart skeptics. By the first week of March, that Boston petition had not only prompted a formal bill before the House of Representatives, it had been approved by Council and now only awaited the governor's signature—which never came. But even if it had been signed, that particular bill would not have freed Massachusetts' slaves. Originally, it did address some of the issues in the Blacks' petition, but in the bill's final draft, all phrases regarding those issues were struck out. It had become merely a bill to end the slave *trade*.[12]

There is no knowing how well informed local Blacks were regarding the details of all those bills and what occurred in House debates. Aside from the occasional newspaper, news often arrived in outlying areas more as verbal headline, filtered by hearsay, than as fully detailed reports. Eventually though, as the truth behind the headlines began to emerge, freedom appeared elusive. In reality, most politicians were not seeking an immediate end to slavery. As a group they were seeking to end the importation of more slaves into Massachusetts. And they were doing so then primarily as a means to smite the British Parliament, show defiance, and threaten the Royal purse.

Even Massachusetts' town authorities in their various statements from 1767 to 1774 focused on the issue of ending the slave trade while tiptoeing around existing slave ownership. They offered colony legislators carefully worded suggestions for some sort of *gradual* emancipation over time, searching for ways to appease slave owners and avoid causing abrupt confiscation of private property.[13]

Then in October 1774, the new assembly of the thirteen colonies, the Continental Congress, eliminated one part of the controversy. As of the beginning of December, all importation and consumption of British-made goods as well as importation of slaves was to cease.

Groups of Blacks in Massachusetts, however, were not about to give up. They continued with their petitions and appeals from time to time over the next six years and prominent abolitionists throughout the colony kept speaking out in pulpits and in print. Blacks in the Kittery-Berwick area and elsewhere were probably still savoring a particularly astute and uplifting newspaper essay that had been prominently placed under the masthead of Salem's *Essex Journal and Merrimack Packet* in August 1774. Writing as "a well-wisher to his brethren who are now in that unhappy state [of slavery]," former slave Caesar Sarter of Newburyport lauded whites' perseverance in pursuing liberty but also reminded them of Blacks natural, God-given right to the same. Sarter's stance was forthright without pleading, and at one point, he chided whites with, "I need not point out the absurdity of your exertions for Liberty while you have a slave in your house."[14]

George H. Moore in his groundbreaking book, *Notes on the History of Slavery in Massachusetts,* chronicles the continuing and valiant struggle of Blacks to bring a straight forward and legal end to their enslavement. But, their efforts proved fruitless. Though few of the petitioners and protestors likely realized it, well before the spring of 1775, the issue of ending slavery in Massachusetts was politically dying, if not already dead, in the seat of government. White men would later offer the excuse that legislators were too distracted by the crisis with British troops in Boston and the possibility of Revolution, as well as appeasing Southern slave-owners in order to protect the slim political fabric of an emerging new nation.

More likely, those legislators—the ones who struck out each emancipation clause in a proposed bill and those who determined the final vote on same—were covetous of their own slaveholding property. With no clear plan on how to dismantle nearly a century and half of human bondage, legislators let each opportunity, each petition and heartfelt appeal from the Blacks slip from their hands. In the end, record after record shows Massachusetts simply "let the matter subside."[15]

---

1. More research is needed on this community's location. Also, some racial intermarriages presented difficulties in identity for this project.

2. Lorenzo Johnson Greene, *The Negro in Colonial America* (New York: Columbia University Press, 1942; reprint, New York: Atheneum, 1969), 126.

3. See Chapter Ten.

4. George Henry Moore, *Notes on the History of Slavery in Massachusetts* (New York: D. Appleton & Co., 1866; reprint, Whitefish, Mont.: Kessinger Publishing, 1988), 113, 124. The correct date re Worcester is 1767, not 1765.

5. Ibid., 125.

6. John Knowlton, comp., "British Shipping Records, Portsmouth, New Hampshire, 1694–1775," (microfilm printout with indexes, 2014, Portsmouth Athenaeum, Portsmouth, N.H.), 5: 489–90; 6: 541, 557, 571, 595, 611. It is not known if any Kittery or Berwick slave owners were involved in such apparent out-shipping.

7. Moore, *Notes on the History of Slavery in Massachusetts*, 126–28.

8. Moore, *Notes on the History of Slavery in Massachusetts,* 130–31.

9. Ibid., 131–35. Sidney Kaplan and Emma Nogrady Kaplan, *The Black Presence in the Era of the American Revolution* (Amherst: University of Massachusetts Press, 1989), 11, 14.

10. Moore, *Notes on the History of Slavery in Massachusetts*, 135.

11. "New England Yearly Meeting Minutes" for 1773 (microfilm), Friends Historical Library, Swarthmore College, Pa.

12. Moore, *Notes on the History of Slavery in Massachusetts,* 140.

13. Ibid., 124–25, 133–34.

14. Kaplan and Kaplan, *Black Presence,* 12.

15. Moore, *Notes on the History of Slavery in Massachusetts,* 144–47, 181–83. Kaplan and Kaplan, *Black Presence,* 11–13.

Chapter Eight

Bravery Knows No Color

Throughout the Kittery/Berwick area, men of African descent stepped forward to risk their lives in America's fight for Independence. Their exact number cannot be determined. Nor is it known, except in a few cases, under what circumstances they did so—free or enslaved. Their record of service, however, reads the same as that of the general Euro-American population: dedication, courage, occasional desertions, injury, and death on the battlefield. What was not the same was Black men's reward for their service. Though they were paid the same as their white counterparts, all were deliberately kept in the lowest ranks. Rarely does one encounter a rank above private and then only as corporal or, much rarer, as sergeant. Concerning naval service of local Black men, none has been found with a rank above seaman.[1]

From 1656 onward, Massachusetts law had excluded "Negroes, Indians and mulattoes" from serving in the military. Over the years, however, wartime expedience made inroads on such a rule. When town draft quotas could not be filled from the white population, Blacks were allowed to be enlisted. Black Will (either the father or the son) appears to have been the first Black (free or enslaved) in this area to serve in the military. He is listed with Kittery militia in 1713 and also in three "marches" or callouts against the Indians during 1725.[2]

For the enslaved man, there were a number of ways he might find himself marching in the ranks. He might have sought permission from his owner to enlist in hopes of earning sufficient military pay to buy his freedom or maybe purchase a bit of farm land or perhaps use the money to purchase tools or a cart to help him start a small business. On the other hand, an enslaved man may have been forced to endure the dangers of war without the least hope of money or freedom.

In colonial times it was quite acceptable for a white man to provide or hire a substitute to save himself or his sons from military draft. If he had an able-bodied slave, he could simply offer him up and save the money. At times, the enlisting of his human property was solely a mercenary matter, a chance to benefit from a substantial enlistment bounty plus the soldier's monthly pay. During the American Revolution, there are many records throughout New England of owners offering their slaves freedom in exchange for military duty or upon its completion.

Likely some such substituting and/or offers for freedom occurred in this area, but no clear references to that have been found. After the American Revolution one Kittery soldier, Prince Frederick, formerly enslaved in the Frost family, stated on his pension application that he "was entered by J. Frost in 1783." Such wording could suggest that Prince might not have enlisted entirely at his own volition.[3]

When William Pepperrell of Kittery led his 1745 expedition against the French at Fort Louisburg, Nova Scotia, local men of African descent, including Cato Farwell, George Black, Thomas and James Hercules, Henry Miles, and John Tobey, were in the ranks. Most of them served in Capt. Richard Cutts's Company from Kittery; others in that of Capt. Peter Staples from the same locale. Also, the grandsons of the first Will Black, Jonathan and Benjamin Black, may have served in that war. A year after it ended they were referred to in a land deed as "common soldiers."[4]

Having a last or surname did not necessarily indicate that a person was free at the time. For Blacks who were not, having one simply indicated that there had been some occasion on which one was chosen or required. The surname on such an occasion might be that of the slave owner or a different one selected by or for the enslaved person.

The above mentioned George Black and Cato Farwell are likely cases in point. It was not uncommon for officers to have a personal slave or two accompany them into a theater of war. An officer might then decide to place a male slave on the muster roll which required a surname and, incidentally, provide the benefit of an enlistment bounty and his slave's wages.

In 1745, a George (who is later known as George Black) and a Cato were among the slaves then being held by William Pepperrell. Cato Farwell is believed to be the same man referred to in one of General Pepperrell's letters from Louisburg. In writing to his wife Mary to ask for various supplies, Pepperrell added that "Catto will need a pair or two of large thick shoes, stockings and woolen shirts or two." The source of the surname Farwell is unknown.[5]

During the French and Indian War (1754–63), local men of African descent again served in the ranks. Thomas Black and Josiah Black are some who have been identified. Record of such service is not always from a muster roll. Sometimes that comes to light in an unusual way. For nineteen-year-old Thomas Black, grandson of Black Will, Sr., such record only comes about as a result of Thomas making a will on August 8, 1757: "I, Thomas Black of Kittery . . . Labourer, being bound on an expedition in His Majesty's Service and not knowing whether ever I shall return and how it may please Almighty God to deal with me, do make this my last will and testament." His brother, Henry, was to have his gun and wearing apparel plus half of his real estate and his sister, Margery, the rest. It remains unknown if Thomas ever returned from that expedition.[6]

Service records for Blacks in this area are far more numerous during the American Revolution. In May 1775, at least two men, Cato and Josiah Black, were among local militiamen sent to reinforce rebel forces surrounding British-held Boston. Within two weeks they were caught up in the horrific Battle of Bunker Hill. Meanwhile, in lower Kittery and neighboring Portsmouth, there was growing alarm over the presence of British warships at the mouth of the Piscataqua River. By late summer, militiamen were at work building and shoring up defense positions on both sides of the river. Men such as Cicaro, owned by Lady Pepperrell; William, owned by Robert Follett; Simon Tobey (mulatto or Indian); and Joseph Black were among Follett's company of militia working on Kittery Point's Fort William (formerly the Battery, now Fort McClary). At Kittery's Seavey Island, now part of Portsmouth Naval

Shipyard, Peter Tobey (likely a relative of Simon) was serving with New Hampshire militiamen in the construction of Fort Sullivan. In a short time, Simon Tobey went to serve there, either as re-assignment or perhaps as a new enlistment. Both men were from Kittery Point.[7]

That Matter of Exclusion

Throughout Massachusetts as well as across the river in New Hampshire, the law of excluding "Negroes, Indians and mulattoes" continued to be challenged (or ignored) as more and more Blacks were being enlisted and moved to defense locations. George Moore in his *Historical Notes on the Employment of Negroes in the American Army of the Revolution* (1862) reveals the controversy over their presence in the ranks as the Continental Army was first being organized at Cambridge, Massachusetts, in 1775. In early June, a few weeks before General George Washington arrived to take command, Major General Artemus Ward ordered the colonels of each regiment to make a detailed return or accounting of their soldiers and to include, among other notations, a description of their "complexion."[8]

Washington was much annoyed at finding Blacks among the troops and he soon issued an order that no Negroes be enlisted. However, he gave no orders regarding those already in the ranks. During the next six months, Blacks' military service continued to be a hot-button issue at Washington's staff meetings as well as in those of Massachusetts legislators and the Continental Congress. Moore's *Historical Notes* proves interesting reading as to the round and round of it all, of those arguing in favor of Blacks serving and those against, of proposals made for inclusion and proposals rejected. Finally in mid-January 1776, Congress ruled that "free Negroes who have served faithfully in the army at Cambridge may be reenlisted therein, but no others." At the time, some officials may have thought the issue was settled but, barely a year later, the war's pressing needs and Black men's continuing determination to serve would prove them wrong.[9]

While Congress continued to deliberate on any over-all policy as to Blacks' military service (free or enslaved), here in Massachusetts the issue was settled as of January 26, 1777. Being instructed by Congress to form fifteen battalions before the end of February, the State instructed its commanding officers of militia companies and regiments to enlist "all [able-bodied] male inhabitants of each town, age sixteen or upward for three years." This time, and for the first time, Blacks, Indians, and mulattoes were *not* excluded. Only Quakers were. From then on, those already in service could remain while many others soon joined their ranks. Apparently there was no segregation at this point. Companies and other units contained men of all "complexions."[10]

Circumstances and Motivation

Little is known about the circumstances under which Kittery and Berwick Blacks enlisted with the Patriot forces in the American Revolution; what or who prompted them to do so and which man was free or enslaved at the time. Pension applications, completed by elderly Black veterans in the early nineteenth century, only reveal some personal and family data plus notations on dates and locations of their wartime service.

In regard to area Blacks who might have fought with or sought refuge with British forces in response to their 1775 offer of freedom, no information on that was encountered in this research. Though many thousands of enslaved Black men, women, and children from New York to Georgia did eventually flee to British protection, opportunities for that to occur in this part of Maine Province would have been quite rare. Once war was declared in 1776, primary theaters of war moved down to New York and southward.

Nevertheless, two possible opportunities do come to mind. In late spring and early summer of 1775, perhaps a few enslaved Blacks in Kittery may have secretly managed to reach one of the British naval vessels which occasionally entered the Piscataqua River or anchored off the Isle of Shoals. That is assuming, of course, that word had already reached this area about Britain offering slaves their freedom. A letter from England containing such an offer had been read at a meeting of Provincial officials in Boston shortly before May 17, 1775, and doubtless, public controversy over it spread rapidly. Another possibility is that some enslaved Blacks from this area may have sought freedom by joining the British in Canada, but to accomplish that they would have had to survive the hazards of a several-weeks journey through unbroken Maine wilderness.[11]

Patriots in Action

For enslaved men such as William, owned by Robert Follett of Kittery Point, there is only a stray bit here and there in records to reveal circumstances of his service. On August 12, 1777, "William Follett, a Creole" was among the crew of the newly built Continental frigate *Raleigh* as it eased down river to Piscataqua Harbor and sailed off into harm's way. More than likely, William had come aboard in June 1776 when Robert Follett was appointed Master of the ship. Robert was discharged from service the following January but his slave remained. However long William's period of service was—until April 1778 or five months after that—he must have come home a changed man, one more impatient than ever to gain his freedom. He had taken part in sea battles, visited a French port when the ship took on supplies, known the thrill of success when *Raleigh* captured a British vessel off Senegal and sailed in parts of the West Indies. Perhaps he was also aboard on the ship's second cruise when, in late September 1778, *Raleigh* had the misfortune to go aground in Maine's Penobscot Bay and fall into the hands of the British Navy. Part of the crew was captured, but William apparently was not among them.

Upon his return to Kittery Point, he found that Robert Follett expected him to continue on in slavery. William may have challenged him on that in some manner. At least that is what one document seems to suggest. On May 24, 1779, Follett made his will and its content reveals a William moving toward self-determination. "In consideration of my Negro man William serving me and my heirs and assigns two years from this date and behaving himself with respect to me and my assigns, grants freedom to sd. Negro who calls himself, William Simmonds." Though doubt remains, it seems likely William waited out that period of delay and then moved across the river. In 1790, the U. S. Census lists a William Simons as Black and living in Portsmouth, New Hampshire.[12]

Two other men of African descent, Peter Tobey and John Caswell, were also among that first crew of the *Raleigh* in 1776. They had enlisted in July, a month or so after the ship was launched. The Continental frigate *Raleigh* was the pride of the Piscataqua region and far beyond. Stoutly built, her 697-ton structure was well designed for battle and doubtless those aboard were eager to see her tested against the British Navy. By mid-November, however, *Raleigh* was still lingering at her mooring and some crewmen's patience was running out.

On Friday, the fifteenth of that month, another new vessel, the armed privateer *Dalton* from Newburyport, Massachusetts, came upriver and dropped anchor off Portsmouth. Compared to *Raleigh*, she was a minnow, a mere 160 tons, but her arrival and her intended mission was a bit of a challenge to the readiness of the frigate. Apparently, *Dalton's* complement of crewmen was not quite complete. The following Tuesday she sailed with the outgoing tide and aboard were various new recruits including Tobey and Caswell. They had chosen the lure of prize money from captured enemy vessels over regular navy service, a most unfortunate choice, as fate would have it.

Barely a month later, *Dalton* was captured by the British battleship HMS *Reasonable* off the coast of Spain and her crew roughly taken off and locked in the battleship's dank and cramped cable hold. Carried to England, they were eventually tried and convicted of high treason and confined to Mill Prison at Plymouth. Among surviving accounts of that capture, the terrible conditions of imprisonment and of eventual escapes and re-captures, there is no mention of Tobey or Caswell. However, one prison journal-writer, probably an officer, noted his annoyance that everyone was put together in the same cell space—"people, officers and negroes."

Finally, in March 1779, diplomatic arrangements were made between America and Britain for freeing *Dalton's* crew. Once safely home, Peter Tobey and John Caswell, along with some other surviving crewmen no doubt became popular storytellers at local gossip sites – taverns, general stores, blacksmith shops, and, of course, at those Sabbath Day noontime gatherings.[13]

Boston was another enslaved man of Kittery Point who served

in the Revolution. Owned by ship captain John Underwood, Boston first comes into records on June 27, 1773, when he married Zilphah, owned by Lady Mary Pepperrell. Three years later, he and Underwood were serving in the Revolutionary War, but in different New Hampshire militia units. As of July 20, 1776, Boston was already enlisted in Colonel Joshua Wingate's Regiment which was headed for Fort Ticonderoga. Bounty for enlistment plus some wages and travel expense had been paid, but to whom—Boston or Underwood—is unknown. In the meantime, Underwood remained behind to serve at Portsmouth's Fort Washington.

By spring 1777, Boston was home safe and sound, but it would not be long before he was placed in harm's way once again. On Wednesday, May 28, Captain Underwood was preparing to ship out on a privateer (name unknown), which was anchored in Kittery Point Harbor. He sent two of his officers to find Boston. After searching for several hours, they found him peacefully spearfishing for plaice (flat-fish) from a float in a creek between the mainland and Cutts' Island. Boston readily responded to their call and came near the shore, but the men insisted on beaching his float. Boston objected until they explained their errand. Returning to the Underwood house, Boston was immediately ordered to board the privateer and, a day or two later, the armed vessel set sail in search of British prey. From then on, records go silent and nothing has been found to tell us of Boston's service on the unnamed privateer or how that experience might have changed his life. Even as a mere crewman, he was legally entitled to a small share of proceeds from the sale of a captured enemy vessel and its cargo. If such occurred, that could have proved a major turning point, a chance to buy his freedom. With his wife Zilphah getting her freedom from Lady Pepperrell by 1779 or shortly before, this chapter of Boston's story could have had quite an upbeat ending.[14]

With further research, perhaps more insights into local Blacks' military service might be found. Certainly there are some intriguing hints here and there among servicemen listed in Appendix Three C. For example, what was Black Private Henry's heroic action that merited him a Badge of Honor (forerunner of today's Purple Heart) during the Revolution? And, what prevented George Patch from getting the "Honor Badge he said he was 'entitled to for faithful service"? What more might be revealed about several men who served throughout the war rather than during the more common short periods of enlistment? What more could be learned about several men who reported being among the troops at war's end when General Washington expressed his thanks for their faithful service?

Even identifying men as of African descent in military records is often difficult, if not impossible, despite General Artemus Ward's 1775 order that soldiers be identified on muster rolls and regimental lists by their "complexion." True, the matter of identity is simple when a listed man has an African-derived first name or an assigned slave name such as Pompey, Caesar, and so forth. Also true if his description is noted as Negro, mulatto, or "complexion Negro, hair wool." However, if a man had dropped the slave name and adopted a completely European-based name, the roll-taker's description of the man as "complexion dark, hair dark" or "complexion brown, hair dark," is not a reliable way to identify him as Black or of African descent. Records of Massachusetts soldiers and sailors are filled with those last two descriptions, but nearly always they are attached to men with entirely British or European names. To add to the confusion, quite often the complexion of the same European-named man is described differently on different muster rolls. All rested on the opinion of the officer doing the roll-taking. On one roll, a man might be listed as "dark," on another he was seen as "tawny," on still another as "light."[15]

By the time of the Revolution, there undoubtedly were a great many mulattoes, people of mixed African, white, and Indian heritage in New England and elsewhere. Though this is mere speculation, one begins to wonder if the total number of Africans and mulattoes in the Revolution may have been much more extensive than is believed. For communities such as Kittery and Berwick, at least, there does remain the unanswerable question as to how many men of color may never be recognized for their service in America's fight for independence because of variations in description and their having an entirely European name.

If, at war's end, Massachusetts' veterans of color believed their dedication and service would alter racism, they were soon disillusioned. Early in March 1785, state regulation came full circle. The new Militia Act once again banned "negroes, Indians or mulattoes" from serving in town "train bands" and the militia. Furthermore, Massachusetts' policy was reinforced in 1793 when the United States Congress restricted military service to "free white males."[16]

---

1. See Appendix Three C.

2. Wilber D. Spencer. "List of Revolutionary War Soldiers of Berwick" (unpublished typescript. NNB459, Maine Historical Society), 7. Lorenzo Johnson Greene, *The Negro in Colonial America* (New York: Columbia University Press, 1942; reprint, New York: Atheneum, 1969), 126–27. Nathaniel B. Shurtleff, ed., *Records of the Governor and Company of the Massachusetts Bay in New England*, 5 vols.in 6 (Boston: William White Press, 1853–54), 398.

3. Town Records for Kittery and Berwick, Town Clerk's Office, contain references on hiring what may have been substitutes for draftees during the American Revolution. The enlistment of Prince Frederick, Appendix Three C, is one example. See Gary Nash, *The Unknown American Revolution* (New York: Viking Penguin Group, 2005), chap. 1.

4. Henry D. Burrage, *Maine at Louisburg in 1745* (Augusta, Me: Burleigh & Flynn, 1910), 61, 68, 69. York County Deeds, Alfred, Me., 25: 267–68.

5. Burrage, *Maine at Louisburg*, 68, 78,100.

6. William M. Sargent, comp., *Maine Wills, 1640–1760* (Portland, Me.: Brown Thurston & Co., 1887), 807. J. L. M. Willis, ed., *Old Eliot: A Monthly Magazine of the History and Biography of the Upper Parish of Kittery, Now Eliot* (Eliot, Me.: Augustin Caldwell, 1897–[1909]), 2: 64.

7. See Appendix Three C.

8. George H. Moore, *Historical Notes on the Employment of Negroes in the American Army of the Revolution* (New York: Charles I. Evans, 1862), 6. New Hampshire also banned Negroes, Indians, and mulattoes from

service, but for some unknown reason, quite a few Blacks from the Kittery area enlisted there early in the Revolution.

9. Moore, *Historical Notes on the Employment of Negroes*, 6–8.

10. Massachusetts, Secretary of the Commonwealth, *Massachusetts Soldiers and Sailors in the War of the Revolution*, 17 vols. (Boston: Secretary of the Commonwealth, Wright & Potter, Printers, 1896–1908), 1: xxiv. Commonwealth of Massachusetts, *Acts and Resolves Public and Private of the Massachusetts Bay*, 5 vols. (Boston: Secretary of the Commonwealth, Wright & Potter, Printers, 1869–86), 2:103.

11. Clark, William Bell, ed., *Naval Documents of the American Revolution* (Washington, D.C.: U.S. Government Printing Office, 1966), 1: 347, 349, 521,612, 615; 2: 462.

12. Oliver P. Remick, *A Record of the Services of the Commissioned Officers and Enlisted Men of Kittery and Eliot, Maine, Who Served Their Country on Land and Sea in the American Revolution, from 1775 to 1783* (Boston: Alfred Mudge & Son, 1901),35, 200, 218. John E. Frost, *Maine Probate Abstracts, 1687–1800*, 2 vols. (Camden, Me.: Picton Press, 1991), 800. See also www.history.navy.mil/danfs/r/raleigh.

13. Remick, *Record of the Services*, 68, 189. See www.awiatsea.com/Privateer/D/Dalton.

14. Joseph C. Anderson, ed., *Vital Records of Kittery, Maine to the Year 1892* (Camden, Me.: Maine Genealogical Society, Picton Press, 1991), 232. Glenn A. Knoblock, *"Strong and Brave Fellows": New Hampshire's Black Soldiers and Sailors of the American Revolution, 1775–1784* (Jefferson, N.C.: McFarland, 2003), 177. York County Court of Common Pleas and General Sessions, box 191: 15.

15. Re complexion variations for same man, see Remick, *Record of the Services*, 58, 74–75, 100, and *passim*.

16. Moore, *Historical Notes on the Employment of Negroes*, 246.

CHAPTER NINE

"Let the Matter Subside"

Results of a Worcester court case in April 1783, marked a turning point for slavery's demise in Massachusetts, yet word of it appears to have been slow in reaching the white public. As far as is known, it occasioned no broadsides, no town criers or newspaper coverage. In this area of Maine, daily life apparently went on as usual. If slave owners discussed the matter in their letters or journals, such have not been found. Certainly there was no mention of that court's decision, or of anything pertaining to anti-slavery, in minutes of Kittery and Berwick Selectmen's meetings. In fact, during all the years of slavery's existence, that dreadful institution was never a topic of discussion in either town's government record books. Even when Massachusetts issued restrictions in the early eighteenth century on freeing slaves and on the activities of Blacks, Indians, and mulattoes, authorities in this area took no official notice.

However, in that spring of 1783 there is little doubt that, via the grapevine, Black men and women in this area were soon aware of a significant sea-change. After all, throughout Massachusetts, they had been watching and hoping in regard to such court cases for several decades. And, this time there seemed great hope in what had occurred in yet another suit for a slave's freedom. Quork Walker of Worcester had sued his owner, Nathaniel Jennison, for false imprisonment and other damages. After many delays and appeals by Jennison, the court finally ruled in Walker's favor. What was unusual and most encouraging in this instance was the judge's instructions to the jury. Telling them they ought to find Jennison guilty, Chief Justice William Cushing said that, in his opinion, slavery was incompatible with the 1780 Massachusetts Constitution because it stated that all men are born free and equal and every subject is entitled to freedom.[1]

One can only imagine how local Blacks reacted to such news. It must have been topic number one at their noontime gathering on Sabbath Days. It was a time of growing uncertainty concerning slavery's continuing legality. And, no doubt, in the weeks and months following results of the Walker court case, more Blacks took the matter in hand to confront slave owners about their freedom and/or for that of their relatives. Nothing remains to tell us of their efforts in Kittery or Berwick, or what may have resulted—which owner yielded easily or which one refused and perhaps caused an enslaved man or woman, or even an entire Black family, to take the great risk of leaving. Nor are we privy to anguished discussions that may have preceded such decisions, especially concerning the elderly or women with numerous small children, whether to take such a risk or be resigned to remain in place for what might come.

After all, that jury decision, based on Judge Cushing's opinion, did not expressly outlaw Massachusetts slavery in 1783. And, state legislators did not follow it up with a law banning the nearly 150-year-old inhuman practice. Instead, authorities left slavery to linger on unsettled legally. Ironically, that same 1780 Massachusetts State Constitution cited for one purpose by Judge Cushing, also offered protection for slave owners in a clause which stated that no man could be deprived of his property without due process. And, according to state tax law, slaves were still considered property. Official printed tax forms continued to show the column "Servants for Life" until at least 1787. Also, the annual poll tax continued to recognize slavery's existence. Its requirements that tax collectors assess "all males age sixteen and older, including Negroes and mulattoes *(except such as are under the government of a master or mistress, that poll being paid by said master or mistress)* [emphasis added]," remained tax law until 1793. Even in the early 1800s there were still remnants of such poll tax wording to indicate that slave-owning might be possible, even if far less likely.[2]

Manumissions

Records elsewhere in Massachusetts tell of slavery's marked decline in numbers by 1783 and that may have been true for Kittery and Berwick. Only about a dozen cases of slave manumission in this area have been documented, but others may have occurred out of public notice or perhaps were never formally transacted. In the earliest case of manumission found here, that of the first Black Will in 1701, there were no restrictions to its being carried out promptly. The next unrestricted manumissions occurred about 1774 for Cesar Sankey from Andrew Neal, and circa 1779 for Cicaro, Phillis, Dick, and his two young children as indicated in Lady Mary Pepperrell's will. However, for other manumissions noted in Kittery and Berwick records, there were impediments.

As mentioned in Chapter Four, Black Will, Sr., managed to obtain Tony's freedom in 1708, but only by placing himself and even his heirs in what amounted to financial hostage to Charles Frost as long as Tony lived. In another case, Bess, enslaved by Robert Elliot, experienced a cruel situation in 1724 when Elliot died at Kittery Point and his property was passed on to Timothy Gerrish. According to terms of the will, Bess was to be freed three years after Elliot's death, but her child, Clear (possibly Clare), would remain as Gerrish's property until age twenty. Come 1727, it is doubtful that Bess would have abandoned her then nine-year-old daughter and sought a life in freedom elsewhere. In all likelihood, the Gerrish household had the advantage of an additional de facto slave, Bess, for the next thirteen years.[3]

Of the numerous slaves held by the two William Pepperrells, only the first William saw fit to free a few of his slaves in a will, but with restrictions. Tobey's release was delayed until one year after Pepperrell, Sr., died and Scipio, whose age is unknown, had to wait until age forty for that. George, aka George Black, was also denied freedom until age forty, which occurred in 1754, two months after his marriage to Beck (Rebecca). Terms of John Morrell's 1756 will, probated in 1763, gave and withheld in regard to one of his slaves. "My Negro Tobey shall be free when he becomes age of 24 years, except he shall remain my wife's servant 'till her decease and then be free." It is anyone's guess as to whether Tobey was old enough to walk away two years later when Mrs. Morrell died.[4]

Robert Follet's legal restraints on William Simmons's freedom in 1779 were mentioned in the previous chapter and those for Sarah of the Samuel Lord household in 1764 are in Chapter Five. As to the last two manumitted Blacks on record, their fate was determined while quite young. In her 1764 will, Martha Lord (widow of Samuel) gave then ten-year-old "Amos called Amos Hall" to her son Samuel until the young Black reached age 30 on January 4, 1784, and further she stated, "it is my will and pleasure that he then become free to act for himself and be at his own dispose forever after." In similar language, Mrs. Lord gave four-year-old "Amey called Amey Hall" to granddaughter, Martha Marshall until Amey would become age 25 on January 8, 1785.[5]

On the record, at least, only four slave owners expressed concern for the future welfare of the persons they were about to set free. Robert Elliot's will did provide a heifer for Bess, and in 1776 Sarah received some used household goods and a few items of Martha Lord's clothing. Lady Mary Pepperrell's 1779 will stands alone in terms of generosity, but given the circumstances of her Black servants by then, that document seems to speak more to self-interest and entrenched slaveowner attitude. Though the woman stated she had "liberated all my slaves," she may have chosen to limit, if not thwart, their opportunity to seek a new and independent life elsewhere. In delaying the payout to them of some money and a few farm animals until after her death, she managed to assure herself of continuing household servants, albeit on hire by 1779 at whatever wage she likely chose.[6]

Last comes the case of Phillis, owned by Mercy Frost, widow of Simon. In Mercy's 1790 will, she stated that "the Negro woman, Phillis, I expect to be supported [by] my children should she stand in need." It is likely Phillis was free by then because shortly after that date, Phillis went to live with her son, Pompey Spring, and his wife Candace in Portsmouth, New Hampshire. That mentioned "need" may never have arisen because even after both Pompey and his wife died in 1807 (within a few months of one another), their estate funds were probably sufficient to care for elderly Phillis until her death.[7]

Exactly when slave ownership came to an end in this area may never be known. The latest notice found of slaves in an estate was that for William Hight of Berwick. His 1782 will listed Dinah, Violet, and Peter and the estate inventory, a year later, cited a blind Negro woman of no value, a Negro boy aged eight, and a Negro girl aged nine, valued at £25 each. In 1784, the "List of Polls and Property Valuation for Kittery" contains a column labelled "Black Persons." Except for listing one such person in the household of Christopher Hammond, the rest of that column is blank. Other Kittery or Berwick lists showing such a column have not been located.[8]

An interesting bit of evidence of local slaves' self-determination and some whites' recognition of slavery's demise is among probate records for Captain Alexander Raitt. He died while in Barbados in 1776 and, having left no will, it took nearly twenty years to settle his Kittery estate. In 1779, the inventory listed an old Negro woman, Susa; a young Negro woman, Violet; and a Negro boy, Pharaoh. There is no record as to their disbursement. They are next mentioned in a 1792 estate accounting: "To three Negroes which were appraised and inventoried through a mistake as they were free by nature and the laws of our land and *all of which have since absconded from their service* [emphasis added]." Once again, we are left with more questions than answers. There is no indication as to when the Black persons decided to leave widow Raitt's household or at what date the inventory mistake was recognized. And, ambiguity of white attitude is certainly apparent in that word "absconded."[9]

Freedom's Reward

Few details remain to tell us of slavery's aftermath hereabouts and what Blacks endured. Still, their experience would have been little different from that elsewhere in Massachusetts. Though public opinion had worked as much as law (if not more so) to bring about slavery's gradual demise, few, if any whites were now calling for an end to prejudice. On the contrary, as more and more Blacks gained their freedom toward the end of the eighteenth century, prejudice evolved into racism. Where once they had been part of normal town life, at least peacefully acknowledged, now, as free persons, white society was closing ranks against them. More and more, the formerly enslaved found themselves relegated to the edges of a community, socially as well as physically. Job opportunities outside of former slave-owner households were scarce and of the most menial and low-paying. Men with talent and trade skills only met discouragement, financially and otherwise, in trying to establish a small business.[10]

Some men in this area managed to overcome that to some degree by moving to less developed parts of Maine such as Limington, the Saco River area, and Harpswell. A few Blacks eventually resettled in Portsmouth and some likely journeyed to larger cities such as Boston, New York, or Philadelphia where growing Black communities were beginning to flourish.

However, venturing beyond ones' original location of enslavement also carried risks. Incidents of kidnapping of unprotected Blacks in New England in order to sell them to farmers in New York or New Jersey or to plantation owners in the South were becoming more frequent. In trying to relocate, Blacks also risked extended homelessness and possible starvation. Finding a welcoming smaller town, even nearby to where one once lived, could sometimes be difficult, if not impossible.

From the mid seventeenth century onward, Massachusetts, like most of New England, had so-called "Warning Out" laws regarding newcomers and strangers entering a town. Those regulated how long (usually a few months) they could remain without connecting into the town through a job, a marriage, or purchasing property. After such time, the "unconnected" were warned to leave or face being escorted out of town by the constable or even suffer a public whipping to further encourage such leaving. Town authorities paid close attention, especially to strangers arriving without any visible means of support. Selectmen were required to care for their own town's poor and homeless, but most definitely not for those from another location. The only references to free out-of-town people of color arriving in this area in slavery's decline, are found in Selectman's minutes of Berwick in 1772 and 1783.[11]

In the earlier case, a homeless "Indian woman named Black Bet, alias Bet Harris," arrived from Arundel on September 25, 1771, and sought shelter at the home of Tristram Warren. At the time Bet was about seven or eight months pregnant. Warren took her in, but, following requirements of the law, he soon notified town selectmen of her presence. Almost immediately, the selectmen ordered the constable to escort Bet back to Arundel, some twenty-five miles away, a ten- or eleven-hour walk over rough paths and roundabout roadways. Once they reached Arundel, however, authorities refused to accept her and a few days later Bet was escorted back to Berwick. Barely waiting a week, Berwick's constable again took Bet back to Arundel, and once again that town refused responsibility. A week later the poor woman was escorted back to Berwick.

After that fifth, arduous trek, authorities apparently abandoned Bet and she again sought shelter at Tristram Warren's house. As he later described the situation, "she was then near the time of travail [giving birth] and in such poor circumstances that I tho't it dangerous to turn her out of doors." Although he proceeded to pay for her medical care and delivery of the baby and for their continued support, he kept appealing to Berwick officials for reimbursement of expenses, but they steadfastly refused. By March of 1772 the selectmen had lost patience and voted to take Warren to court, but he managed to get there ahead of them. On Tuesday, April 14, he filed a petition in York County Court for a resolution. There followed a series of court delays in the case as requested by first one town and then the other. Finally, in January 1773, the court brought both towns' representatives together and the judge ruled that Arundel was Bet Harris' "legal place of settlement." That town was ordered "to reimburse the Petitioner for his expenses and charges and take care of the said Black Bet alias Bet Harris for the future." What occurred afterward regarding this woman and her child is still to be discovered.[12]

The second incident in Berwick is more concise, though no less informative. On November 8, 1783, Selectmen took note that Black men, Thomas Halls and Peleg Burnell and their families "are not inhabitants of this town and have come to reside here, if they continue here [they are] likely to become town charges." Berwick's constable was then ordered to warn Halls and Burnell "to depart immediately with their families or they may expect to be dealt with as the law directs and the constable is to report [back] within ten days." Again the record goes silent, leaving only speculation as to an outcome, how long those destitute families wandered from one unwelcoming town to the next. Perhaps, like some other New England Blacks, they eventually ignored or defied the law and settled in a remote wilderness area of a town.[13]

Subsidence

In one guise or another, actual or de facto, slavery lingered in both Kittery and Berwick for many years, if not several decades after 1783—just as it did in various other small Massachusetts towns and rural communities. Some slave owners refused to accept a court determination in a single case as indicating a change in the law; others recognized its legal implications, but probably managed to discourage their long-time servants from leaving. Responsibility for slavery's slow decline must also lie with communities at large. Their continuing acceptance of the status quo and apparent indifference to a growing and pernicious climate of racism undoubtedly served to erode or discourage the initiative and enterprise of many Blacks.

Evidence of slavery's lingering in one form or another in this locale is suggested, though not expressly stated, in yearly poll tax records and in the U.S. Census for 1790 to 1810. As to poll taxes, the term *Servant* was used to indicate, as the previously mentioned Massachusetts law required, that a master or mistress was being billed for the tax on persons under their governance. Poll tax records for Kittery from 1782 to 1808 contain listings such as "Daniel Bartlett, son John, and Servant—3 polls; John Hill and Servant—2 polls; James Neal and Servant—2 polls; Capt. Elisha Shapleigh and Servant—2 polls," and so forth.[14]

Use of the term *Servant* could be enigmatic as to race, but in this instance, there is the possibility, if not likelihood, that it refers to persons of African descent. One indicator is the fact that, in each case, the family surname, if not also the actual listed person, was connected with slave-owning in Kittery at some time. Also, given the discouraging economic and societal conditions facing Blacks as slavery waned, the term Servant could indicate persons who continued to remain with a former owner or his family. Only adult males were included for a poll tax, so it is anyone's guess as to how many servant women and children were present but unaccounted for. As yet, such poll tax records for Berwick have not been found, but undoubtedly they would show similar servant data.[15]

As to the 1790 U. S. Census, there was a column for "Slaves," but Massachusetts left it blank. Instead a column, "All Other Free Persons," was inserted to indicate Blacks, Indians, or mulattoes who were either living independently or living with a white family. For Kittery, twelve white households each had one unnamed, gender-not-indicated "Other Free Person." Four others each had two such "Persons." And, as in poll tax lists, most of those white family names harkened back to the era of slavery. Of course, in the case of the 1790 Census, there is no indication if those "Other Free Persons" were or had ever been enslaved.

For Berwick, that Census listed a total of forty-two "Other Free Persons" (OFP) among twenty-six white households. In most there was only one, but nine households had more: two in four, three in four, and five in one. (Oddly enough, that last household with five OFP was for Humphrey Chadbourne, descendant of the same named man whose 1667 estate listed the race-undesignated "five men and mades" for sale.) There were no OFP listed as head of household. However, in the U. S. Census of 1800, Berwick had five such householders plus a total of twenty-seven of their relatives and others.

Of particular interest in both Kittery and Berwick 1790 Census data relating to OFP as part of white households, is the appearance of some white family names not encountered in any earlier document relating to slavery. Given the happenstance nature of even finding documentation of slave owning and the fact that evidence of it in a family could easily remain hidden (even forever), one cannot help wondering if the 1790 Census data might link those additional white family names to slaveholding at some point. That first U. S. Census also lists households of independent people of color in Kittery, though none in Berwick (at least none that can be identified). Among thirteen such households in Kittery, only four are those of former slaves. We see Sambo and his household of four (probably wife Phillis and two children) living near or with Minister Stevens at Kittery Point. Just across the road, down at the cove, is Cicaro (spelled Sessoro by the census taker) and wife Phillis who, by the 1800 Census, will assume Pepperrell as her surname. Further away, near the head of Spruce Creek, perhaps close to today's intersection of Haley Road and Route One, is the indomitable Mary (Molly) Miles caring for her family of four "Persons." Then closer to the center of Kittery (near today's Depot Square) lives formerly enslaved man, Jack Roberts and family of five.

Upper Kittery (now Eliot) was the locale for the other nine households of persons of color. Jack Hanscom and his family of four is there. And near him, on what remains of the first Black Will's hundred acres, are the homes of Will's descendants: Henry, Henry, Jr., James, Catherine, and Margery. Also part of that community or near it are the dwellings of Amy Marsh and John Patch and relatives. By that time, however, facial hues must have altered and/or amnesia was beginning to set in regarding slavery's past existence in Kittery. In the upper Kittery group, all but the Hanscoms were apparently recognized as white by the census taker and not listed as "Other Free Persons."

All told, according to 1790 census takers' efforts (said by some contemporaries to have been somewhat lacking in accuracy and biased as to a fair and accurate accounting of Blacks), there was a total of 101 "Other Free Persons" in the Kittery/Berwick area, 62 of whom lived in white households. By the Census of 1800 the total OFP population dropped to 67, with 20 as part of white households. Ten years later, numbers were about the same, and by 1820, all reference to ethnicity in census for this region was dropped when Maine was separated from Massachusetts and officially became a slave-free state.[16]

Full details of what has been found in poll tax and census records up to 1810 regarding persons of color in Kittery, Berwick, and Eliot are presented in Appendix Three A. Also provided are notations from other records regarding a few such persons who were present in 1820 and 1837, including some then still living as part of white households. As if to echo the early beginning of slaveholding here, records for the 1837 Distribution of Federal Surplus Revenue shows mulattoes Mehitable Patch and Eunice Hall as part of a Shapleigh household in Eliot (formerly upper Kittery).[17]

Try as one might, there is no way to end this part of local history on an upbeat note. There must have been some formerly enslaved local Blacks or their immediate descendants who later thrived, who successfully battled racism to find a good-paying job or become an entrepreneur and gain a respected place in the community. *But they must have done so only by moving elsewhere.* During this research, no evidence was found of such accomplishment in any part of Kittery or Berwick in slavery's aftermath. Just a few people of color—Henry Black, Sr. and Jr., and occasionally members of the Patch family including Paul, George, and John—had enough wherewithal to be listed as taxpayers in Kittery. Of the two families, only the Henry Blacks remained consistently on tax lists over the years. But from what scant records exist, it appears their farming, sheep-tending, and yarn spinning kept them generally in the lowest levels of income.

A newly discovered record book of Daniel Pierce, a Kittery physician and store and tavern-keeper, reveals the difficulties for Blacks living independently in this region in the latter eighteenth and early nineteenth centuries. Some, such as Jack Black and Susanna Black (not related to the Henry Blacks), were reduced to poverty and their accounts with Pierce were paid "by Town order." Henry Black, Jr., and his aging father, with some assistance from the Town, did manage to pay their medical and other bills at Peirce's store a few times in cash. However, as commonly done by other residents, they did so primarily by trade, exchanging bushels of apples, barrels of cider, and, on at least one occasion, forty-eight skeins of yarn spun by Henry Jr.'s daughter, Mary.[18]

Dr. Pierce's records also reveal the unfortunate circumstances for enslaved Blacks as well as those who may or may not have still been under slavery's yolk at the beginning of the nineteenth century. On

October 18, 1784, Dr. Pierce paid a nighttime visit to the house of Capt. Dennis Fernald "for a Negro woman" and six days later returned to deliver her of a male child.[19] Widow Mrs. William Lewis paid for Dr. Pierce's dressing a leg wound "for a Negro woman" in November 1792 by having an unidentified Negro man haul wood for Pierce.[20] Elizabeth Rogers, a single woman and long-time slave owner of Dinah and probably Venus, mostly paid for the doctor's visits for the Black women between 1785 and 1800 by having Venus do various work for Pierce.[21]

If Dr. Pierce's earlier account book could be found (referred to in the extant one), quite likely we would gain even more insight into the nature of slavery in this area as well as conditions of everyday life for free and newly free Blacks.

---

1. Leon A. Higginbotham, Jr., *In the Matter of Color: Race and the American Legal Process* (Oxford: Oxford University Press, 1978), 91–95. George Henry Moore, *Notes on the History of Slavery in Massachusetts* (New York: D. Appleton & Co., 1866; reprint, Whitefish, Mont.: Kessinger Publishing, 1988), chaps. 8, 9 and *passim*. The Act of 1768 against buying and selling slaves only referred to "inhabitants of Africa."

2. Reference to each year's tax laws are in Commonwealth of Massachusetts, *Laws of the Commonwealth of Massachusetts Passed from the Year 1780 to the End of the Year 1800,* 2 vols. (Boston: Manning & Loring, 1899).

3. William M. Sargent, comp., *Maine Wills, 1640–1760* (Portland, Me.: Brown Thurston & Co., 1887), 256. John E. Frost, *Maine Probate Abstracts, 1687–1800*, 2 vols. (Camden, Me.: Picton Press, 1991), 106.

4. Re "George," see Chapter 10 and William Pepperrell, Sr. and Jr., in Appendix Two. Frost, *Maine Probate Abstracts,* 559.

5. Source of the surname Hall is unknown. York County Probate Court Records, Alfred, Me., docket 12221.

6. Sargent, *Maine Wills,* 256. Frost, *Maine Probate Abstracts,* 959.

7. Joseph C. Anderson, ed., *York County, Maine, Will Abstracts 1801–1858* (Camden, Me.: Maine Genealogical Society, 1997), 89. Re

"Pompey/Pomp" see Chapter Ten. Frost, *Maine Probate Abstracts*, 819, 831. MS2400, Maine Historical Society.

8. Frost, *Maine Probate Abstracts,* 819, 831. MS2400, Maine Historical Society.

9. Frost, *Maine Probate Abstracts,* 776, 1059–60.

10. Maine Historical Society, *Proceedings and Collections of the Maine Historical Society* (Portland, Me., 1923 to date), 5th Series, 3: 401–2. Joanne Pope Melish, *Disowning Slavery: Gradual Emancipation and "Race" in New England, 1780–1860* (Ithaca, N.Y.: Cornell University Press, 1998), chap. 5, esp.164.

11. Robert Kelso, *History of Public Poor Relief in Massachusetts* (Boston: Houghton Mifflin, 1923), 57–59.

12. Berwick Town Records, 1755–88, 188, 190. General Sessions of the Peace, Maine State Archives, 11: 478, 485, 494.

13. Berwick Town Records, 1755–88, 440.

14. Kittery Tax Lists 1782–84, 1795, MS1189, Maine Historical Society.

15. Lorenzo Johnson Greene, *The Negro in Colonial America* (New York: Columbia University Press, 1942; reprint, New York: Atheneum, 1969), 332.

16. Heads of Families at the First U. S. Census, 1790 – Maine. Regarding inaccuracies in census, see Lawrence S. Glatz, "Maine's Black Population in the Census of 1790 and 1800" (Portland, Me.: L.S. Glatz, 2014), Maine Historical Society.

17. "Misc. Papers Relating to Kittery, Maine," in J. L. M. Willis, ed., *Old Eliot: A Monthly Magazine of the History and Biography of the Upper Parish of Kittery, Now Eliot* (Eliot, Me.: Augustin Caldwell, 1897–[1909]), 1: 139, 143. Kittery Tax List 1807, misc. collections, Kittery Town Clerk's Office. "Eliot, Maine, Town Records 1837–1842," MS1289, Maine Historical Society, contains a detailed listing of residents of Eliot households for distribution of the Federal Surplus Funds.

18. Daniel Pierce Record Book, Paul Taylor Collection, box 3, folder 29, Fogler Library, University of Maine. From his house which still exists on what is now Picott Rd. in Kittery, Dr. Pierce carried out his medical and legal practice as well as maintaining an active general store

and public house. The time period of his extant records appear to be from the 1770s until his death in 1803. For individuals, see 42–43 (Susanna Black), 266–67 (Jack Black), 66–67, 118, 180–81, 244–45, Henry Black, Jr.). See also 206.

19. Ibid., 4.
20. Ibid., 40–41.
21. Ibid., 128–29, 136.

Chapter Ten

Lives of Consequence Revealed:

Biographical Notes on the Lives of Blacks, Mulattoes, and Indians in Early Kittery and Berwick

The biographical notes presented in this chapter record the lives, to the best of our knowledge, of Blacks, mulattoes, and Indians living in our area of study from the seventeenth century to 1820. Compiled from fragments of information teased from many different source, these brief sketches provide a glimpse into the lives of individuals who heretofore have only left a shadowy mark on the historical record.

John Eldridge Frost's monumental two-volume work, *Maine Probate Abstracts, 1687 to 1800*, and William M. Sargent's *Maine Wills, 1640 to 1760* were the starting points of this inquiry. Considering the neglect of the topics of slavery and Black persons in this area's published histories, I was astonished at what those volumes contained. Within a relatively short time I had gathered a list of one hundred slave owners and references to what appeared to be one hundred or more enslaved Blacks. Determining an exact number for the latter persons was difficult because of wording variations among given estate documents—that problem of slave-naming and generic references as discussed in Chapter Three.

Once it became evident from those records that Kittery Point information could not be easily studied separately from the rest of the original Parish of Kittery (including what became Berwick), the search for sources greatly expanded. Although Frost's *Maine Probate Abstracts* is the most up-to-date work, I decided to do some checking of the original records in the York County Court House, examining both the handwritten record books of the Probate Registrar as well as the docket papers of identified slave owners. That latter task necessitated the unfolding of each item, large and small—often tiny strips of paper containing executors' afterthoughts—and then carefully refolding them to fit the small docket envelope. (Doing all that went against the grain, but such is the state of their availability. It is most regrettable that those valuable, data-rich papers for the seventeenth and eighteenth centuries have not been given proper archival treatment and safely stored in a facility such as Maine Archives or the Maine Historical Society.)

Patience-testing and ever so time-consuming as that re-checking and docket-examining process was, it proved worthwhile in locating enslaved Blacks not accounted for in published works. Except for a few new findings in the Registrar's books, most others came to light by reading (frequently with a magnifier) every faint, tiny, handwritten word in docket papers while seeking the words "Negro" or "mulatto." Most often, those words appeared at the end of an inventory line item on farm animals or, like an afterthought, at the bottom of an inventory. (The word *slave* was never used.) Curiosity and/or hunch sometimes caused me to inspect dockets of persons not otherwise known to be connected with slavery and occasionally that proved worthwhile.

Beyond doing all of the above, every effort was made, where possible, to follow a given enslaved Black's later progress as property of whomever were the heirs. Everett S. Stackpole's *Old Kittery and Her Families* (Lewiston, Me.: Press of Lewiston Journal Company, 1903) was the primary source for locating potential heirs' names. As to non-white families, Stackpole did not identify any as such. Under the surname "Black," two men of York are listed along with the families of William Black, Senior and his sons, William and Joshua. Regarding slavery, Stackpole only refers to it in passing and to the facts that the William Pepperrells, Sr. and Jr., owned slaves and that William Whipple was involved in the slave trade. (Whipple later was a signer of the Declaration of Independence.)[1]

Other obvious sources of data, such as town vital records and church records, were useful, but considering the number of Blacks apparently in the population over the years, those records appear meager. Between 1723 and 1784, Town officials recorded thirteen marriages among known enslaved, and about the same number for other Blacks, free or status unknown. After a careful read-through of Kittery and Berwick church records (the few extant originals and type-scripts otherwise) over the same time period, they show forty baptisms. Only a couple of those were designated as infants. Nothing was found in cemetery records regarding enslaved Blacks.

York County Deeds (YCD) or registered transfers of property were sometimes a source, but not in a normal way. The index does not show the type of property exchanged. Nor does it list persons without a surname. YCD was only helpful when some other data bit from elsewhere on a slave owner suggested a consultation of his or her property transactions. Several times it was merely a hunch that sent me leafing through page after page of those indices regarding an other-wise-known slave owner to then be rewarded with discoveries. Perhaps, if all volumes of York County deeds from the beginning up to about 1790 were to be searched using the on-line posting of the volumes at the Internet Archives Digital Library of Free Books, more enslaved Blacks might very well be discovered.

As to other sources consulted—white family histories and those for town, county, Massachusetts colony, and related New Hampshire historical material— results specific to Kittery and Berwick Blacks were spotty to nil. However, reading through them greatly expanded my understanding and helped develop a framework for this project's presentation. Published abstracts of court records up to 1718 in Neal Allen's *Province and Court Records of Maine* were most helpful, but it was necessary to read through all six volumes because of incomplete indexing. Original court records beyond that date in Maine Archives in Augusta were forthcoming in some cases.

In sum, there was little that was orderly or quick in seeking data on early Blacks in this locale. Since I never knew where such might be hidden, most any relevant or seemingly relevant book or archival material was explored.

What never ceased to be amazing in this research was the uncanny way in which evidence surfaced to reveal the presence of Blacks and of slave owning beyond what were found in formal records. Had the Negro Bilhah not decided to attend prayer meeting at the Kittery Point meetinghouse on Wednesday, September 2, 1744, we would not otherwise know of her existence. Had the Indian servant Eunice and her infant not come to that same church with owner, Isaac Chapman, two months earlier, we would not know of them. And, there would not be such additional evidence of enslaved Indians in this community. If Jane Frost (Mrs. Charles, Jr.) had not bought shoes for an enslaved man named Kittery in 1733, he would have remained out of our sight. Had Rachel not been murdered and Toney not have committed one and had various escaped men not been advertised for, they would not have been found for this history. If Sambo had not obtained the money to purchase Phillis, she, too, would be absent here. In addition, most of the owners of the above enslaved would not have otherwise been discovered.

Evaluating the Data

There is concern regarding some of the information presented here. The data reveals what is in the record, but uncertainty remains a problem, more so among the list of Blacks. For many persons, their status as enslaved is clearly evident in a document, but for numbers of others, it is unknown what their status was or had been when encountered in the records. Occasionally, one cannot be certain of a person's ethnicity, but he or she has been included and appropriately marked pending further research. At the end of each enslaved person's listing are names of some other Blacks who were in the same household at some time.

In the case of slave owners and other white persons possibly involved in such practices (see Appendix Two), there may sometimes be errors in identity. Determining which of three John Hills, two Samuel Fernalds, or several John Frosts, for example, is being references in a given document sometimes can be problematic. Since there was often more than one enslaved Black in a household, slave-owner information has been presented separately. When consulting the list given in this chapter of named persons of color, and a slave owner is mentioned, it is best to consult Appendix Two for supplementary information.

Given the sometimes random and unexpected documentation of a slave's presence, questions arise concerning every slave owner as to the possible further extent of his or her involvement in slavery. That is especially so for owners whose will had unspecified statements such as "all my Negroes," "any four of my Negroes," or "all my Negroes except those I dispose of in this will." Another factor in establishing the number of slaves in a household could also be hidden in gift giving. Wills often contain the phrase "in addition to what I have already given him" (or her), but a list of specifics are not included. Since there was no gift tax, there is no searchable source that could fill such a void.

For complete citations of the sources referenced here, see the list of Abbreviations and Short Titles on pp. 162–66.

List of Blacks, Mulattoes, and Indians in Early Berwick and Kittery

Adam – May 29, 1764: "Ran away from Benjamin Fernald, age about 17 years, a short, thick fellow, 5'1" tall, born New England, speaks good English. Had on big sea jacket, grey stocks, stripped woolen shirt, frequently wears a wig. Six dollars reward." (*New Hampshire Gazette*, June 1, 1764) (K)

Amos – *See* Amos Hall.

Amy – Nov. 7, 1742: child Amy, daughter of Sarah "servant" of Lt. Samuel Lord, baptized. Died ca.1743. (FSCRB, 58; Lord, "Black Sara") (B)

Amy/Amey – *See* surnames Black, Freeman, Hall, Marsh, Wittam.

Bash – 1778 estate inventory of Ichabod Goodwin: "an old Negro woman called Bash we apprehend of no value." 1789 estate account mentions "boarding old Negro woman [for] 49 weeks." (*MPA*, 766, 946) (B) *See also* Phillis.

Beck – *See* Rebecca.

Bess – 1752 inventory of Capt. Charles Frost: a "Negro girl Bess at £20." (YCPCR, docket 6304) (KE) *See also* Silas.

Bess – Mar. 11, 1764: "Mr. Nathaniel Sparhawk, Jr. his Negro (Sambo) and Mr. Ebenezer Dearings Negro woman Bess their intentions of marriage entered and published by Mr. Nathaniel Sparhawk's order." Apr. 21, 1776: "Daughter Negro servant Col. Sparhawk Sambo baptized." (*VRK*, 22; FPCR, 456) (KP) *See also* Sambo.

Bess – 1718 will of Robert Elliot gave Negro woman, Bess, her freedom in three years after his death and a three-year-old heifer. "Bess's child Clear [*sic*] be free at age 20." Elliot's 1724 inventory lists Bess at £20 and a Negro girl age 3 or 4 at £9. (*MW*, 256; *MPA*, 106) Note: Black Bess was witness to Robert Eliot's deed in New Castle, N.H., Dec. 12, 1713. (YD, 15:40) (KP)

Bet/Bett – *See* Bet Harris.

---

*	Ethnicity uncertain.	##	Free	00	Status unknown
NG	Gender not given.	(B)	Berwick	(K)	Kittery
(KE)	Eliot area	(KP)	Kittery Point		

Bilhah 00 – Sept. 2, 1744: "Bilhah a Negro [female] owned covenant and baptized." (FPCR, 361) (KP)

Black, Amey 00 – Born 1731, daughter of Joshua & Mary Black. Used surname Wittam prior to brother, Joshua's, 1763 estate distribution. (*VRK*, 8; *MPA*, 2: 316) (KE)

Black, Andrew Wood 00 – Nov. 1805 m. Sukey (Susanna) Mitchell. (*VRK*, 261) (K) *See also* Andrew Wood.

Black, Benjamin 00 – Born 1719, son of Joshua & Mary Black. Oct. 3, 1747, noted as "a common soldier" when purchasing 5 ¾ acres in Kittery from his brother, Jonathan Black. Property was part of land formerly leased to Anthony Freeman by grandfather, William Black, Sr. (*VRK*, 84; YCD 26: 267–68) (KE)

Black, Cato 00 – Served American Revolution, Capt. T. Fernald's Co. Militia. (Remick, 59) (K)

Black, Charles 00 – Served American Revolution (*FPAA*, 21) (K)

Black, David 00 – Aug. 29, 1787, treated by Dr. Pierce at home of Henry Black, Jr. (Daniel Pierce Record Book, 180) (KE)

Black, Dinah 00 – Oct. 31, 1737: Richard Black m. Black Dinah. May 18, 1740, "Dinah Blisk or Black, wife of Richard Blisk or Black a negro owned covenant and baptized." (*VRK*, 100; *NEHGR* 151 [1997]: 354) (KP)

Black, Dublin 00 – Served American Revolution, 1777–80, Continental. (*MSSWR* 2: 94; *FPAA*, 21) (B)

Black, Elizabeth 00 – ca. 1727, listed daughter of Will Black. (*MW*, 290) (KE)

Black, Flora – *See* Flora Hubbard.

Black, George 00 – Mar. 7, 1792, m. Charlotte Frost. (*VRB*, 32, 134) (B)

Black, George – *See* George.

Black, Henry 00 – Born Dec. 1, 1716, son of Joshua and Mary Black. Possibly the Henry on 1771 Mass. tax list, total property value £5. (*VRK*, 84; Pruitt TX) (KE)

Black, Henry, Jr. 00 – Born 1758, served American Revolution, m. Sarah Spinney, May 23, 1782. Tax lists 1782–95 show a Henry Black and son, Nathan. 1801 will of Elizabeth Ferguson indicates Henry Black is looking after her sheep. (*VRK*, 162; Remick, 59; Kittery Taxes, Coll. 1189, MeHS; YCPCR, docket 5634, pension W15985) (KE)

Black, Jack 00 – His children treated for illness by Dr. Pierce in 1792, 1793. Bills paid by Town of Kittery. (Daniel Pierce Record Book, 266) (K)

Black, Joab 00 – Born Kittery 1753. Served American Revolution. D. 1822, wife listed as Lydia Merrill. (Mass. Pension, S-37592; MOCA, 53.) (K)

Black, Jonathan 00 – Born 1720, son of Joshua and Mary Black. Oct. 3, 1747, listed as "a common soldier of Kittery" in sale of 5¾ acres to brother, Benjamin. This was part of his grandfather, William Black, Sr.'s land once leased to Anthony Freeman. Likely that Jonathan served in 1745 Louisburg Expedition. 1749 deed cites him as a mariner. (*VRK*, 84; YCD 26: 267; 28: 3) (KE)

Black, Jonathan 00 – (Perhaps same as above) Feb. 1745: Convicted of stealing heifer from William Whipple of Kittery. Sentenced to fifteen stripes and fine of £4. Unable to pay and was sentenced to do service for Whipple [who] "is empowered to dispose of sd Black in service to any of His Majesty's subjects for a term of three years." (YCGSP, 11: 379) (K)

Black, Joseph 00 – Enlisted 1778 at age 18. Was Drummer in 1779 in Lt. Raitt's militia. Continental 1779–80. (Remick, 59; *MSSWR* 2: 98) (KE)

Black, Joshua 00 – Son of Will Black, Sr., d. ca. 1756. Joshua and wife, Mary, cited Apr. 1733 for church non-attendance. Court excused fine due to Mary's illness. Probate inventory 1756 for Joshua: house, barn, 8 acres, linen wheel, Irish wheel, woolen wheel, flax comb, cards, 3 lb. sheep wool, 67 lb. flax, 12 lb. woolen yarn. Also, 2 cows, a heifer, mare, 4 stears [*sic*], ten sheep, 15 lambs, 1 sow. Total: £77.12.4. (*VRK*, 84; Stackpole, 297; YCGSP, 11: 5; YCPCR, docket 1191) (KE)

Black, Joshua, Jr. 00 – Son of above Joshua and Mary, b. Dec. 27, 1724; d. May 3, 1742. Distribution of estate 1756 to brother, Thomas Wittam, sisters Amey Wittam and Margery Black. (Stackpole, 297; *MPA*, 565) (KE)

---

*	Ethnicity uncertain.	##	Free	00	Status unknown
NG	Gender not given.	(B)	Berwick	(K)	Kittery
(KE)	Eliot area	(KP)	Kittery Point		

Black, Josiah 00 – Served on jury Jan. and Oct., 1708. Josiah Black convicted Apr. 1754 fighting with Benjamin Woodman. Given 3 stripes and fined 5 shillings. (*PCRM*, 224, 347. YCGSP, 11: 575) (K)

Black, Josiah 00 – Born Jan. 4, 1750, served American Revolution 1775–79, m. Mercy Cookson. Buried Limington, Me. (Revolutionary War Veterans, MOCA.) (K)

Black, Josiah 00 – Apr. 1784 m. Mary Patch; listed as Blacks. He is listed as of Harpswell, Me., at marriage. (*VRK*, 163. 240) (K)

Black, Katherine 00 – Born 1734, daughter of Joshua and Mary Black. (*VRK*, 84) (KE)

Black, Kittery 00 – Served American Revolution. (Remick, 60) (K)

Black, Mary 00 – Born 1722, daughter of Joshua and Mary Black (*VRK*, 84) (K)

Black, Margery 00 – 1756, received portion of father, Joshua's estate. (*MPA*, 1:565) (K)

Black, Molly 00 – Aug. 29, 1787, treated by Dr. Pierce at home of Henry Black, Jr. (Daniel Pierce Record Book, 180) (KE)

Black, Nathan 00 – *See* Henry Black.

Black, Olive 00 – *See* James Whittam.

Black, Phillis – *See* Dan Hill.

Black, Richard 00 – Oct. 27, 1728: "Richard Blisk or Black (a Negro) owned covenant." Sept. 15, 1734, "Richard Blick or Black, Negro" baptized. On Oct. 31, 1737, m. Black Dinah of Kittery. 1759 will of William Pepperrell states that Richard's house was just west of Battery [Fort McClary] between river and the highway. On June 25, 1785, at Lady Mary Pepperrell's request, Sir William Pepperrell, 2nd's representative, John Sparhawk, gave a belated deed for this property to Richard Black's daughter Zilpah and stated that property had already been paid for by Richard. (FPCR, 232, 46, 362, 366; *VRK*, 100; *MW*, 845; YCD 48: 211–12) (KP) *See also* Sylvia, Titus.

Black, Richard, Jr. 00 – Mar. 13, 1742: "Richard Blisk or Black, infant son of Richard Blisk, baptized." Served American Revolution. (FPCR, 357; Remick, 28, 60) (KP)

Black, Richard 00 – Mar. 31, 1757: m. Mary Miles. (*VRK*, 125) (KP)

Black, Samuel 00 – Served American Revolution, "dark complexion," m. Sally Billings. Mar. 18, 1791: On Register of American Seamen, District of York, 1796, age 31, Certificate no. 20. (Remick, 60; "Kittery and York Misc. Accts., 1758–1844," folder 10, MS352-0741, Maine State Library) (K)

Black, Sara Ann 00 – Died Dec. 6, 1815, aged 91. (*OER*, 1:77) (KE)

Black, Sarah 00 – Born 1730, daughter of Joshua & Mary Black. Married Nicholas Collins, May 18, 1754. (*VRK*, 84; YCPCR, docket 1191; Re her child with Collins, YCCCP, Feb. 26 1754) (K)

Black, Sarah 00 (KE) – *See* George Patch.

Black, Silva 00 – Oct. 4, 1747: Infant daughter of Richard Black [Sr.] bapt. (*NEHGR* 151 [1997]: 366) Apparent misspelling for Zilphah. *See also* Richard Black [1728] above. (KP)

Black, Sip 00 – 1795, 1796 tax lists—one poll, no other property. ("Kittery and York Misc. Accts., 1758–1844," folders 6,7, MS 352-0741, Maine State Library) (K)

Black, Susanna 00 – Aug. 24, 1787, treated by Dr. Pierce for unknown illness. Bill paid by Town. (Daniel Pierce Record Book, 42) (K) *See also* Susanna.

Black, Thomas 00 – Born 1735, son of Joshua & Mary Black. His will, made Aug. 8, 1757, when leaving for "an expedition in His Majesty's service," names brother Henry and sister Margery. Thomas likely one of the four men whom Pepperrell enlisted Aug. 8, 1757, for First Reg. York County. (*VRK*, 84; Stackpole, 297; *MW*, 807; *OE*, 4: 177–78) (KE)

Black, Titus 00 – Oct. 28, 1744: Infant son of Richard Blisk [Black] baptized. (*NEHGR* 151 [1997]:326) (KP)

Black, Will – *See* Will and Will, Jr.

*Blake, Timothy 00 – 1716, m. Joanna Mitchell. (*VRK*, 145) Note: According to Stackpole, 297, some Blacks of Kittery began using surname "Blake." (K)

Blisk – *See* Richard Black.

---

* Ethnicity uncertain.	## Free	00 Status unknown
NG Gender not given.	(B) Berwick	(K) Kittery
(KE) Eliot area	(KP) Kittery Point	

Booker, Lucy – *See* Peter Tobey.

Boston – Apr. 23, 1746: baptized at home of John Ricker. (FSCRB, 65) (B) *See also* Candace and Maria.

Boston (aka Boston Underwood) – Owned by Capt. John Underwood, Boston, m. Zilphah, owned by Lady Mary Pepperrell, on July 11, 1773. Served N.H. militia bound for Ticonderoga July 20, 1776. Boston began serving aboard Underwood's privateer vessel in May 1777. (*VRK*, 232; *NHPSP*, 14:345, 473; Knoblock, 177; YCCCP, box 191:15) (KP) *See also* Phillis.

Boston – 1768 inventory of the estate of William Wentworth lists Negro man at £18. Notation in 1769 account: "to supporting a Negro of the intestate quite super annuated [*sic*] and useless from intestate's death till this time, named Boston." (*MPA*, 619, 644) (K)

Boston – Owned by William Rice ca.1760. Described by Rice's granddaughter, Sarah R. Goodwin, as "a man of great dignity & good sense. He had one of the noblest foreheads I ever saw. After my grandmother died [Boston] came to Portsmouth & set up a house. He died of consumption about age fifty." (Sarah Parker Rice Goodwin, "Pleasant Memories," MSS 4, box 9, folder 2: 3, Strawbery Banke Museum, Portsmouth, N.H.) (K) *See also* Dinah.

Bridget ## – *See* Henry Miles. (KP)

Burnells, Peleg – *See* Addendum.

Caesar – 1777 will of Tilly Haggin gave son, John, a Negro boy, Caesar, "who he has with him." (YCPCR, 13: 87) (B) *See also* Sandy.

Caesar/Ceasar – 1769 will of John Rogers gave Negro Ceasar to wife, Susanna, for her life and afterward to whichever son that Ceasar chose for a master. 1774 inventory of John's estate only lists "old bed and bedding for Negro, 20 shillings." (*MPA*, 705, 709) (K)

Caesar/Seasar – Nov. 18, 1737, Black Ceasar m. Black Dinnah. Dec. 29, 1741, Caesar and wife, Dinah, owned covenant and were baptized. (*VRK*, 100; FPCR, 357) (KP)

Caesar/Cesar – Sept. 24, 1724: Will of Charles Frost, Jr., gave Cesar to Mrs. Frost (Jane) for her lifetime and then to son, Elliott. (*MW*, 257, 264) (KE) *See also* Hector, Prince, Pompey.

Caesar/Cesar. (a.k.a. Caesar Sankey) – Mar. 7, 1756, will of Andrew Neal, Jr., gave Negro boy, Cesar, to son, James Neal, but to also serve Andrew's wife, Dorcas and son, Andrew 3rd. Neal, Sr., also said that if James neglects his mother's care, she may take Cesar away from him. If Andrew settles in Berwick, then Cesar shall serve him for two years and be returned "as well clothed as when he took him." Cesar listed at £30 in 1758 inventory. (*MW*, 814–16; *MPA*, 483) By 1774, this man, then listed as Caesar Sankey, is attending Quaker Meetings with James Neal family. Entry in Dover Meeting Minutes indicates Neal manumitted him before 1777. Caesar m. Sara Sharp on Nov. 23, 1774. Their son, Simon, b. Jan. 31, 1776. Quakers disowned Caesar Feb. 22, 1777, for serving in the Revolution. About this time, James Neal recalled, "I some years since permitted him [Caesar] to go and labor for himself although his wages was given to me. I purposed and have since applied the same to his use in purchasing a piece of land with house in Berwick on Oak Hill for which a deed is taken in his name." (Min. Dover Meeting, ii: 123, 139) Apr. 16, 1774, David Allen sells thirty-six acres on Oak Hill to "Negro man called Ceaser, lately servant to James Neal of Kittery" for £16.10.0. Deed does not refer to the name Sankey and Caesar did not sign deed. Thus, he is not found in the index to YC deeds. (YCD, 76: 24) In 1830, at age 74, Caesar was in Pomfret, N.H., and applied for military pension S11424. (Knoblock, 194) (KE)

Caesar/Cezar – *See* Cezar Rogers.

Caesar/Seaser – May 26, 1718: Sareth S. Mendum of Kittery sold "one Negro man aged about thirty-five called Seaser to William Pepperrell for £35." (vol. 8, John S.H. Fogg Autograph Collection [Coll. 420], MeHS) (KP)

Callile (Carlisle), Abraham 00 – Dec. 9, 1784, m. Abigail Patch, "both Blacks of Kittery" (*VRK*, 163) (K)

Candis/ Candace – Apr. 23, 1746: baptized at home of her owner, "Mr. Rickard." Mentioned as singing with other Blacks in the North Berwick Church. (FSCRB, 65; Lord, "Black Sara") Note: Possibly the Candace in *Black Portsmouth*, 98–105.) (B)

---

*	Ethnicity uncertain.	##	Free	00	Status unknown
NG	Gender not given.	(B)	Berwick	(K)	Kittery
(KE)	Eliot area	(KP)	Kittery Point		

Carlisle, Cato 00 – Served American Revolution on first cruise of *Ranger*, 1777. (Remick revised, 66) (K)

Cato/Catto – Oct. 24, 1745, letter, William Pepperrell to wife asking for supplies to be sent to Louisburg encampment: "Catto will need a pair or two of large thick shoes, stockings and woolen shirts . . . ." (Burrage, 100. Author states, without giving source, that this man was same as Cato Farwell) (KP)

Cato – Dec. 27, 1741: Cato owned covenant and baptized. (*NEHGR* 151 [1997]: 357) (KP)

Cato – Winter 1754, was in Nathaniel Sparhawk's household. (*Collections and Proceedings of the MeHS*, Series Two, 9: 245) (KP)

Cato – "Two Dollars Reward. Ran away from me the subscriber, the 26th of August last, a Negro man named Cato about 25 years of age, 5 feet high, speaks good English, carried with him a light coloured sustain coat, grey homespun breeches, striped woolen shirt. William Haley, Kittery." (*Freeman's Journal*, Sept. 13, 1776) (KP)

Cato – 1781 estate inventory for Madam Jane Frost lists Negro boy Cato, age 16, at £250. (YCPCR, 8: 160) (KE)

Cato – Apr. 18, 1761, codicil to will of Lt. Samuel Lord gave Negro man, Cato, to Nathan Lord. (YCPCR, docket 12272) (B) *See also* Enos.

Cato – *See* Cato Black, Cato Carlisle, Cato Rogers, Cato Sams, Cato Farwell.

Cato – May 1764: "Ran away from William Wentworth. Speaks good English, about age 30, brought up on a farm, straight limbed fellow, has stammer if spoken to suddenly, sometimes wears a dark wig, 5' 8" tall, had on old bearskin coat, two checked shirts, three pair stockings and felt hat. Six dollars reward." Included warning to ship masters of law against transporting runaway servants. (*New Hampshire Gazette*, June 1, 1764) (K)

Celia – 1759 estate inventory of Capt. John Shapleigh lists Celia at £30. His will gave wife Dorcus "services of a Negro woman while she keeps my children." (*MPA*, 507) (KE) *See also* Prince, Primus.

Celia – June 17, 1763: Sarah Frost deeds to daughter Abigail Frost "Celia, Negro girl, during the term of her life reserving to myself the labour and services of said Negro when I shall stand in need [of her] during my life." (misc. box, fol. 14, Coll. 1991, MeHS; YCD, 40:53) (KE)

Celinda – (b. July 9, 1737) Daughter of Libby owned by Timothy Gerrish. (Kittery Town Records, Book 2:135) (KP)

Charlotte – *See* Charlotte Frost.

Charles – *See* Charles Black.

Chaunce / Chance – Oct. 3, 1742, Chance, Mr. Abraham Lord's Negro owned covenant and baptized. 1772 will of Capt. Abraham Lord gave son, David Lord, a Negro man, Chaunce. (*MPA*, 777; FSCRB, 58) (B) *See also* Dinah.

Cicaro / Cisero / Cicero – Mar. 24, 1764, "Negro servt Lady Pepperrell Cicaro baptized." July 7, 1765, "baptized privately daughter of Cicaro and Phillis, servants of Lady Pepperrell and Col. Sparhawk." (FPCR, 448–49) Served American Revolution 1775. (Remick, 72) Jan. 18, 1779, will of Lady Mary Pepperrell states that she has "since" liberated all her slaves" and she gives Cisero and Zilpah 20 shillings each and a good cow, 2 sheep, and £6 sterling each. (*MPA*, 959) Cicaro received this legacy Jan. 1790 and was paid wages totaling £7.5.5 for Mar. and Jan. (YCPCR, docket 14801) It appears that sometime after being freed, Cicaro worked in the Nathaniel Sparhawk household and ca. 1790 he and Phillis, cited above, went with Sparhawk's widow to live in the William Jarvis household in Boston. (Mary Pepperrell Sparhawk Jarvis Cutts, *The Life and Times of Hon. William Jarvis of Weathersfield, Vermont* [New York: Hurd & Houghton, 1869], 428–29) The Kittery Point site of Cicaro's house and a nearby cove called Phyllis's Notch, "so named from a colored woman who once lived nearby" can be seen in a map and photograph published by Everett S. Stackpole (Stackpole, 48, 59) (KP) *See also* Phillis, Phyllis.

Clear – 1718 will of Robert Elliot states "I give Bess child Clear [*sic*] her freedom at 20 years old and Bess her time three years after my death." Estate inventory of 1724 lists Negro girl, age 3 or 4, at £9. (*MW*, 256; *MPA*, 106) (KP)

Cloe – Feb. 29, 1756: Cloe, Negro girl, admitted to full communion. July 30, 1772: "Cloe, Negro woman, belonging to Edmund Wilson m. Prince belonging to Mark Adams." (K3PC, 17, 28) (K)

---

*	Ethnicity uncertain.	##	Free	00	Status unknown
NG	Gender not given.	(B)	Berwick	(K)	Kittery
(KE)	Eliot area	(KP)	Kittery Point		

Coffe – May 26, 1676: Edward Bushnell, merchant at Boston sold Negro man named Coffe who is "now in custody of John Holden at Scotland on the Island of Barbados" to Maj. Nicholas Shapleigh of Kittery "for goods and considerations." (SCD 9: 336) (KE)

Coffee – *See* Cuff.

Collins, Nicholas 00 – *See* Sarah Black.

Cookson, Mercy 00 – *See* Josiah Black.

Cudgis 00 – Sept. 17, 1747, m. Deb. (*VRK*, 219) (K)

Cuff/Coffee – Apr. 18, 1722, Cuff, Capt. E. Plaisted's Negro, owned covenant and baptized. July 3, 1743, Cuff received into the church. Was suspended from communion for fornication Mar. 29, 1744, repented Apr. 4, 1746, and "church voted in favor of his restoration." 1750 will of Elisha Plaisted gave Negro man, Coffee, to son, William Plaisted, but son died before inheriting. (FSCRB, 57, 59; William Plaisted, unpublished will, ca. 1750, Dottie K. coll., OBHS) (B) *See also* Membor.

Cuff – 1778 inventory estate of Sarah Gerrish, "a Negro man Cuff £100." (73, fol.12, Elizabeth K. Hobbs Collection [Coll. 73], MeHS) (K)

Cumbo – 1746, "Cumbo [*sic*] Negro woman of Capt. Bartlett baptized." (K3PC, 77, 87) (K)

Cyrus – Dec. 27, 1741, "Cyrus owned covenant and baptized." Apr. 26, 1742, "Admitted to full communion, Cyrus a Blackamore." (FPCR, 48, 357) (KP)

Cyrus – In 1740, Charles Frost mortgaged property including Cyrus, age 3, valued at £35 and three other Negroes to Sir William Pepperrell for £800. Mortgage discharged 1742. (FPCR, 357. YD 22:72) (KE) *See also* Dinah, Deborah, Phillis.

Dan – *See* Dan Hill.

Deborah – In 1740, Charles Frost mortgaged property including Deborah valued at £60 and three other Negroes, to Sir William Pepperrell for £800. Mortgage discharged 1742. Deb [*sic*] m. Cudgis on Sept. 17, 1747. (YD 22:72; *VRK*, 219) (KE) *See also* Cyrus, Dinah, Phillis.

Diana – 1748 will of Jonathan Dam gave Diana to his wife, Sarah. Inventory lists "Negro woman Diana £125." (*MW*, 596; *MPA*, 319) (KP) *See also* Kittery.

Diana – *see* Addendum. (KP)

Dick – Will of Lady Mary Pepperrell, June 18, 1779, states that she "has since liberated all her slaves and that Dick [a slave] has since died leaving two children." Nov. 17, 1776, "bapt. a daughter for Dick's wife, [child's name] Margery." (*MPA*, 959; *NEHGR* 151[1997]: 456) (KP) *See also* E. Tobey, Cicaro, Zilphah.

Dillo – Mar. 19, 1725, unrecorded will of Andrew Neal gave "little Negro girle Dillo" to wife Katherine. His 1742 est. inventory lists a Negro girl at £100. (*OE* 3: 20–21; *MPA*, 215) (KE) *See also* Quash.

Dinah – *See* Dinah Black.

Dinah – Was age 18 when purchased by William Rice ca. 1760. She later went to Portsmouth, married John Gibson, and died in 1825. (Sarah Parker Rice Goodwin, "Pleasant Memories," mss 4, box 9, Strawbery Banke Museum; *Black Portsmouth*, 105) (K) *See* Boston.

Dinah – Aug. 18, 1765: "Admitted Negro woman Dinah, servt. Thomas Fernald." (Record Book, Second Church, Coll. 1189, MeHS) (K)

Dinah – 1772 will of Capt. Abraham Lord gave wife, Margaret, the Negro woman, Dinah. (*MPA*, 777) (B) *See also* Chaunce.

Dinah – 1763 will of Thomas Rogers gave Negro girl, Dinah, to his daughter, Elizabeth. Between 1784 and 1800, Dinah was treated for various illnesses by Dr. Pierce. (*MPA*, 738; Daniel Pierce Record Book, 128–29, 136) (K) *See also* Quam and Venus.

Dinah – 1764 inventory of Elisha Hill lists Negro woman, Dinah, at £35. (*MPA*, 582) (B) *See also* Peter.

Dinah – 1782 will of William Hight gave, after his wife's death, Negro Dinah to son, Temple Hight. William's 1783 inventory lists "a Negro woman blind at no value and a Negro boy age 8, a Negro girl age nine at £25." (*MPA*, 819, 831) (B) *See also* Violet, Peter.

Dinah – Aug. 12, 1740, Charles Frost mortgages property including Dinah, age 5, valued at £35 and three other Negroes to Sir William Pepperrell for £800. Mortgage discharged 1742. (YD 22:72) (KE) *See also* Cyrus, Deborah, Phillis.

*	Ethnicity uncertain.	##	Free	00	Status unknown
NG	Gender not given.	(B)	Berwick	(K)	Kittery
(KE)	Eliot area	(KP)	Kittery Point		

Dinah 00 – Nov. 18, 1737: "Black Dinnah" m. Black Seasar." (*VRK*, 100) (KP)

Dublin – *See* Dublin Black.

Edward – *See* Edward Sams.

Enos – 1762 estate of Lt. Samuel Lord gave Negro boy, Enos, to John Lord. 1769 inventory of Capt John Lord lists Negro boy, Enos, at £30. 1771 estate account mentions "expense of tending Enos a Negro boy who died." (YCPCR, docket 12272; *MPA*, 641, 670) (B)

Esquire – 1691 will of Charles Frost of Kittery gave Negro boy, Esquire, to son, John Frost, after John became of age. (*MW*, 116–17) (KE) *See also* Tony, Prince.

Eunice – July 1, 1744, "Eunice Indian serv't Isaac Chapman [and?] infant baptized." (*NEHGR* 151 [1997]: 361) (KP)

Fan/ Fannie – 1761 will of Capt. Noah Emery: "Negro woman Fan shall serve with my son Noah, he paying to each of his brothers £50 for their shares in her." In 1762 inventory, "Fannie" listed at £40. (*MPA*, 535, 538) (KP)

Farwell, Cato 00 – At Louisburg 1746. Listed in Kittery Companies of R. Cutts and P. Staples. Said to be same as the "Catto" listed above. (Burrage, 68, 76, 100) (K)

Flora – 1749 estate of Madam Jane Frost lists Negro woman, Flora, at £250. (*MPA*, 368) (KE) *See also* Pompey.

Flora – *See* Flora Hubbard.

Florer -1770 will of John Hill gave Negro woman, Florer, to his wife, Sarah, "while she remains a widow. Otherwise Florer given to whichever children or grandchildren that Sarah chooses." His 1772 inventory lists "Florer and her bedding" at £15. 1772 will of Sarah gave Florer to daughter, Abigail (Mrs. Thomas Wallingford). (*MPA*, 678, 680, 684; YCPCR, docket 9270) (B) *See also* Peter, Jo.

Follett, William – *See* William Simmonds.

Fortune 00 – Apr. 18, 1791, "Had Negro man Fortune pulling down the chimney." (Diary of Benjamin Gerrish of Berwick, 1792, 14, Coll. 1009, MeHS) *See also* Fortune March

Foy, Susanna – *See* William Mitchell.

Frederick, Prince 00 – Served American Revolution. "Entered by J. Frost 1782–1783." Described at enlistment as "age 42, a farmer, complexion Negro, hair wool." (Remick, 101). See also *SSPRWM*, 272; *MSSWR*, 4: 26) (K)

Freeman, Amey 00 – Nov. 20, 1736, m. Lambo (Sambo) Marsh. Probably daughter of Anthony and Mary Freeman. (*VRK*, 79) (KE)

Freeman, Anthony, Sr. – *See* Tony.

Freeman, Anthony, Jr. 00 – Born Apr. 21, 1720, son of Anthony and Mary Freeman. (*VRK*, 84) (KE)

Freeman, Mary 00 – *See* Tony. (KE)

Frost, Charlotte 00 – *See* Black, George. (B)

George – 1733 will of William Pepperrell gave daughter, Mary Watson, "Negro man servant George or £100 instead as she chooses [and] if sd Negro serves her faithfully until age 40 he is to be freed." Feb. 24, 1742: "George and Scipio owned covenant and baptized." Served Pepperrell's 1st Reg. 1745 at Louisburg. When George Black m. Beck Oct. 4, 1751, William Pepperrell was listed as owner of both Negroes. Dec. 9, 1751, William Pepperrell, Jr., carried out father's wishes and issued certificate of freedom to George. (*MW*, 344; *NEHGR* 151 [1991]:124; Burrage, 68; *VRK*, 124; YCD 29: 116) (KP) *See also* Tobey, Scipio, Rebecca.

Greg – 1751 estate of William Whipple lists Negro men Greg and Pompey at £60. (*MPA*, 363) (K) *See also* Pompey.

Hall, Amey – 1764 will Martha Lord states, "to [25 year-old] granddaughter Martha Marshall my servant girl Amey called Amey Hall to serve her . . . till she [Amey] be 25 on 8 January 1785 and it is my will and pleasure that she become free and be at her own dispose." (YCPCR, docket 12221) Note: an Amey Hall m. Uriah Williams in 1788. (*VRB*, 131) (B)

Hall, Amos – 1764 will Martha Lord gave son, Samuel Lord, "my servant boy Amos called Amos Hall . . . till he be 30 years of age on 4 January 1784 and . . . then he should become free to act for himself and be at

---

*	Ethnicity uncertain.	##	Free	00 Status unknown
NG	Gender not given.	(B)	Berwick	(K) Kittery
(KE)	Eliot area	(KP)	Kittery Point	

his own dispose forever after." (YCPCR, docket 12221) (B) Note: Amos probably went to Abraham Lord, as brothers, Samuel and John Lord, died before their mother.

Halls, Thomas – *See* Addendum.

Hannah – Feb. 28, 1685: Francis Hooke filed a quit claim on Hannah and Tom who were part of a Barbados estate inherited by wife, Mary. 1706 inventory of Mrs. Francis Hooke lists Negro woman, Hannah, at £25. (YCD, 4:53–54; *MPA*, 50) (KP) *See also* Tom and unnamed boy re Hooke.

Hannah – 1752 estate Nicholas Shapleigh lists "an old Negro woman Hannah" at 20 shillings. In 1738 and 1746 Hannah is listed as Negro woman of Maj. Shapleigh. Likely the same "Hannah Negro woman" who is listed as a member of the Upper Parish congregation in 1746. (*MPA*, 380; R2PC, 77, 84; Stackpole, 202) (KE) *See* Sampson.

Hanscom, Jack 00 – Died Jan. 3, 1822, Black, buried at Raitt family cemetery. (*NEHGR* 97 [1943]:272) (KE)

Hanscom, John 00 – Oct. 1, 1815, colored member of Eliot Church, age 80. (*OER* 1: 77) (KE)

Hanscom, Margaret 00 – Oct. 1815, colored member of Eliot Church, age 60. (*OER* 1: 77) (KE)

Hanscom, Peggy (Mrs. Jack) 00 – Died Sept. 30, 1822, buried Raitt family cemetery. (*NEHGR* 97 [1943]:292) (KE)

Harry – 1742 inventory of estate of James Fernald lists Harry at £100. (YCPCR, docket 5726) (KP) *See also* Richard.

Harris, Bet ## – Sept. 25, 1771, Indian woman named Black Bet, alias Bet Harris, pauper, came from Arundel to Berwick and "fell into" house of Tristram Warren. He notified Selectmen who refused her care. Over the next three weeks, Bet was taken back and forth several times between the two towns by constables as neither town wanted responsibility. When last sent back to Berwick, she was taken in by Warren because "she was then near time of travail [about to give birth] and under such poor circumstances . . . it was dangerous to turn her out of doors." Bet remained there at least until Apr. 1772 when Warren went to court to be reimbursed for her care. Both towns tried disclaiming but the county court ruled in Jan. 1773 that Arundel assume care of Bet and reimburse Warren. Arundel officials agreed to do so the following Mar. (YCGSP, 11: 478, 485,

394; Berwick Town Records 1751–1788, 180, 190, Town Clerk's Office, Berwick; Town Records of Kennebunkport, 1678–1822, 225, Town Clerk's Office, Kennebunkport) (B & Arundel)

Hector – Apr. 30, 1695, Charles Frost letter details young Indian named Hector sent to him after escaping from capture by Indians. 1724 will of Charles Frost lists Negro man Hector. (*OE* 4: 89; *MW*, 257, 264) (KE) *See also* Prince, Pompey, Caesar, unnamed girl re Frost.

Henry – *See* Black, Henry.

Hercules (Arckle), James ## – Served at Louisburg, 1745, in R. Cutts and P. Grant's companies. (Burrage, 69, 74) (KP)

Hercules (Arcules, Arckle), Thomas ## – Jan. 4, 1725/26: Thomas Hercules "free Negro" accused Henry Miles, mulatto, of selling spirits without a license. Thomas and wife, Mary, fined for non-attendance at church. Were reported to court by William Pepperrell and Timothy Gerrish. Apr. 1745, re fight with Nathaniel Todd of Kittery, both men found guilty and fined. Served 1745 at Louisburg Siege, R. Cutts Co. (YCCCP, box 24: 19; YCGSP, 9: 109, 10: 575; Burrage, 61, 69, 74) (KP)

Hetty – In the household of Capt. Elisha Shapleigh at least from the Revolution to her death in 1863. Her tombstone is inscribed: "Hetty – d. Jan. 15, 1863, aged near 100 years. A faithful friend and servant." This marker is the only one found for a slave in the entire Kittery/Berwick region. (Meade and Staples, "Cemetery and Bible Records of Eliot, Maine," pamphlet, EL44, MeHS; U.S. Census, 1810) (KE)

Hill, Dan 00 – June 20, 1798: m. Phillis Hill "alias Black." (*VRB*, 42) Note: original record book in minister's handwriting does not say "alias Black." (Coll. 1499, MeHS) (B)

Hill, Phillis 00 – (B) *See* Hill, Dan.

Hubbard, Flora (Black) 00 – (B) *See* March, Fortune.

Indians – *See* Eunice, Sarajohn, Bet Harris, and unnamed Indian re William Pepperrell.

---

*	Ethnicity uncertain.	##	Free	00	Status unknown
NG	Gender not given.	(B)	Berwick	(K)	Kittery
(KE)	Eliot area	(KP)	Kittery Point		

Jack – 1755 estate of Rev. John Newmarch lists Negro man, Jack, at £26. (*MPA*, 433–34) (KP)

Jack – 1715 will of Ichabod Plaisted gave Negro man, Jack, to wife, Mary Plaisted. (*PRPNH*, 1: 759–63) (B) *See also* Sambo.

Jack – *See* Jack Robert, Jack Hanscom, Jack Black.

Jess 00 – March 1752, m. "Combo (or Merear) by Mr. Rogers." (*VRK*, 131) (K)

Jo – 1770 will of John Hill gave wife, Sarah, a Negro man, Jo, as long as she remains a widow. Otherwise, Jo goes to whichever children or grandchildren Sarah chooses. John's 1772 inventory lists Jo and his bedding at £16. Sarah's 1772 will gave Jo to daughter, Abigail (Mrs. Thomas Wallingford.) Jo baptized Sept. 6, 1772. (*MPA*, 678, 680, 684; YCPCR, docket 9270; FSCRB, 105) (B) *See* Peter and Florer.

Joe – 1756 will of John Morrell gave Negro Joe to wife, Hannah, during her lifetime. Afterward he was to go "to whichever of my sons Joe shall choose for a master." (*MPA*, 559) (B) *See also* Tobey.

Joel – *See* Joel Black.

Joseph 00 – Apr. 1779 grant of administration re estate of Joseph, a Negro of Berwick who died intestate. Dominicus Goodwin posted bond of £200 with sureties for Caleb Emery and Daniel Grant to administer estate. No other papers in docket. (*MPA*, 77; YCPCR, docket 10596) (B)

Joseph – *See* Joseph Black.

Joshua – *See* Joshua Black.

Josiah – *See* Josiah Black.

Juba – Dec. 26, 1754, letter of Nathaniel Sparhawk mentions Juba as a cook in his Kittery Point household. Feb. 24, 1795, funeral for Juba Sparahawk [*sic*] in Portsmouth. (MeHS Coll. 2nd series, 9: 241; SJCR, 414) (KP)

Kittery – 8 July 1748, will of Jonathan Dam gave Negro boy, Kittery, to son, Simon Dam. (*MPA*, 319) (KP)

Kittery – 1733/34 account of Jane Frost with Timothy Gerrish, shoemaker of Kittery. Debit: "1 pr. shoes for Kittery 12 shillings." Credit: "by Kittery's work 17 days £4/5/0." (folio 8, Elizabeth K. Hobbs Collection, Coll. 73, MeHS) (KE) *See also* Prince.

Kittery – *See* Kittery Nowell.

Lambo – *See* Lambo Marsh, a.k.a. Sambo.

Leroy 00 – July 4, 1742, Leroy owned covenant. (FPCR, 358) (KP)

Libby – Midwife, Grace Foye (Mrs. James), testified that on July 9, 1737, she "delivered a Negro woman named Libby belonging to Timothy Gerrish, Esq. of a white female child born of her body named Celinda and further say that I have at sundry times before delivered the same Negro woman of six black children." Sarah Amee also witnessed Celinda's birth. (Kittery Town Record, Book 2: 135–36) (KP)

Lidia – June 21, 1752, Lidia, servant girl of Maj. [Richard?] Cutts, baptized. (*NEHGR* 151 [1997]: 444) (KP)

Long, Lydia 00 – Died Feb. 19, 1824, buried Raitt family cemetery. (*NEHGR* 97 [1943]:272) (KE)

Long, Sally 00 – Died Nov. 10, 1820, buried Raitt family cemetery. (*NEHGR* 97 [1943]:272) (KE)

Lord, Violet 00 – Jan. 16, 1816, "Violet March woman of color baptized." Nov. 24, 1788, m. Fortune March. 1817 will of Mrs. Joshua Hubbard (Dorcus) gave "my Black girl Violet March all my day apparel, small feather bed and bedding, one chest, Kitchen table, all my kitchen chairs, one iron pail, full kettle and decent mourning [clothes]." (*VRB*, 27; K2PC, 142; YCPCR 2: 374) (KE) *See also* Violet.

Lucy – *See* Lucy Perkins.

March, Fortune 00 – Nov. 24, 1788, m. Violet Lord. Feb. 10, 1798, m. Flora Hubbard. (*VRK*, 27, 254; *VRB*, 41) (B and K) *See also* Fortune above.

March, Violet – *See* Violet Lord.

Margery – (b. Nov. 17, 1776) Daughter of Dick owned by Lady Pepperrell. (*NEHGR* 151 [1997]: 456) (KP)

Margery – *See* Margery Black.

---

*	Ethnicity uncertain.	##	Free	00	Status unknown
NG	Gender not given.	(B)	Berwick	(K)	Kittery
(KE)	Eliot area	(KP)	Kittery Point		

Marie/Merea – Apr. 23, 1746, baptized at home of her owner, "Mr. Rickard." She sang in choir with other Blacks in North Berwick Church. (FSCRB, 65; Lord, "Black Sara") (B)

Marsh, Amey/Ammey 00 – 1801 will of Elizabeth Ferguson, "to Ammey Marsh $20 together with my home spun wearing apparel & two bushels Indian meal." (Likely Mrs. Lambo Marsh.) (YCPCR, docket 5634) (K)

Marsh, Anthony 00 – Born Sept. 14, 1746, son of Lambo and Amey (Freeman) Marsh. (*VRK*, 84) (K)

Marsh, Lambo/Sambo 00 – Nov. 20, 1736, m. Amey Freeman. Aug. 12, 1738. (*VRK*, 4, 100, 129, 84; *NEHGR* 97[1943]: 272) Note: *VRK*, 4, shows earliest transcript listing "Sambo Marsh." (K)

Marsh, Lydia 00 – Born Apr. 7, 1741, daughter Lambo/Sambo and Amey (Freemen). Lydia Marsh m. Jack Black of Dover, N.H., Nov. 1, 1781. (*VRK*, 84, 160) (K)

Marsh, Molley 00 – *See* Pharo Nowell. (K)

Marsh, Sarah 00 – Born Aug. 12, 1738, daughter Lambo (Sambo) and Amey (Freemen) Marsh. (*VRK*, 84) (K)

Marten, Isaac 00 – Served American Revolution (*FPAA*, 23) (B)

Mary 00 – *See* Thomas Hercules. (KP)

Membor – 1750 will Elisha Plaisted gave son, William Plaisted, "my Negro man Coffee and my woman Negro, Membor [*sic*]." (Dottie K. Spencer papers, OBHS; Spencer, "Solders") William died two years before father so perhaps Membor went to William's widow, Jane. (*See* Lord, Jane, re burial of an "old colored woman.") (B) *See also* Coffee.

Merear (or Combo?)** – Jan/Feb 1751, m. Parris. March 1752, m. Jess by [Rev.] Mr. Rogers. (*VRK*, 131, 219) (K)

Merrill, Lydia 00 – *See* Joab Black.

Mezsa – Mar. 14, 1738/39, bill of sale, "Abraham Cross of Kittery to James Fogg of Kittery for £130. Negro woman named Mezsa." (Box 9.6, John S.H. Fogg Autograph Collection [Coll. 420], MeHS) (KE)

Miles, Hannah 00 – *See* Henry Miles. (KP)

Miles, Henry ## – Jan. 1, 1723, m. Bridget "a free Negro woman." Son, James, b. Mar. 5, 1726, daughter, Hannah, b. Sept. 10, 1729. (*VRK*, 71) In 1726, mulatto Henry Miles accused of selling beer without license.

Henry and Bridget attended First Parish Church, and beginning in 1728 Henry hired for £7 per year to ring the bell, sweep the church "keeping it clean and sanded and keeping the dogs out." In 1742, he also carried in the christening basin as needed, looked after the church barn and burial grounds. In 1759, widow Bridget on church poor list. (Records of First Parish Church, Kittery, transcript: 18, 20, 38, 41, 89, church office, First Congregational Church, Kittery Point, Me.) In 1726, mulatto Henry Miles accused of selling beer without a license. (YCCCP, 24: 19) Served at Louisburg, 1745, in R. Cutts Company. (Burrage, 61) In 1757, William Pepperrell sued widow, Bridget, for her husband's debt of £52. Henry listed as joiner. (YCCCP, box 126:36) (KP)

Miles, James 00 – *See* Henry Miles (K)

Miles, Mary (a.k.a., Molly) – (b. May 9, 1718 – d. Mar. 7, 1827) Enslaved by Col. William Pepperrell. *See* Chapter Five for full details. (KP)

Mingoe – Dec. 7, 1663, William Ellington purchased from father-in-law, Thomas Booth of York, "one Negro boy Mingoe and one sorrel horse for three score pounds." (*YD* 1:159) (KE) *See also* Addendum.

*****Mitchell, Joanna** – *See* Timothy Blake.

*****Mitchell, William** (b. 1754–d. 1827) – Served American Revolution, "Dark complexion," m. Susanna Foy. His daughter Susanna (Sukey) m. Andrew Wood Black, 1805. Daughter Martha m. Henry Black. (Remick, 149; *VRK*, 261) (K)

Molly – *See* Mary Miles.

Morse, Molly 00 – *See* Pharo Nowell.

Ned – May 1770, Ned, Negro man belonging to Thomas Hutching, admitted to full communion. 1772 will of Thomas Hutching gave Ned to wife, Martha, while she remains a widow. Afterward Ned goes to daughter, Hannah (Mrs. Samuel Clough). The 1774 inventory of Hutching estate lists Negro man £30. (K3PC, 26; *MPA*, 709, 712) (K)

Ned (of York) – *See* Rachel.

Newport – August 1776, "Ran away from Tilly Higgin. Age about 34, 5'5" tall, speaks good English. His face is scar'd [*sic*] in his temples which was

---

*	Ethnicity uncertain.	##	Free	00	Status unknown
NG	Gender not given.	(B)	Berwick	(K)	Kittery
(KE)	Eliot area	(KP)	Kittery Point		

done in Guinea. Reward five dollars." (*Continental Journal*, Sept. 9, 1776) (B)

Nowell, Kittery 00 – Served American Revolution as cook's mate on privateer *America*, 1780. (Remick, 155) (K) *See also* Pharo Nowell.

Nowell, Pharo 00 – Oct. 1784: m. Molly Marsh, both listed as "blacks." (*VRK*, 163) (K) Note: Remick says may be same as Kittery Nowell, but gives no reason for that supposition.

Parris 00 – Feb. 1751 m. Merear (or Combo) "Both Negroes." (*VRK*, 220) (K)

Patch, Abigail 00 – (K) *See* Abraham Callile.

Patch, George 00 – Born 1759. Served American Revolution 1776–88, "Dark complexion." "Discharged by General Washington, entitled to honorary badge for faithful service." Married Sarah Black, Feb. 23, 1782. He died 1816. (Remick, 159; *SSPRWM*, 999, Pension 15163; *VRK*, 160) (KE)

Patch, Mary 00 – *See* Josiah Black.

Patch, Robert 00 – 1775 in Capt. Leighton's Co., 1778 in Continental service, "dark complexion." (Remick, 161)

Peggy – *See* Hanscom.

Pepperrell – *See* Phillis, wife of Cicaro.

Perkins, Lucy – 1771 account est. of Capt. John Lord lists "expenses for Lucy Perkins, a lame Negro servant." (*MPA*, 670) (B) *See also* Enos.

Peter – 1705, William Pepperrell advertises for runaway, Peter, "age about 20 speaks good English, of a pretty brown complexion, middle stature" had on mixed gray coat, white home spun jacket & breeches, colored stockings, French fall [faille] shoes, black hat." Recaptured in South Carolina and sent back to Pepperrell in April 1706. Advertisement of 1714 for Peter, a runaway from a Boston owner, was "formerly a servant to William Pepperrell of Kittery." Described as "a slim fellow, not very tall, goes a little lame, has lost his fore-front teeth." (*Boston News Letter*, Dec. 10, 1705, Apr. 22, 1706, Mar. 14, 1714) (KP)

Peter – 1782 will of William Hight gave Negro, Peter, to wife, Mary, for her lifetime; afterward to son, Temple Hight. 1783 estate inventory of

William lists Negro boy aged 8 at £25. (*MPA*, 819, 831) (B) *See also* Violet, Dinah.

Peter – 1764 inventory of Elisha Hill lists Negro man, Peter, at £40. (*MPA*, 582) (B)

Peter – 1770 will of John Hill gave Negro boy, Peter, to wife, Sarah, while she remains a widow. If she re-marries, Peter goes to children or grandchildren of her choice. 1772 inventory of John's estate lists Negro Peter at £25. In 1772 will of widow, Sarah Hill, she states "my executors shall sell my Negro boy Peter in payment of my debts." (*MPA*, 678, 680, 684) (B) *See also* Florer and Jo.

Peter – Nov. 29, 1741, "Peter Mr. Nathan Lords Negro baptized." (FSCRB, 54) (B)

Peter – Sept. 23, 1745, Charles Frost III gave Negro boy, Peter, to son, Charles. Apr. 1762 Charles Frost IV sold Peter, "age 18 or 19 to Nathaniel Sparhawk of Kittery for £45 [to be] his slave during the life of sd Negro." (YCD 28: 5; 37: 100) (KE)

Peter – *See* Peter Tobey.

Pharaoh – 1779 inventory estate of Alexander Raitt lists Negro boy, Pharaoh, at £120. Raitt's 1793 estate account – "to three Negros which were appraised and inventoried as slaves through a mistake as they are free by nature and the laws of our land, and which have since absconded from their services." (*MPA*, 776, 1059, 1060) (KE) *See also* Susanna, Violet, Pharo Nowell.

Pharo – *See* Nowell.

Philis – 1778 inventory estate of Ichabod Goodwin lists a young Negro woman, Philis, and her child at £60 (*MPA*, 766) (B) *See also* Bash.

Phillis – Undated order (1740s?) to James Kerswell from Andrew Pepperrell: "Please to make ye Negro Phillis one pr [size] 3 shoes and charge by acct, William Pepperrell." (14, Correspondence, Pepperrell Papers, 1701–1795 [Coll. MS093], Portsmouth Athenaeum) (KP)

Phillis – Age one in 1740, valued at £15, she is listed along with three other Negroes in property mortgaged by Charles Frost to Sir William

---

*	Ethnicity uncertain.	##	Free	00	Status unknown
NG	Gender not given.	(B)	Berwick	(K)	Kittery
(KE)	Eliot area	(KP)	Kittery Point		

Pepperrell for £800. (YCD, 22:72) Note: Frost paid off the mortgage a year later. Jan. 23, 1744, Charles gave Phillis to his unmarried daughter, Jane Frost. (YCD, 22:72; 28:5) (KE) *See also* Cyrus, Deborah, Dinah.

Phillis – 1775 will of Rev. Josiah Chase gave Negro girl, Phillis, to his wife, Sarah, as long as she remains a widow. Otherwise Phillis goes to his daughter, Sally. If Sally has no children, then she goes to son, Cotton Chase. (*MPA*, 774) (KE)

Phillis – Nov. 17, 1778, Mary Underwood with husband, John's permission, sold Negro woman, Phillis, to Sambo, a slave owned by Rev. Benjamin Stevens at Kittery for £60. (*MPA*, vi, 727) (KP) *See also* Boston.

Phillis – July 18, 1742, "Pompey William Whipple's servant and Phillis both Negroes owned covenant and baptized." (FPCR, 358) (KP)

Phillis – 1767 inventory Simon Frost list a Negro woman, Phillis, at £15. July 14, 1771, Pomp son of Phillis, Negro of Mercy Frost, baptized. Mercy's 1790 will states, "The Negro woman Phillis I expect to be supported [by] my children in case she should stand in need." Later, Phillis went to Portsmouth to live with son, Pomp. (*MPA*, 732; R2PC, 112; *YCMWA*, 89; *Black Portsmouth*, 98–105) (KE). *See also* Plato, Scipio, Pomp, Pompey.

Phillis – *See* Phillis Hill.

Phillis – Jan. 8, 1764, "Negro servt Phillis Col. [Nathaniel] Sparhawk owned covenant." Small cove at Kittery Point known as "Phillis' Notch" is apparently named after her. Original mss of 1810 Kittery Census lists Phillis Pepperrell. (FPCR, 448–49; Stackpole, 59; Misc. mss. Coll., Kittery Town Clerk's Office) *See also* Cicaro.

Phillis – Nov.23, 1755, "Phillis Negro servt. of Maj. Cutts baptized." (FPCR, 446) (KP)

Phillis – Apr. 20, 1748, Prince and Phillis the servants of "Mr. Rickers" baptized. (FSCRB, 70) (B)

Phillis – July 4, 1742, Leroy and Phillis owned covenant. (FPCR, 358) (KP)

Phyllis – *See* Phillis.

Plato – 1767 estate inventory of Simon Frost lists Negro man, Plato, at £50. (*MPA*, 610) (KE) *See also* Phillis, Scipio, Pompey.

Pomp – July 27, 1758, "Ran away the 24th of this instant July, from his Master Dennis Fernald of Kittery . . . a mulatto boy named Pomp about 21 years of age, five feet eight inches high a short thick set straight fellow . . . and at the same time a white girl about 16 years of age . . . four dollars reward for both or two dollars each." (*OE* 1: 144. Original source not given) (K)

Pompey – Baptized Mar. 4, 1739. (FSCRB, 49) (B)

Pompey – "Ran away from Ichabod Goodwin of Berwick, a Negro man named Pompey, a short thick fellow, had on homespun doubt-breast light color jacket with pewter buttons, one of his ears was cut; there [also] went a white boy, 14 years of age. Reward of four Pounds. (*Boston Post Boy*, Jan. 1, 1748; July 24, 1749) Goodwin again advertises for "Pomp" noting "It is said he has changed his clothes since he ran away." (Ibid., July 24, 1749) Another advertisement (Ibid., July 29, 1750) mentions that Pompey "speaks good English, had on a pair of Pot Hooks" (iron slave collar). Reward was increased to £10. Masters of vessels were warned not to aid escaping slaves. (B) *See also* William Nason.

Pompey/Pomp – 1767 estate inventory of Simon Frost lists Negro boy, Pompey, one year old at £6. July 14, 1771, Pomp [*sic*] son of Phillis, Negro woman of Mercy Frost (Simon's widow), baptized. Later, it appears that he was given to Frost's daughter, Sarah (Mrs. Alpheus Spring), and Pompey took that surname and moved to Portsmouth, N.H. (*MPA*, 610; R2PC, 112; *Black Portsmouth*, 98–105) (KE) *See also* Phillis, Hector, Cesar.

Pompey – July 18, 1742, "Pompey William Whipple's servt. and Phillis both Negroes owned covenant." In 1751, estate of William Whipple lists Negro men Pompey and Greg "both at £60." (FPCR, 358; *MPA*, 363) (K) *See also* Greg.

Pompey – 1738 will of John Dennett of Kittery gave Pompey to wife, Mary, during her life and then to son, Thomas Dennett. Pompey mentioned as first item in will. (*MW*, 456; YCPCR, docket 4310) (K)

Pompey – 1724 will of Charles Frost (wife Jane) gave Pompey to son, John, after his mother's death. (*MW*, 257) (KE)

---

*	Ethnicity uncertain.	##	Free	00	Status unknown
NG	Gender not given.	(B)	Berwick	(K)	Kittery
(KE)	Eliot area	(KP)	Kittery Point		

Pompey – 1749 estate of Madam Jane Frost lists ten-year-old Negro boy, Pompey, at £250. (*MPA*, 36) (KE) *See also* Flora.

Pompey 00 – July 22, 1775, Pompey, a laborer, did "with force and arms" steal two young sheep then in the care of one Tilton at Kittery which were property of Lady Mary Pepperrell. He could not pay fine of 35 shillings so Pepperrell or her agent could put him into service to someone for four months. Pompey was also sentenced to ten stripes on naked back and a fine of 20 shillings. Was to remain committed [jailed] until sentence performed. (YCGSP, 11: 542–43) (K)

Primus – Oct. 1759 inventory of Capt. John Shapleigh lists Primus at £35. (*MPA*, 507) (KE) *See* also Celia, Prince.

Primus – Born May 2, 1774, son of Rachel, "a Negro woman and servant of Capt. Dennis Fernald. (*VRK*, 135) (K)

Prince – Apr. 20, 1748, Prince and Phillis the servants of "Mr. Rickers" are baptized. (FSCRB, 70) (B)

Prince – 1759 will of Capt. John Shapleigh gave Prince as "one of my young Negroes" to Mrs. Shapleigh (Dorcus). 1769 will of their son, John, gave his wife, Sybilla, Negro man, Prince. (*MW*, 858; *MPA*, 937) (KE) *See also* Celia, Primus.

Prince – Jan. 11, 1772, Prince, owned by Mark Adams, m. Cloe, owned by Edmund Wilson. (K3PC, 28) (K)

Prince – 1691 will of Charles Frost gave Negro boy, Prince, to son, Nicholas Frost, "after son becomes of age." However, Nicholas died ca.1699 and quit claim to his estate gave "a Negro boy" (Prince?) to Charles, Jr. Charles Jr.'s 1724 will gave 'Peinc' (illegible, probably Prince) to Charles III, after his mother, Jane's, death. 1733 account of Jane Frost with Timothy Gerrish, shoemaker of Kittery, shows debit for shoes for Negroes, Prince and Kittery. Credit 1734 "to 17 days' work by Prince and Kittery." (*MW*, 116–17; YD 7:20–21; *MW*, 257, 26; fol. 8, Elizabeth K. Hobbs Collection, Coll. 73, MeHS) (KE) *See also* Tony, Esquire, Pompey, Kittery, Hector, Cesar.

Prince – May 29, 1772, "Negro man, named Prince ran away from his master, John Higgins of Berwick. He is a well set fellow, about 25 years of age, has a scar in his forehead over his left eye: had on a Kersey round tail'd jacket of a dark color, a woolen under jacket and moose skin breeches . . . four dollars reward." (*Essex Gazette*, June 16–23, 1772) (B)

Prince – *See* Prince Frederick.

Quamino – Feb. 1736, a slave belonging to Tobias Leighton convicted of stealing leather and sheep skins from Nathan Bartlett and sentenced to fifteen stripes on naked back and fine of 22 shillings. (YCGSP, 10: 129) (KE)

Quam – 1763 will of Thomas Rogers gave Negro boy, Quam, to son, John Rogers. (*MPA*, 738) (K) *See also* Dinah.

Quash – 1725 will of Andrew Neal gave son, John, the Negro man, Quash. No male Black listed in Neal's 1742 estate inventory. (*OE* 3: 20–21; *MPA*, 215) (K) *See also* Dillo.

Rachel – *See* Rachel Sanke.

Rachel 00 – (K) *See* Edward Sams.

Rachel – May 3, 1774, "Negro woman and servant" of Capt. Dennis Fernald, gave birth to son, Primus. July 1776, Rachel, Negro woman belonging to Capt. Fernal [*sic*], m. Ned, Negro belonging to Capt. Blaisdel of York. (*VRK*, 135; K3PC, 18) (K)

Rachel – In 1694, she was killed by owner, Nathaniel Keen (Kene, Cain) of Kittery. Accused of murder, he was tried and found guilty only "of cruel beating and hard useage" and fined £5 plus court costs of £5.10.0. It appears he may not have paid the fine, but only the court costs. (*PCRM*, 4: 34, 35; Lorenzo Johnson Greene, *The Negro in Colonial America* [New York: Columbia University Press, 1942; reprint, New York: Atheneum, 1969], 234) (K)

Raitt, Susanna 00 – Died Jan. 24, 1821, buried at Raitt family cemetery. *See also* Susanna. (*NEHGR* 97 [1943]:272) (KE)

Rebecca a.k.a Beck – Nov. 29, 1741, "Rebecca Black: Col. Pepperrell's servant owned covenant." Oct. 4, 1751, "Beck" married George Black "both Negroes of Sir William Pepperrell." (*NEHGR* 151 [1997]: 357; *VRK*, 124) (KP) *See also* George Black, Deborah, Dinah, Cyrus.

Regin/Riggins, Cato 00 – Nov. 28. 1754, "Cato Regin and Rachel Sanke Negroes married." (K3PC, 14) (K)

---

*	Ethnicity uncertain.	##	Free	00	Status unknown
NG	Gender not given.	(B)	Berwick	(K)	Kittery
(KE)	Eliot area	(KP)	Kittery Point		

Rice, Eliza (Elizabeth) 00 – On 1810 special list of Blacks in Kittery. Not listed as OFP on U.S. Census 1810. (Misc. Coll., Kittery Town Clerk's office.)

Richard – *See* Richard Black.

Richard – 1742 estate inventory of James Fernald of Kittery lists Richard at £150. (YCPCR, docket 5726) (K) *See also* Harry.

Robert, Jack 00 – 1801 will of Elizabeth Ferguson, "to Jack Robert, so called, $20 and two bushels Indian meal. Dec. 17 1813, "Died Jack Roberts, a black man about ninety years old." (YCPCR, docket 5634; "Journal of William Fogg," *OE* 3: 8) (KE)

Rogers, Cato 00 – Served American Revolution (Remick, 171) (K)

Rogers, Cezar – Christopher and Thomas Hammond are said to have jointly owned a slave named Cezar Rogers. 1784 List of Polls & Tax Assessments for Kittery has a column headed "Black Persons" and Christopher is listed as having one. For all other residents that column is blank. (*OE* 3: 141; "A List of Polls and the Estates . . . of the Town of Kittery, . . . 1784," Coll. 2400, MeHS) (KE)

Rose – 1747 will of Mrs. Jeremiah Wise (Mary Shipway), "It is my will that my Negro Slave Rose shall work for my daughter, Sarah Plaisted, 52 days a year until her Negro wench is able to do work for her." (*MW*, 6) (B)

Sambo – 1715 will of Ichabod Plaisted gave Sambo to son, Samuel Plaisted, if Sambo lived "until my son comes of age." (*PRPNH*, 1: 759–63; *PCRM*, 5: xxvii) (B)

Sambo – Mar. 11, 1764, "Mr. Nathaniel Sparhawk, Jr. his Negro (Sambo) and Mr. Ebenezer Dearings Negro woman Bess their intentions of marriage. Entered and Published by Mr. Nathaniel Sparhawk's order." Apr. 21, 1776, "Daughter Negro servant Sambo owned by Col. Sparhawk baptized." (*VRK*, 227; FPCR, 456) (KP) *See also* Phillis.

Sambo – Nov. 17, 1778, Mrs. John (Mary) Underwood sells to Sambo, a slave owned by Rev. Benjamin Stevens of Kittery Point, a Negro woman called Phillis "with all her appurtenances" for £60. (*MPA*, vi, 727; Eliza Buckminster Lee, *Memoirs of Rev. Joseph Buckminster, D.D. and of His Son, Rev. Joseph Stevens Buckminster* [Boston: William Crosby & H. P. Nichols, 1849], 54) (KP)

Sampson – 1707 estate of John Shapleigh lists Negro man, Sampson, at £35. 1752 estate of John's son, Nicholas Shapleigh, lists "an old Negro man Samson at 20 shillings." (*MPA*, 52, 380) (KE) *See also* Hannah.

Sams, Cato 00 – Served American Revolution, 1778. (Remick, 172) (K)

Sams, Edward 00 – Served American Revolution, 1776–81, wife Rachel. (Remick, 28, 172) (K)

*Samuel – 1694 will of Francis Hooke, "My will and desire is that my boy Samuel be brought up in the fear of God and disposed of to a religious family when my wife dies." Hooke had no known children. (*MW*,108) (KP)

Sandy – 1777 will of Tilley Haggin gave Negro boy, Sandy, to son, Edmund Haggin. (YCPCR 13: 87) (B) *See also* Caesar.

Sanke, Rachel 00 – Nov. 28, 1754, "Cato Regin and Rachel Sanke Negroes married." (K3PC, 14) (K)

Sankey, Cesar – *See* Caesar.

Sankey, Simon – *See* Caesar Sankey.

Sara/Sarah – Nov. 7, 1742, "Sarah the serv't of Lt. Samuel Lord owned covenant and baptized and Amy her child baptized." (FSCRB, 58) 1764 will of Martha Lord (Mrs. Lt. Samuel) "I give to my maid servant Sarah three of my kitchen chairs, a pine chest, a small iron pot and kettle, also one bed and bedding . . . also my common & daily or everyday wearing apparel together with my old black gown & black hood and apron for mourning. It is also my will and pleasure that at my decease she be discharged from slavery and become a free woman to be at her own dispose if she sees fit to accept of it." Martha died 1776. (YCPCR, docket 12221) William F. Lord, in "Black Sara" (1897), states she was born ca. 1720 and purchased at age 4 by Capt. Samuel Lord for a pair of oxen. Later, she married an unidentified man who died ca.1742. Child died six months later. Sarah died ca.1793 and funeral held at North Parish Church. Buried Lord Cemetery, Berwick. (Lord, "Black Sara" (B) *See also* Amey and Amos Hall, Enos, Cato.

Sara 00 – Pre 1727, wife of Will Black, Sr. (YCPCR, 3: 264) (KE)

---

*	Ethnicity uncertain.	##	Free	00	Status unknown
NG	Gender not given.	(B)	Berwick	(K)	Kittery
(KE)	Eliot area	(KP)	Kittery Point		

Sara – *See* Sara Sharp.

Sarahjohn – Indian woman, age 20, ran away from Ichabod Goodwin. Described as "fat, thick, short woman, she carried away with her a silk crepe gown, was seen to pass through Hampton . . . Reward £5." (*Boston Post Boy,* July 9, 1750) (B)

Scipio – Nov. 29, 1754, letter of Nathaniel Sparhawk gave instructions for making a "large double breasted jacket (blue or red) for Scipio." (Maine Historical Society, *Proceedings and Collections,* 2nd series, 9: 241) (KP) *See also* Scipio re Pepperrell estate; possibly the same person.

Scipio – 1767, Simon Frost estate inventory lists Negro boy Scipio age 7 at £25. Frost's 1775 estate account "credits for sale of Scipio a Negro lad, £20 and £30" [*sic*]. (*MPA*, 610, 732) (KE)

Scipio – 1733 will of William Pepperrell, Sr., "Scipio is to be free at age 40." Feb. 28, 1742 "George and Scipio Negroes" owned covenant and baptized, (*MW*, 350; FPCR, 357) (KP) *See also* Tobey, Beck.

Seaser – *See* Caesar.

Selah – July 12, 1770, Negro Selah was baptized at home of her owner, Daniel Ferguson.

(R2PC,112) (KE)

Sharp, Sara 00 – *See* Caesar (Sankey).

Silas – 1752 inventory of Captain Charles Frost lists Negro boy, Silas, at £37.6.8. (YCPCR, docket 6304) (KE) *See also* Bess.

Silas – *See* Silas Sparhawk.

Simmonds, William (a.k.a. William Follett) – May 24, 1779, Robert Follett states, "in consideration of my Negro man William serving me and my heirs and assigns two years from this date and behaving himself with respect to me and my assigns, grants freedom to sd. Negro who calls himself William Simmonds." Served American Revolution, 1775, as "William" in Robert Follett's militia and listed as William Follett, "Creole, dark complexion" on USS *Raleigh* in 1776. Likely he was on board in 1775 when Robert Follett served as that ship's Master. 1790 Census lists a William Simmons in Portsmouth, N.H. (*MPA*, 800; Remick, 200, 218; *NHGR* 2 [1904–5]: 184) (KP)

Simon – *See* Simon Tobey.

Simpson, Lit 00 – Died Apr. 10, 1830, buried at Raitt family cemetery. (*NEHGR* 97 [1994]: 272) (KE)

Sparhawk, Silas 00 – 1810 original manuscript of Census of Kittery, lists Silas as colored and living alone. (Misc. mss., Coll. Kittery Town Clerk) (KP)

Spinney, Sarah 00 – *See* Henry Black, Jr. (K)

Susanna – 1779 inventory of Alexander Raitt lists "an old Negro woman Susanna at £30. 1793 estate account states, "to three Negroes which were appraised and inventoried as slaves, through a mistake as they were free by nature and the laws of our land and all of which have since absconded from their service." (*MPA*, 776, 1059–60) (KE) *See also* Violet and Pharaoh.

Sylvia – *See* Sylvia Black.

Titus – Feb. 21, 1741, "Titus a negro servant of Elihu Gunnison owned covenant." 1752 estate papers of Elihu Gunnison lists Negro man, Titus, at £40 and detailed expenses regarding his clothing and his various work used to offset that. The 1769 estate inventory of Margery Gunnison lists "Negro named Titus £30." Accounts also include "Negro's board, his cleaning house before funeral, credits include fish caught by Negro and leasing Negro for a day." Later accounting includes "a Negro who died 10 April 1771 inventoried at £30." (FPCR, 357; *MPA*, 381, 421, 658, 669) (KP) *See also* unnamed maid and boy re Gunnison.

Titus – *See* Titus Black.

Tobey – *See* Joe.

Tobey – The 1756 will of John Morrell states, "my Negro Tobey shall be free when he comes age of 24 years, except he shall remain my wife [Hannah's] servant till her decease and then be free." Hannah Morrell died 1765. (*MPA*, 559) (B)

Tobey – In 1733, according to the will of William Pepperrell, Sr., a mulatto named Tobey is to be freed one year after Pepperrell's death. (*MW*, 350) (KP) *See also* Scipio.

---

* Ethnicity uncertain.	## Free	00 Status unknown	
NG Gender not given.	(B) Berwick	(K) Kittery	
(KE) Eliot area	(KP) Kittery Point		

Toby, E. – The 1790 estate account for Lady M. Pepperrell paid to "E. Tobey, a child of Dick's, her 20 shillings." Note: one of the two children mentioned in Pepperrell's 1779 will. (YCPCR, docket 14801) (KP) *See also* Margery.

Tobey, John 00 – Served at Louisburg, 1745, R. Cutts Company. "John Tobey mulatto found frozen to death at Kittery." (Burrage, 61, 69; *Boston Post Boy*, Jan. 13, 1772) (K)

Tobey, Peter 00 – Served American Revolution. "Dark complexion, an American," on *Raleigh*, 1776. "A Negro who lived at Capt. John Lawrence's at [Kittery] Point and died there about 1840." Married Lucy Booker of York 1783. (Remick revised, 18; *VRK*, 270) (K)

Tobey, Simon 00 – Served American Revolution, Capt. R. Follet Co. Militia 1775 and also at Kittery's Fort Sullivan. (Remick revised, 189; *NHPSP*, 17: 33) (K)

Tobey/Tobbey, Thanks 00 – Died Nov. 24, 1837, buried Raitt family cemetery. (NEHGR 97 [1943]: 272) (KE)

Tom – *See* Thomas Black.

Tom – Oct. 31, 1750, John Frost's note to "brother Gerrish" asks him to come help Tom drive off cattle safely as far as the rode . . . and over the creek . . . ." In 1768, John Frost's will states, "My Negro Tom is to be sold to pay my debts."(fol. 9, Elizabeth K. Hobbs Collection, Coll. 73, MeHS; *MPA*, 626) (KE)

Tom – Feb. 28, 1685, Francis Hooke files quit-claim deed re Tom and Hannah who were part of a Barbados estate inherited by wife, Mary Hooke. Dec. 13, 1685, Capt. Francis Hooke and wife mortgage their Kittery Point property (house, land, livestock, a Negro man, Tom or Thomas, and vessels) to Henry Dearing of Boston for £150. In April 1686, Tom was delivered to Dearing. (YCD, 4: 53–54; YD, 4: 133–34) (KP)

Toney – In June 1756, Toney, a slave in the household of Samuel Johnson of Kittery," was tried and convicted of murdering Johnson's five-year-old daughter, Mary. Toney claimed to be a victim of mistreatment so severe that it made him lose his will to live. Not wanting to commit the sin of suicide, he reasoned that killing someone else would force others to kill him. He turned himself in to the York County Sheriff and gave a detailed confession. He was hanged July 29, 1756. (Records of Massachusetts Court of Judicature, Boston, vol.1775–56: 250; *Boston Evening Post,* Aug.

11, 1755, June 28, 1756; Daniel Allen Hearn, *Legal Executions in New England, 1623 to 1960* [Jefferson, N. C.: McFarland, 1999], 143–44) (K)

Tony (a.k.a. Anthony Freeman) – 1691 will of Charles Frost of Kittery gave Negro man, Tony, to son, Charles, Jr., after his mother, Mary's, death. (*MW*, 116) Nov. 13, 1708, Charles Frost, Jr., signs formal notice that he has "Dismissed, Discharged and Set free my Negro man called Tony." This was at the request of Will Black who was required to give a surety deed or mortgage against his one hundred acres to Charles Frost if Will failed to provide for Tony in all personal and legal matters. (YD, 7:113–14) Amey, daughter of Anthony Freeman and wife Mary, was born Apr. 16, 1716. Son, Anthony, born Apr. 21, 1720 (*VRK*, 79). Will Black's 1727 will states that Antony Freeman still owes "for 2 acres which I promised him where his house now stands." (YCPCR, 3: 264) In 1737, Abe Cross sued Tony for three weeks' lease of oxen for ploughing. (YCCCP, box 66: 29) (KE) *See also* Esquire, Prince.

Tony – Aug. 23, 1773, "Mr. John Riker's Negro Tony died." (*NEHGR* 74: 186) (B)

Trysell – Deed of sale, Feb. 1, 1749, John Perry of Kittery to James Gowen of Kittery for £112.10.0, a certain Negro man about twenty-one years of age named Trysell. (*Sprague's Journal of Maine History*1 [1913]: 224) (KE)

Underwood – *See* Boston.

Venus – Apparently enslaved by Elizabeth Rogers. Was treated by Dr. Pierce between 1784 and 1802. Her labor was used to pay his account. (Daniel Pierce Record Book, 128, 129, 136) (K) *See* Dinah.

Violet – *See* Violet Lord.

Violet – The 1779 inventory est. of Alexander Raitt lists young Negro woman, Violet, at £90. In 1793 estate account "to three Negroes which were appraised and inventoried as slaves through a mistake as they were free by nature and laws of our land and all which have since absconded from their service." (*MPA*, 776, 1059–60) (KE) *See also* Susanna, Pharaoh.

*	Ethnicity uncertain.	##	Free	00	Status unknown
NG	Gender not given.	(B)	Berwick	(K)	Kittery
(KE)	Eliot area	(KP)	Kittery Point		

Violet – The 1782 will of William Hight gave, after death of his wife, Mary, Negro girl, Violet, to son Temple Hight. The 1783 estate inventory of William lists a blind Negro woman no value, a Negro boy aged 8, a Negro girl aged 9 at £25. (*MPA*, 819, 831) (B) *See also* Dinah, Peter.

Whittam – *See* Wittam.

Will (a.k.a. Black Will, William Black) – The May 1683 settlement of Maj. Nicholas Shapleigh's estate (inherited by nephew, John Shapleigh) gave "a Negro man called Will to be Mrs. (Alice) Nicholas Shapleigh's for her life." (YD, 3:126) Deed in 1685 refers to "land [Mrs. Shapleigh's] Negro lives on . . . reserved to his sd Negro's use being about three acres." (YD, 4:43, 52, 88) That same year, the funeral expenses for James Chadbourne, Sr., include £1.10.0 paid to Black Will for unspecified labor or services. (YCPCR, docket 2642) In 1690, Will is accused of being father of a child with Alice Hanscom. (*PCRM* 4:48–49, 64–66) Dec. 5, 1696 Black Will buys one hundred acres in Kittery from James Gowen for £25.7.0. (YD, 6: 43) Feb. 13, 1700, Black Will is formally emancipated by John Shapleigh. (YD, 6: 88) In 1704, "William Blacket" [*sic*] seeks tax abatement of 10 shillings due to ravages of Indian warfare in Kittery. (Stackpole, 176) In 1703, Town of Kittery granted fifty acres to William Black. (YD, 11: 107) Note: this appears to be a clearing of the records on land that Will already owned as part of his 100 acres. At Will's request, Charles Frost emancipates Negro, Tony (a.k.a., Anthony Freeman), Nov. 13, 1708. On the same date, Black Will mortgages his one hundred acres to Charles Frost as a surety in event that Will fails to provide for Tony's personal and legal needs. (YD, 7:113, 114) Jan. 1712, Black Will is accused of having an illegitimate child by a white woman, Elizabeth Brooks, but court finds no evidence and he is acquitted after paying court fees of £1.6.0. (*PCRM*, 3:126) Served in Militia 1713 and on three "marches" in 1725, James Grant's Co. (Spencer, *Statistics,* 7) In 1719, Will sells 25 acres to Elisha Andrews of Berwick. (YCD, 12: pt.:12; also 11:76) May 5, 1721, Town of Kittery re-confirms and clarifies terms of Will's ownership of the 100 acres he bought from James Gowen in 1696. (Kittery Town Records, 2: 58, Town Clerk's Office, Kittery) The term *grant* was used, but it was not a grant.) Jan. 1728, his will refers to wife, Sarah, and to money that Anthony Freeman [a.k.a., Tony] still owes him for 2 acres "which I promised him where his house now stands." Inventory missing. (*MW*, 290–91) (KE)

Will, Black, Jr. ## – Born 1690, son of Black Will and white woman, Alice Hanscom. Nov. 22, 1714, Black Will, Jr., and Elizabeth Turbot published intention to marry. (*PCRM*, 4: 48–49, 64–66) In 1715, Will, Jr., accused of having a bastard child by Elizabeth Turbot. He is goaled and posts bond but fails to appear in court on Apr. 1716. (*PCRM*, 5: 126, 169, 171) Jan. 1, 1722, "Will Black, Jr. aka William Negro" mortgaged eighty acres of land to John Furbish and William Leighton with promise to repay by May 1 of that year. Feb. 12, 1724, Furbish sells to Leighton "1/2 of 55 acres of land for £23, it being part of the 80 acres formerly in possession of Will Black, Jr." (YCD, 11: 107; 16:8) In 1754, Will, Jr., then of North Yarmouth, Me., got a £30 mortgage from Simon Frost on ten acres in Kittery. Mortgage discharged 1756 for £23.8.8. (YCD, 12:14; 31: 163) (KE)

Will – The 1744 estate of Sarah Moore (wid. of John d.1733) lists Negro, Will, at £200. (*MPA*, 303) (KP)

Will – The 1751 estate of Capt John Moore (wife Deborah) lists a Negro man, Will, at £26. (*MPA*, 303, 364) (KP) Note: Uncertain if different from "Will" above. No family connection found between these Moores.

William – *See* William Simmonds.

Williams, Uriah 00 – In Berwick ca.1756. Black, Served American Revolution. Married Amy Hall 1788. (*VRB*, 131. Spencer: 47) (B) *See also* website of OBHS.

Wittam, Amy – *See* Amy Black.

Wittam, James 00 – Born 1756, served American Revolution, 1776–83, on privateer *Queen of France*. Married Olive Black 1783. Died 1833. Of Harpswell at time of marriage. Was in Eliot 1790. (Remick revised: 203. *VRK*, 240. Pension S35131) (KE)

Wittam, Naomi 00 – May 25, 1751, m. Nathaniel Freeman of York. (*VRK*, 220) (K)

Wittam, Thomas 00 – In 1763, receives share of brother, Joshua Black's estate. (*MPA*, 1: 565) (K) *See* Thomas Black.

*	Ethnicity uncertain.	##	Free	00	Status unknown
NG	Gender not given.	(B)	Berwick	(K)	Kittery
(KE)	Eliot area	(KP)	Kittery Point		

Wood, Andrew 00 – Sept. 20, 1781, m. Margery Black, b. 1739, daughter of Joshua & Mary Black. (*VRK*, 84, 160) (K) *See* Andrew Wood Black.

Zilpah – *See* Silva Black.

Zilpah/Zilphah – July 11, 1773, Zilpah owned by Lady Mary Pepperrell married Boston owned by Capt. John Underwood. Jan. 18, 1779, Lady Mary Pepperrell's will states, "whereas I have liberated all my slaves, I verify the same viz. Cicero, Zilpah and Dick and wheras Dick has since died leaving two chn [children], I give twenty shillings to each and to Cicero and Zilpah a good cow, 2 sheep and £6 sterling each." Legacy received Jan. 1790. (*VRK*, 232; *MPA*, 959; YCPCR, docket 14801) (KP)

UNNAMED BLACK PERSONS

Unnamed man – Owned ca.1742 by unknown neighbor of Samuel Lord. Man was husband of Sarah. (Lord, "Black Sara") (B)

Unnamed child NG 00 – Bapt. May 18, 1740, child of Richard and Dinah Black. (FPCR, 45) (KP)

Unnamed woman – Wife of Lady Pepperrell's slave, Dick, and mother to at least one of his two children. (*NEHGR* 151 [1997]: 456) (KP)

Unnamed girl and boy – 1768 inventory of **John Adams** lists mulatto girl at £9 and mulatto boy, age seven at £7.10.0. (*MPA*, 632) (KP)

Unnamed man 00 **and infant** ## – Jan. 1710, **Joanna Barnes** (possibly Mrs. Henry) of Kittery was accused of having a mulatto child "by a Negro man." (*PCRM*, 4: 389; 5:123) (K)

Unnamed person NG – 1771 MA Tax, **Samuel Bracket, Jr.**, one slave. (Pruitt TX) (B)

Unnamed group, 3 NG – 1735 estate of **Mary Brown** lists three Negroes at £90. (*MPA*, 185) (B)

Unnamed group, 2 or more NG – **Moses Butler** is said to have owned two or more slaves. "Two of them lived with him after emancipation as long as he lived." (George H. Butler, *Thomas Butler and His Descendants* [New York: Trow's Printing and Bookbinding Co., 1886], 14) *See also* U.S. Census 1790, 1810. (B)

*Unnamed group of five – 1667 estate of **Humphrey Chadbourne** list "five servant men and mades [*sic*] at £40." (YD, 2: 31) (B)

Unnamed girl – 1768 estate of **James Chadbourne** lists a Negro wench at £28.4.8. (YCPCR: 2642; Stackpole, 201) (KE)

Unnamed infant NG – July 1, 1744: "Eunice, Indian serv't **Isaac Chapman,** infant baptized." (*NEGHR* 151 [1997]: 361) (KP)

Unnamed man – Jan. 6, 1751, inventory for **Joseph Curtis,** one Negro man £ 0. [*sic*] He was listed second on the same line with a horse, valued together at £40. (YCPCR, docket 3811) (K)

Unnamed group, 4 males, 4 females – 1674 inventory of **Robert Cutts** lists "three negro men, two of them old and decrepit at £45, two negro women at £30, two negro women children at £20, one Negro lad at £16. (*PCRM*, 2: 292) (K)

Unnamed person NG – 1771 MA Tax, **William Dearing**, one slave. (Pruitt TX) (KP)

Unnamed woman – Oct. 24, 1784, gave birth to a male child at house of **Dennis Fernald.** (Daniel Pierce Record Book, 4) (K)

Unnamed boy – Born Oct. 24, 1784, at house of **Dennis Fernald.** (Daniel Pierce Record Book, 4) (K)

Unnamed man – In 1773 estate inventory of **John Fernald 3rd**, a Negro man at £40. (*MPA*, 701) (K)

Unnamed two people NG – 1771 MA Tax, **Samuel Fernald,** two slaves. (Pruitt TX) (K)

Unnamed person, NG – 1771 MA Tax, **Samuel Fernald,** one slave. (Pruitt TX) (KE)

Unnamed girl – 1724 estate inventory of **Charles Frost** lists Negro girl. (*MPA*, 106)

Unnamed man – 1770 List of Personal Estates shows **Charles Frost,** 4th has a Negro man. (*NEHGR* 55 [1901]: 254–55) (KE)

Unnamed person NG – 1771 MA Tax, **John Frost**, one slave. (Pruitt TX) (KE)

***Unnamed boy** – 1663 estate inventory of **Nicholas Frost** lists servant boy 7¾ years at £14. (*PCRM*, 2: 383) (KE)

---

*	Ethnicity uncertain.	##	Free	00	Status unknown
NG	Gender not given.	(B)	Berwick	(K)	Kittery
(KE)	Eliot area	(KP)	Kittery Point		

Unnamed person NG – 1771 MA Tax, **Joseph Gerrish**, one slave. (Pruitt TX) (KP)

Unnamed 3 men – 1756 estate of **Timothy Gerrish** lists three Negro men at £21.16.8. No will found. (YCPCR, docket 6590) (KP)

Unnamed 6 children NG – Pre-1737, midwife, Grace Foye, testified that "I have at sundry times before delivered the Negro woman [Libby, belonging to **Timothy Gerrish**] of six Black children." (Kittery Town Records, Book 2: 135) (KP)

Unnamed child NG – 1778 estate of **Ichabod Goodwin,** "Phillis and her child at £60." (*MPA*, 766, 946) (B)

*****Unnamed female and boy** – 1752 estate of **Elihu Gunnison** lists "expense of shoes and clothes, etc. for a servant maid and servant boy." (*MPA*, 421) (KP)

Unnamed group NG – 1777 will of **Tilley Haggin** gave wife "all my Negroes except what I dispose of in this will." (YCPCR, 13: 87) (B)

Unnamed person NG – 1771 MA Tax, **John Hamilton**, one slave. (Pruitt TX) (B)

Unnamed person NG – 1771 MA Tax, **Moses Hanscom,** one slave. (Pruitt TX) (KE)

Unnamed person NG – 1771 MA Tax, **Benjamin Hill,** one slave. (Pruitt TX) (K)

Unnamed child NG – 1764 estate inventory **Elisha Hill** lists Negro child at £25. (*MPA*, 582) (B)

Unnamed two persons NG – 1771 MA Tax, **John Hill, Jr.,** two slaves. (Pruitt TX) (B)

Unnamed boy – 1706 estate inventory of **Mrs. Francis Hooke** (Mary) lists a mulatto boy, two years old, at £5. (*MPA*, 50) (KP)

Unnamed woman – 1713 estate inventory of **Phillip Hubbard** lists Negro woman at £35. (*MPA*, 66) (B)

Unnamed girl – 1781 estate inventory of **Caleb Hutchings** lists a Negro "garl" at £9. (*MPA*, 799. YCPCR, docket 10020) (K)

Unnamed person NG – 1771 MA Tax, **James Hutchings** one slave. (Pruitt TX) (K)

Unnamed male – Samuel Johnson advertises runaway Negro man aged 25, "had on white woolen shirt, blue broadcloth jacket, old felt hat, blue yarn stockings and old shoes." "Reasonable reward" offered. (*Boston Weekly Post Boy*, Sept.18, Oct.2, 9, and 16, 1749) (K)

Unnamed person NG – 1771 MA Tax, **Richard Keating**, one slave. (Pruitt TX) (K)

Unnamed woman – 1725 estate of **John Leighton**, Negro woman at £20. (*MPA*, 191) (B)

Unnamed person NG – 1771 MA Tax, **Samuel Leighton** one slave. (Pruitt TX) (B)

Unnamed boy – 1748 estate inventory of **Tobias Leighton** list a Negro boy at £350. (*MPA*, 319) His estate sale advert included "a likely Negro Man." (*MPA*, 319; *Boston Post Boy*, July 29, 1751) (B)

Unnamed girl – 1749 estate inventory of **William Leighton** lists Negro girl at £65. (*MPA*, 338) (B)

Unnamed woman 00 – Aug. 7, 1792, treated for leg injury by Dr. Pierce at house of **Mrs. William Lewis.** (Daniel Pierce Record Book, 40) (K)

Unnamed man 00 – Sent twice by **Mrs. William Lewis** for a days' hauling of wood in Nov. 1792 and again in Feb. 1793 as payment for Dr. Pierce's treating Lewis' Negro woman. (Daniel Pierce Record Book, 41) (K)

Unnamed woman – 1782 estate account of **Jane Lord,** widow of Ebenezer re expense for care of aged Negro woman and her burial. (*MPA*, 817; YCPCR, 13: 254) (B)

Unnamed man – 1761 will of **John Lord** gave a Negro man to son Tobias Lord. (*MPA*, 533) (B)

Unnamed person NG – 1733 inventory estate of **Nathan Lord** lists "one Negro" at £100. (*MPA*, 165) (B)

Unnamed woman – 1733 estate inventory of **Ebenezer More** (Moore) lists a Negro woman at £60 and "Negro's bed and cabin" at £1. (*MPA*, 171) (KP)

Unnamed person NG – 1771 MA Tax, **John Morrell**, one slave. (Pruitt TX) (B)

---

*	Ethnicity uncertain.	##	Free	00	Status unknown
NG	Gender not given.	(B)	Berwick	(K)	Kittery
(KE)	Eliot area	(KP)	Kittery Point		

Unnamed person NG – 1771 MA Tax, **Peter Morrell,** one slave. (Pruitt TX) (B)

Unnamed person NG – 1771 MA Tax, **Benjamin Parker,** one slave. (Pruitt TX) (K)

Unnamed girl – July 17, 1765, daughter of Cicaro and Phillis baptized. Owned by **Lady Pepperrell**. (FPCR, 449) (KP)

Unnamed woman – Nov. 1776, wife of **Lady Pepperrell's** slave, Dick, and mother of daughter, Margery, and also possibly of female, E. Tobey. (*NEHGR* 151 [1997]: 456) (KP)

Unnamed Indian NG – Notice that a "Negro man slave and an Indian who ran away from **William Pepperrell** of Kittery were captured in South Carolina and returned to Kittery." (*Boston News-Letter,* Apr. 22, 1706) (KP) *See* Peter.

Unnamed woman – 1719 Bill of Lading to **William Pepperrell,** one Negro woman at 50 shillings. (vol. 8, John S.H. Fogg Autograph Collection [Coll. 420], MeHS) (KP)

Unnamed group, at least four NG – 1759 will of Sir **William Pepperrell** allows wife Mary "to choose any four of my Negroes." (*MW*, 845) (KP)

Unnamed girl – 1778 estate inventory of **Mrs. Elisha Plaisted** (Hannah) lists a 9 year-old Negro girl at £20. In 1779 account, "by 16 the young Negro girl fetched more than she was appraised at after being kept one year . . . thereby adding £8." (*MPA*, 764, 775) (B)

Unnamed person NG – 1735 estate account for **Samuel Plaisted** lists a debt of £70 owed to Hugh Hall "for a Negro." (YCPCR, 5: 28–29) (B)

Unnamed girl or woman – 1747 will of Mrs Jeremiah Wise of Berwick mentions her daughter, **Sarah Plaisted** has a "Negro wench." (*MW*, 6) (B)

Unnamed man, woman and girl – 1762 estate of **Samuel Pray** lists a Negro man at £47.10.0, a Negro woman at £37.10.0 and a Negro girl at £42.10.0. (*MPA*, 546) (K)

Unnamed group, boys and girls, (possibly 39 total) – "Kittery, 14 June 1752 – Arrived this day the BETSY, Samuel Lamphier Commander, from the coast of Guinea with a quantity of boys and girls of the blackest sort. All persons who incline to be purchasers may apply to me the Subscriber, where they shall be dealt with on reasonable terms. **Alexander Raitt**."

(*Boston Post Boy*, June 29, 1752) According to Portsmouth Naval Office records, the *Betsy* arrived with thirty-nine Negroes. (BSRPP, 1: 33) (K)

Unnamed group girls (estimate at least 3) – 1771 will of **Joseph Ricker** states "To wife Mary the use of one of my Negro girls for life . . . to sons Tristram and Joseph Ricker . . . Negros and residue [of estate] equally divided." (*MPA*, 689) (B)

Unnamed person NG – 1771 MA Tax, **Noah Ricker**, one slave. (Pruitt TX) (B)

Unnamed two people NG – 1771 MA Tax, **Thomas Rogers,** two slaves. (Pruitt TX) (K)

Unnamed person NG – 1771 MA Tax, **William Rogers**, one slave. (Pruitt TX) (K)

Unnamed person NG – "June 26, 1769, Mrs. Downing Woodman's son and **Mrs. Sheepley's (Shapleigh**) Negro of Kittery were drowned." (*NEHGR* 74 [1920]:125) (KE)

Unnamed group, 3 men, 1 woman, 1 child NG – 1683 inventory of **Nicholas Shapleigh.** (YD 5: 15–16) (KE)

Unnamed person, NG – Mar. 18, 1787, treated for throat illness by Dr. Pierce at house of **Henry Sherburne.** (Daniel Pierce Record Book, 206) (K)

Unnamed woman, boy, and girl – 1719 estate inventory of **Josiah Skillings** lists Negro woman at £30, Negro boy aged 4 at £20, and Negro girl aged 3 at £15. (*MPA*, 85) (K)

Unnamed girl – Apr. 21, 1776: "Daughter of Negro servant Sambo [owned by] **Col. Sparhawk** baptized." (FPCR. 456) (KP)

Unnamed man and a boy – Dec. 16, 1754, letter from **Nathaniel Sparhawk** mentions sale of a "Negro fellow" for £300 and of "the least Negro boy but one for £200 all." (Maine Historical Society, *Proceedings and Collections*, 2nd series, 9: 244) (KP)

Unnamed group six girls – Nov. 29, 1754, **Nathaniel Sparhawk** shipped six "new Negro girls" to Kittery Point with detailed instructions for their

---

*	Ethnicity uncertain.	##	Free	00	Status unknown
NG	Gender not given.	(B)	Berwick	(K)	Kittery
(KE)	Eliot area	(KP)	Kittery Point		

care and confinement until sold. (Maine Historical Society, *Proceedings and Collections*, 2nd series, 9:240–45) (KP)

Unnamed man – 1757 will of **Benjamin Stacy** gave a Negro man to wife Sarah Stacy. (*MW*, 839) (KP)

Unnamed man – 1768 will of **John Tetherly** gave "my Negro man," value £13.6.8, to brother, William Tetherly. (*MPA*: 625) (KP)

Unnamed man – 1747 estate inventory of **Samuel Tetherly** lists a Negro man at £200. (*MPA*, 293) (KE)

Unnamed three people NG – 1771 MA Tax, unidentified owner – three slaves. (Pruitt TX) (K)

Unnamed three people NG – 1771 MA Tax, unidentified owner – three slaves. (Pruitt TX) (K)

Unnamed person NG – 1771 MA Tax, unidentified owner – one slave. (Pruitt TX) (B)

Unnamed girl – 1743 estate inventory of **John Walker** lists a Negro girl at £25. (*MPA*, 237) (K)

Unnamed girl – 1752 estate inventory of **Nahum Ward** lists a Negro girl at £40. (*MPA*, 371) (K)

Unnamed person NG – 1771 MA Tax, **Joseph Weeks Jr.**, one slave. (Pruitt TX) (K)

Unnamed man – 1688 probate inventory for **Thomas Wills** lists Negro man at £12. (YCPCR, 1: 7; *MPA*, 25) (K)

Unnamed person NG – 1771 MA Tax, **E. Wise**, one slave. (Pruitt TX) (B)

Unnamed woman 00 – 1720 account for mulatto woman who purchased three quarts of rum at the William Pepperrell store and paid for them with two deer skins and three raccoon skins. (box 1, folder 8, William Pepperrell Papers, 1698–1801(MS028), Portsmouth Athenaeum) (KP)

ADDENDUM:

NO DOCUMENTATION

The following appears in "Slavery in Maine," *Maine Historical Society Quarterly* 27 (fall 1987). Ref. to Thomas Bolt of Kittery selling Negro boy, **Mingo**, to son-in-law, Francis Hooke of Kittery. (This is wrong father-in-law for Hooke and extensive search has not revealed such a sale. See documented **Mingo** and **William Ellingham** in above list.)

NO DOCUMENTATON

The undated story of a slave named **Dinah**, who set fire to her owner's house on Gerrish Island, mentioned in *On the Trail of the Maine Pioneer* (1916), compiled by members of the Maine Federation of Women's Clubs (p. 233). The author gives no references or sources for this story. My research has been unproductive.

MISC. – In ca.1738, **Cato**, owned by Francis Littlefield of Wells, stole goods at Kittery from the Rev. John Newmarch, Samuel Newmarch, and Samuel Hixon. He was convicted and ordered to restore goods and pay a £4 fine or suffer fifteen stripes. He was also to pay the above men triple the value of stolen goods or was to be sold for the same sum by those men for a term of six years. Cato was "committed until sentence be performed." (YCGSP, 10: 147–48)

MISC. – "During recent snow storm a Negro man froze to death in Berwick." (*Boston Post Boy*, Jan. 28, 1758). At Kittery "a few days ago a white man and a Negro going into the water to wash themselves were both drowned and were found clasped in each other's arms." (*Boston Post Boy*, Mar. 7, 1769)

MISC: On Nov.8, 1785, Berwick Town officials ordered Constable Woods to see that Blacks, **Thomas Halls** and **Peleg Burnells** and their families, newly come to Berwick, were to leave town within ten days because they were poor and likely to become "charges" on the town. (Berwick Town Record Book, 1751–88, Part 2: 440). *See also* **Black Bet** above.

---

1. Stackpole, 250, 255.

CHAPTER ELEVEN

Conclusion

For all but a very few of the close to five hundred Black persons encountered in this research, we will never know who they were. In the realm of public history, their true identity, their rightful name connection to their ancestry was destroyed by the institution of slavery. Today, for untold numbers of American families of color, there now exists a disheartening genealogical wall blocking the pathway to many of their earliest New England ancestors and also to their African or Native American roots before the era of slavery. Today's genetic science has caused some cracks in that wall but, for most seekers, it will likely never be surmounted for specific details.

Still, within the framework of what has been found for Kittery and Berwick, there is the reward of bringing some unknown or little known Black men and women into bright light: William Black, Sr. and Jr., Caesar Sankey, Molly Miles, and others. However, for most Blacks cited here, only a faint, momentary light was possible, for Zilphah, Bilhah, Cuff, Richard Black, the many Phillises, Caesars, Pompeys, and numerous others bearing such meaningless names. Even the no-named, the numerous off-handedly cited "Negro" or "mulatto" woman, man, boy, or girl add a strobe light's flash to displace what was once total darkness.

What sort of life did they lead? At times that question could be answered in details specific to Blacks of Kittery or Berwick. In most other instances lack of data or disjointed bits of data necessitated going outside to see inside, to borrow from the larger New England rural scene and then rely on probability and inference to try revealing the story—personally, always a disappointing choice.

Although the search for data for this book was extensive, it was not perforce exhaustive. Further effort is needed to try to locate personal papers, reminiscences, or family stories of early Blacks in this region. More research is needed on the specific location and composition of the eighteenth-century Black community in what is now Eliot. All indications are that Black Will's original 100 acres were located somewhere south of Goodwin Road and back of the Marshwood Middle School property.

Much more work, in particular, needs to be done in following the trail of Kittery and Berwick merchant traders and ship captains involved in or connected in some manner with the early slave trade—not only for possible revelations on Blacks arrival here, but the possible extent to which some men such as Nathaniel Sparhawk, Alexander Raitt, and others connected with Pepperrell & Company were transporting slaves from West Africa to Caribbean and southern colonies. Careful checking of early port records for those areas might prove worthwhile.

Recently, printouts of each frame of a British microfilm of early shipping records (1694–1775) for the Port of Portsmouth, New Hampshire, were made and comprehensively indexed by John Knowlton, former librarian at the Library of Congress. This monumental accomplishment and valuable resource is now available in the collections of the Portsmouth Athenaeum. Those records show direct involvement in slave imports for the above men and possible involvement for others. Clearly evident is the fact that a majority of ships in those records constantly sailed in slavery's commercial path. And, much of their out-going cargo, of lumber, barrel staves, fish, cattle, clothing, and so forth, served to supply and encourage the growing slave-based economy to the southward.[1]

Given the sometimes random and unexpected documentation, questions arise concerning every one of the 186 slave owners and the 60 possible slave owners as to the further extent of his or her involvement in slavery. That is especially so for owners whose will had unspecified statements such as "all my Negroes" or "any four of my Negroes" or "all my Negroes except those I dispose of in this will." A possible factor in establishing the number of slaves could also be hidden in gift giving. Wills often contain the phrase "in addition to what I have already given him" (or her), but a list of specifics are not included. Since there was no gift tax, there is no searchable source that could fill that void.

As can be seen in Appendix One, some families were very much involved in slave owning and, as mentioned above, several were also involved in the maritime slave trade. Those families owning five or more enslaved Blacks among their members over the years, as far as is known, include Cutts (8), Fernald (12), Frost (38), Gerrish (10), Goodwin (5), Hill (5), Lord (12), Pepperrell (19+), Plaisted (8), Ricker (9), Shapleigh (12), and Sparhawk (11+). The majority of other families are recorded as owning one or two enslaved Blacks. And—it cannot be repeated too often—in probably most slave-owning families, at times there existed unknown numbers of children and young teenage Black laborers who likely would never be documented in any way.

In the final analysis, however, it is *impact*, not simply quantity, which matters. Wherever an enslaved Black person existed in early Kittery and Berwick, their labor, abilities, and innate wisdom had significant, even at times crucial, impact on the lives of white people around them. And, such impact not only involved the day-to-day life of a slave owner and his family, but it may very well have been key to the startup and/or continuance of financial prosperity for various owners. Of course, what aided individual families and businesses inevitably increased the well-being and economic development of an entire community.

Regrettable and totally inexcusable as the institution of slavery was, it only does further injustice to continue to dismiss its impact, its consequence, based only on numerical comparisons with large New England towns or with southern plantations.

Today, in this Maine area, miles of old stone walls, forest-free, wide-open farm lands, old mill sites, crumbling wharves and surviving seventeenth- and eighteenth-century houses whisper of long-ago Blacks' presence and accomplishments, but there are no plaques or monuments to make that known. All that remains are a few, scattered,

marker-less slave burial sites, nearly all of them more rumor than veri-
fied. Aside from the known burial site for Sarah of the Lord household,
only one inscribed tombstone has been found for a Black person held
in slavery. In Eliot within the stone walls of a Shapleigh family burial
ground stands the marker for Hetty, "Died Jan. 15, 1863 aged near
100. Faithful friend and servant." Shapleigh family records mention
her as the "colored woman" originally held by Capt. Elisha Shapleigh.[2]

How very strange is the fact that the only known physical objects
to remind us of the era of human bondage in this Maine region of old
Massachusetts are one tombstone and a small, battered table.

1. John Knowlton, comp., "British Shipping Records, Portsmouth, New
   Hampshire, 1694–1775" (microfilm printout with indexes, 2014,
   Portsmouth Athenaeum, Portsmouth, N.H.), *passim*. See also Anne
   Ferrow, Joel Lang, and Jennifer Frank, *Complicity: How the North
   Promoted, Prolonged, and Profited from Slavery* (New York: Ballantine
   Books, 2005).

2. Re burials, see Edwin H. Vetter, *A Pictorial Tour of Historical Markers,
   Plaques, and Landmarks in Eliot, Maine* (Eliot, Me.: E. Vetter, 1999),
   75, 78. See also "Capt. Elisha Goodwin's Record Book," *New England
   Historical and Genealogical Register* 97 (1943): 272; Miss Melvil F.
   Leeds and Mrs. Harold J. Staples, comps., "Cemetery and Bible
   Records of Eliot, Maine" (typescript, n.d.), Mge EL44, Maine Histori-
   cal Society.

Abbreviations and Short Titles

A.R.	American Revolution
B	Berwick
b.	born
Black Portsmouth	Mark J. Sammons and Valerie Cunningham. *Black Portsmouth: Three Centuries of African-American History.* Durham, N. H.: University of New England Press, 2004.
BSRPP	John Knowlton, comp. "British Shipping Records, Portsmouth, New Hampshire, 1694–1775." Microfilm printout with indexes, 2014. Portsmouth Athenaeum, Portsmouth, N.H.
Burrage	Henry S. Burrage. *Maine at Louisburg in 1745.* Augusta, Me.: Burleigh and Flynt, 1910.
d.	died
Daniel Pierce Record Book	Daniel Pierce Record Book, box 3, folder 29, Paul Taylor Collection, Fogler Library, University of Maine, Orono
FPAA	Eric G. Grunset, ed. and comp. *Forgotten Patriots: African American and American Indian Patriots in the Revolutionary War.* Washington, D.C.: National Society, Daughters of the American Revolution, 2008.
FPCR	First Parish Church Records, Kittery
FSCRB	Joseph C. Anderson II, ed. *Records of the First and Second Church of Berwick, Maine.* Maine Genealogical Society Special Publication no. 33. Camden, Me.: Picton Press, 1999.
K	Kittery
KE	Eliot
Kittery Taxes	Miscellaneous manuscript collection, Kittery Town Clerk's Office
Knoblock	Glenn A. Knoblock. *"Strong and Brave Fellows": New Hampshire's Black Soldiers and Sailors of the American*

	Revolution, 1775–1784. Jefferson, N.C.: McFarland, 2003.
K2PC	Kittery Second Parish Church
K3PC	Kittery Third Parish Church Baptisms, Marriages
KP	Kittery Point
KTR	Kittery Town Records, Town Clerk's Office, Kittery, Me.
Lee, *Memoirs*	Eliza Buckminster Lee. *Memoirs of Rev. Joseph Buckminster, D.D. and of His Son, Rev. Joseph Stevens Buckminster.* Boston: William Crosby & H. P. Nichols, 1849.
Lord, "Black Sara"	W.F. Lord, "Black Sara." Unpublished manuscript, January 22, 1897. Old Berwick Historical Society.
m.	married
MeHS	Maine Historical Society, Portland
MHGR	S. M. Watson, ed. *The Maine Historical and Genealogical Recorder.* 9 vols. Portland, Me:. Printed for the editor, 1884.
MHS	Massachusetts Historical Society, Boston
Min. Dover Mtg.	Minutes of the Dover [Quaker] Meeting, Collection of the Dover Public Library, Dover, N.H.
MOCA	Maine Old Cemetery Association
MPA	John E. Frost. *Maine Probate Abstracts, 1687–1800.* 2 vols. Camden, Me.: Picton Press, 1991.
MSSWR	Massachusetts, Secretary of the Commonwealth. *Massachusetts Soldiers and Sailors of the War of the Revolution: A Compilation from the Archives.* 17 vols. Boston: Secretary of the Commonwealth, Wright & Potter Print Co., State Printers, 1896–1908.
MW	William M. Sargent, comp. *Maine Wills, 1640–1760.* Portland, Me.: Brown Thurston & Co., 1887.
NEHGR	*New England Historical and Genealogical Register*
NHPSP	Isaac W. Hammond, comp. and ed. *New Hampshire Province and State Papers.* Vols.14–15. *Rolls of the Soldiers in the Revolutionary War, 1775, to May 1777.* Manchester, N. H.: Parsons B. Cogswell, 1885–86. Vols. 16-17. *Rolls and Documents Relating to Solders*

	in the Revolutionary War. Manchester, N.H.: John B. Clarke, 1887–89.
OBHS	Old Berwick Historical Society, South Berwick, Me.
OE	J. L. M. Willis, ed. *Old Eliot: A Monthly Magazine of the History and Biography of the Upper Parish of Kittery, Now Eliot.* Eliot, Me.: Augustin Caldwell, 1897–[1909].
OER	J. L. M. Willis, ed. *Old Eliot.* Reprint. 3 vols. Somersworth, N.H.: New England History Press, 1985.
OFP	Other Free Persons (i.e. Black) in white households
PCRM	Maine Historical Society. *Probate and Court Records of Maine.* 6 vols. Portland: Maine Historical Society, 1928–75.
PRPNH	Albert Stillman Batchellor et al., eds. *Probate Records of the Province of New Hampshire.* 9 vols. State Papers, vols. 31–39. Concord, N. H.: State of New Hampshire, 1907–41.
Pruitt TX	Bettye H. Pruitt, ed. *The Massachusetts Tax Evaluation List of 1771.* Boston: G. K. Hall, 1978.
Remick	Oliver P. Remick. *A Record of the Services of the Commissioned Officers and Enlisted Men of Kittery and Eliot, Maine, Who Served Their Country on Land and Sea in the American Revolution, from 1775 to 1783.* Boston: Alfred Mudge & Son, 1901.
Remick revised	Oliver P. Remick's personal copy of his book cited above with marginal notes and corrections, Rare Book 30295, Portsmouth Athenaeum, Portsmouth, N.H.
R2PC	Joseph E. Frost. "Eliot, Maine, Congregational Church Baptisms, 1721–1831 [and other church records]." Unpublished typescript, 1983. Portsmouth Athenaeum, Portsmouth, N.H.
SCD	William Blake Trask et al. *Suffolk Deeds.* 14 vols. Boston, Mass.: Rockwell & Churchill Press, 1880–1906.
SJCR	Records of St John's Church, Portsmouth, N.H., 1795–1884. 3 vols. Portsmouth Athenaeum.

Spencer, *Burials*	William D. Spencer. *Burial Inscriptions and Other Data of Burials in Berwick, York County, Maine, to the year 1922.* Sanford, Me.: Averill Press, 1922.
Spencer, "Soldiers"	Wilber D. Spencer. "List of Revolutionary Soldiers of Berwick, Maine." Unpublished typescript NNB459, Maine Historical Society.
Spencer, *Statistics*	Wilbur D. Spencer. *Statistics of Berwick, Maine including Tax List of 1700, Militia Lists, and List of Revolutionary War Soldiers.* Augusta,, Me.: 1943.
SSPRWM	Carleton Edward Fisher and Sue G. Fisher. *Soldiers, Sailors, and Patriots of the Revolutionary War, Maine.* Louisville, Ken.: National Society of the Sons of the Revolution, 1982.
Stackpole	Everett S. Stackpole. *Old Kittery and Her Families.* Lewiston, Me.: Press of Lewistown Journal Co., 1903.
VRB	John E. Frost and Joseph C. Anderson. *Vital Records of Berwick, South Berwick, and North Berwick, Maine, to the Year 1892.* Maine Genealogical Society Special Publication no. 12. Camden, Me.: Picton Press, 1993.
VRK	Joseph C. Anderson II and Lois Ware Thurston, eds. *Vital Records of Kittery, Maine, to the Year 1892.* Maine Genealogical Society Special Publication no. 8. Camden, Me.: Picton Press, 1991.
YCCCP	York County Court of Common Pleas and General Sessions, Maine State Archives, Augusta, Me.
YCD	York County Deeds, Office of the Registrar, Alfred, Me.
YCGSP	York County General Session of the Peace, Maine State Archives, Augusta, Me.
YCPCR	York County Probate Court Records, Alfred, Me.
YCMWA	Anderson II, Joseph C., ed. *York County, Maine, Will Abstracts, 1801–1858.* Maine Genealogical Society Special Publication. 2 vols. Camden, Me.: Picton Press, 1997.
YD	John T. Hull, ed. *York Deeds.* Portland, Me.: Thurston & Co., 1887.

Appendix One

Statistical Information and Data Compilation

Black Persons Encountered in Documents:	443+
Enslaved females:	102+
Enslaved males:	125+
Enslaved, no gender stated:	94+
Females, slave status unknown:	46
Males, slave status unknown:	65
Females encountered as free:	4
Males encountered as free:	4
Free, no stated gender:	3

If the above total of 443 persons is expanded in number by occasional references in documents to groups—"all my Negroes," or "any four of my Negroes," or other such phrases—the final tally would undoubtedly be higher. Also, if it were possible to account for enslaved Black persons not qualified to be counted on yearly poll taxing and census taking before 1790, i.e. children and persons under age 16, persons over the age of 40 (45 some years) and, in the case of poll taxing, women, perhaps the total enslaved population of this Kittery-Berwick region during the era of slavery might have reached close to 1,000 or even more.

Regarding Slave Ownership

Number of documented slave owners:	186
Number of additional persons who might have been slave owners:	60
Documented slave owners who appear to have owned just one slave:	97
Documented slave owners owning two or more slaves:	89

Caution is the watchword in regard to the list that follows here. Overall, the evidence does not lend itself to normal statistical analysis as to quantities of the enslaved at a given time. Although information on persons is presented as found, there is always that nagging concern of possible duplications due to generic references. Meaningful population statistics for a particular date or period of time are impossible due to the fact that enslaved Blacks only appear in records *after* they had been in place for some unknown period of time. Also, if one considers incomplete census data and the probable large number of Black children never accounted for over the years, even estimated Black population figures are questionable.

DATA COMPOSITE – EARLY KITTERY & BERWICK ENSLAVED BLACKS
With Evaluation When Known

Date	£Amt.	Name	F	M	NG	Loc.	Owner	Misc.
1663	60	Mingoe		x		KE	W. Ellington	"and one sorrel horse"
1667*	40	men & women	x	x		B	Chadbourne	"five men & mades" (estimated as three males and two females)
1674	45	three men		x		K	R. Cutt	
1674	30	two women	x			K	" "	
1674	16	a boy		x		K	" "	
1674	20	two children	x			K	" "	
1676	--	Coffe		x		KE	N. Shapleigh	
1682	90	NN	x			KE	N. Shapleigh	1 woman
		NN		x		KE	" "	2 men
		NN			x	KE	" "	"one little Neager"
1683	--	Will		x		KE	" "	
1685	--	Tom		x		KP	F. Hooke	
1688	12	NN		x		K	T. Wills	
1691	--	Esquire		x		KE	C. Frost	
1691	--	Prince		x		KE	" "	
1691	--	Toney		x		KE	" "	
1694	--	Rachel	x			K	N. Keen	
1695	--	Hector		x		KE	C. Frost	
1705	--	Peter		x		KP	W. Pepperrell	
1706	25	Hannah	x			KP	M. Hooke	
1706	5	NN		x		KP	M. Hooke	age 5
1706	--	NN			x	KP	W. Pepperrell	"an Indian"
1707	35	Sampson	x			B	J. Shapleigh	
1713	35	NN	x			B	P. Hubbard	
1715	--	Jack	x			B	I. Plaisted	
1715	--	Sambo		x		B	I. Plaisted	
1718	35	Seaser		x		KP	S, Mendum	
1719	30	NN	x			K	J. Skillings	
1719	20	NN		x		K	" "	
1719	15	NN	x			K	" "	age 3
1719	50s	NN	x			KP	W. Pepperrell	
1719	--	Molly	x			KP	" "	
1720	2 Oxen	Sarah	x			B	S. Lord	
1720	--	NN	x			KP	00	
1722	--	Cuff		x		B	E. Plaisted	

* ethnicity uncertain   ** more than one   NN no name   00 slave status unknown
UNO unknown owner

DATA COMPOSITE – EARLY KITTERY & BERWICK ENSLAVED BLACKS
With Evaluation When Known

Date	£Amt.	Name	F	M	NG	Loc.	Owner	Misc.
1724	20	Bess	x			KP	R. Elliot	
1724	9	Clear	x			KP	" "	child
1724	--	Caesar		x		KE	C. Frost	
1724	--	Pompey		x		KE	" "	
1724	--	NN	x			KE	" "	
1725	20	NN	x			B.	J. Leighton	
1725	--	Dillo	x			KE	A. Neal	
1725	--	Quash			x	KE	" "	
1727	--	Sara	x			KE	00	
1733	100	NN			x	B	N. Lord	
1733	100	George		x		KP	W. Pepperrell	
1733	--	Tobey		x		KP	" "	
1733	--	Scipio		x		KP	" "	
1733	60	NN		x		KP	E. Moore	"Negro's bed & cabin £1"
1734	--	Kittery	x			KE	J. Frost	
1735	30	NN			x	B	M. Brown	
1735	30	NN			x	B	" "	
1735	30	NN			x	B	" "	
1735	70	NN			x	B	S. Plaisted	
1736	--	Quamino		x		KE	T. Leighton	
1737	--	Celinda	x			KP	T. Gerrish	
1737	--	Libby	x			KP	" "	
c. 1737	--	child			x	KP	T. Gerrish	
c, 1737	--	child			x	KP	" "	
c. 1737	--	child			x	KP	" "	
c. 1737	--	child			x	KP	" "	
c. 1737	--	child			x	KP	" "	
c. 1737	--	child			x	KP	" "	
1738	130	Mezsa	x			KE	A. Cross	
1738	--	Pompey		x		K	J. Dennett	
1740	60	Deb	x			KE	C. Frost	
1740	--	Phillis	x			KP	W. Pepperrell	
1740	--	Phillis	x			KE	C. Frost	
1740	35	Dinah	x			KE	C. Frost	
1740	35	Cyrus		x		KE	C. Frost	
1741	--	Cyrus		x		KP	W. Pepperrell?	
1741	--	Rebecca	x			KP	" "	

* ethnicity uncertain ** more than one NN no name 00 slave status unknown
UNO unknown owner

DATA COMPOSITE – EARLY KITTERY & BERWICK ENSLAVED BLACKS
With Evaluation When Known

Date	£Amt.	Name	F	M	NG	Loc.	Owner	Misc.
1741	--	Peter		x		B	N. Lord	
1742	100	Harry		x		KP	J. Fernald	
1742	--	Chaunce		x		B	A. Lord	
1742	--	NN			x	B	S. Lord	
1742	--	NN			x	B	UNO	
1742	30	Pompey		x		K	W. Whipple	
1742	--	Phillis	x			K	" "	
1742	150	Richard		x		K	J. Fernald	
1742	--	Leroy		x		KP	00	
1742	--	Phillis	x			KP	00	
1743	25	NN	x			K	J. Walker	
1744	200	Will		x		K	S. Moore	See 1751
1744	--	Eunice	x			KP	I. chapman	Indian
1744	--	infant			x	KP	" "	
1744	--	Bilhah	x			KP	00	
1745	--	Peter		x		KE	C. Frost	
1745	--	Catto		x		KP	W. Pepperrell	
1745	--	Maria	x			B	Mr. Ricker	
1746	--	Boston		x		B	" "	
1746	--	Candis	x			B	" "	
1746	--	Cumbo	x			K	Capt. Bartlett	
1747	200	NN		x		KE	S. Tetherly	
1747	--	NN	x			B	S. Plaisted	
1747	--	Cudgis		x		K	00	
1747	--	Rose	x			B	M. Wise	
1748	112	Trysell		x		KE	J. Perry	age 21
1748	350	NN		x		B	J. Leighton	
1748	125	Diana	x			KP	J. Dam	
1748	--	Kittery		x		KP	" "	
1748	--	Pompey		x		B	I. Goodwin	
1748	--	Phillis	x			B	Mr. Ricker	
1748	--	Prince		x		B	" "	
1749	65	NN		x		B	W. Leighton	
1749	--	NN	x			B	J. Lord	
1749	250	Flora	x			KE	J. Frost	
1749	250	Pompey		x		KE	J. Frost	
1749	--	NN		x		K	S. Johnson	

* ethnicity uncertain   ** more than one   NN no name   00 slave status unknown
UNO unknown owner

DATA COMPOSITE – EARLY KITTERY & BERWICK ENSLAVED BLACKS

With Evaluation When Known

Date	£Amt.	Name	F	M	NG	Loc.	Owner	Misc.
1750	--	Membor	x			B	E. Plaisted	
1750	--	Tom		x		KE	J. Frost	
1750	--	Sarajohn	x			B	I. Goodwin	Indian
1751	30	Greg		x		K	W. Whipple	
1751	26	Will		x		K	J. Moore	See 1744 – same?
1751	--	Parris		x		K	00	
1751	--	NN		x		K	J. Curtis	
1752	40	NN	x			K	N. Ward	
1752	--	Jess		x		K	00	
1752	20	Bess		x		KE	C. Frost	
1752	--	Lidia	x			KP	Major Cutts	
1752	40	Titus		x		KP	E. Gunnison	
1752	--	NN	x			KP	" "	
1752	--	NN		x		KP	" "	
1752	38	Silas		x		KE	C. Frost	
1752**	--	NN			x	KP	A. Raitt	shipment of 39 Negroes
1752	20s	Hannah	x			KE	N. Shapleigh	old
1754	300	NN		x		K	N. Sparhawk	
1754	--	Cato		x		KP	" "	
1754	--	Juba	x			KP	" "	
1754	--	Scipio		x		KP	" "	
1754	--	NN		x		KP?	N. Sparhawk	
1754**	--	NN		x		KP?	" "	least boy but one."
1754**	--	NN	x			KP	" "	six girls
1755	26	Jack		x		KP	Rev. Newmarch	
1755	--	Phillis	x			KP	Maj. Cutts	
1756	26	three men	x			KP	T. Gerrish	
1756	--	Cloe	x			K	E. Wilson	
1756	--	Joe		x		B	J. Morrell	
1756	--	Tobey		x		B	" "	
1756	--	Toney		x		K	S. Johnson	
1757	--	NN		x		K	B. Stacy	
1758	30	Cesar		x		B	A. Neal	
1758	--	Pomp		x		KE	D. Fernald	
1759	35	Primus		x		B	J. Shapleigh	
1759	30	Celia	x			KE	J. Shapleigh	
1759		Prince		x		KE	J. Shapleigh	

* ethnicity uncertain   ** more than one   NN no name   00 slave status unknown
UNO unknown owner

DATA COMPOSITE – EARLY KITTERY & BERWICK ENSLAVED BLACKS
With Evaluation When Known

Date	£Amt.	Name	F	M	NG	Loc.	Owner	Misc.
1759	--	NN			x	KP	W. Pepperrell	unknown quantity
c1760	--	Boston		x		K	W. Rice	
c1760	--	Dinah	x			K	" "	
1761	40	Fan	x			KP	N. Emery	
1761	--	NN		x		B	J. Lord	
1761	--	Cato		x		B	S. Lord	
1762	47	NN		x		K	S. Pray	
1762	42	NN	x			K	" "	girl
1762	37	NN	x			K	" "	woman
1763	--	Celia	x			KE	S. Frost	
1763	--	Quam		x		K	T. Rogers	
1763	--	Dinah	x			K	T. Rogers	
1763		Hetty	x			KE	J. Shapleigh	
1764	--	Cicaro		x		KP	M. Pepperrell	
1764	25	NN			x	B	E. Hill	
1764	40	Peter		x		B	E. Hill	
1764	35	Dinah	x			B	E. Hill	
1764	--	Phillis	x			KP	N. Sparhawk	
1764	--	Sambo		x		KP	" "	
1764	--	Adam		x		K	B. Fernald	
1764	--	Bess	x			KP	E. Dearing	
1764	--	Cato		x		K	W. Wentworth	
1764		Amy Hall		x		B	M. Lord	
1764	--	Amos Hall	x			B	M. Lord	
1765	--	Dinah	x			K	T. Fernald	
1765	--	NN	x			KP	M. Pepperrell	
1767	15	Phillis	x			KE	S. Frost	
1767	25	Scipio		x		KE	S. Frost	
1767	50	Plato		x		KE	" "	
1767	6	Pompey		x		KE	" "	one year old
1768	18	NN		x		K	W. Wentworth	
1768	13	NN		x		KE	J. Tetherly	
1768	9	NN	x			KP	J. Adams	
1768	7	NN		x		KP	" "	age 7
1768	--	Boston		x		K	W. Wentworth	
1768	--	NN	x			KE	J. Chadbourne	
1769	30	Enos		x		KE	J. Lord	

* ethnicity uncertain   ** more than one   NN no name   00 slave status unknown
UNO unknown owner

DATA COMPOSITE – EARLY KITTERY & BERWICK ENSLAVED BLACKS
With Evaluation When Known

Date	£Amt.	Name	F	M	NG	Loc.	Owner	Misc.
1769	--	Caesar		x		K	J. Rogers	
1769	--	NN			x	KE	Mrs. Shapleigh	
1770	15	Florer	x			B	J. Hill	"and her bedding"
1770	--	Selah	x			KE	D. Ferguson	
1770	--	NN			x	KE	C. Frost 4th	
C1770	--	Hetty	x			KE	Elisha Shapleigh	
1771	--	NN	x			B	J. Ricker	
1771	--	NN			x	B	" "	plus unknown quantity
1771	--	Lucy Perkins	x			B	J. Lord	
1771	--	NN			x	B	S. Brackett	
1771	--	NN			x	KP	W. Dearing	
1771	--	NN			x	K	S. Fernald	
1771	--	NN			x	K	" "	
1771	--	NN			x	K	" "	
1771	--	NN			x	K	S. Fernald, Jr.	
1771	--	NN			x	K	J. Frost	
1771	--	NN			x	KP	J. Gerrish	
1771	--	NN			x	B	J. Hamilton	
1771	--	NN			x	K	M. Hanson	
1771	--	NN			x	B	B. Hill	
1771	--	NN			x	B	J. Hill, Jr.	
1771	--	NN			x	K	J. Hutchings	
1771	--	NN			x	K	R. Keating	
1771	--	NN			x	B	S. Leighton	
1771	--	NN			x	B	J. Morrell	
1771	--	NN			x	B	P. Morrell	
1771	--	NN			x	K	B. Parker	
1771	--	NN			x	B	N. Ricker	
1771	--	NN			x	K	T. Rogers	
1771	--	NN			x	K	" "	
1771	--	NN			x	K	W. Rogers	
1771	--	NN			x	K	UNO	
1771	--	NN			x	K	" "	
1771	--	NN			x	K	" "	
1771	--	NN			x	K	" "	
1771	--	NN			x	K	" "	
1771	--	NN			x	K	" "	

* ethnicity uncertain   ** more than one   NN no name   00 slave status unknown
UNO unknown owner

DATA COMPOSITE – EARLY KITTERY & BERWICK ENSLAVED BLACKS
With Evaluation When Known

Date	£Amt.	Name	F	M	NG	Loc.	Owner	Misc.
1771	--	NN			x	K	" "	
1771	--	NN			x	K	J. Weeks, Jr.	
1771	--	NN			x	B	M. Wise	
1772	25	Peter		x		B	J. Hill	
1772	16	Jo		x		B	J. Hill	"and his bedding"
1772	--	Prince		x		B	J. Higgins	
1772	--	Dinah	x			B	A. Lord	
1772	--	Prince		x		K	M. Adams	
1773	40	NN		x		K	J. Fernald	
1773	--	Boston		x		KP	J. Underwood	
1773	--	Tony		x		B	J. Ricker	
1773	--	Zilphah	x			KP	M. Pepperrell	
1774	--	Rachel	x			K	D. Fernald	
1774	30	Ned		x		K	T. Hutchings	
1774	--	Primus		x		K	D. Fernald	
1775	--	Phillis	x			KE	J. Chase	
1775	--	Pompey		x		K	00	
1776	--	Cato		x		KP	W. Haley	
1776	--	NN	x			KP	N. Sparhawk	
1776	--	Dick		x		KP	M. Pepperrell	
1776		Margery		x		KP	M. Pepperrell	
1776	--	NN	x			KP	M. Pepperrell?	Dick's wife
1776	--	Newport		x		B	T. Haggin	
1777	--	Caesar		x		B	" "	
1777	--	Sandy		x		B	" "	
1777	--	NN			x	B	T. Higgin	unknown quantity
1778	100	Cuff	x			K	S. Gerrish	
1778	60	Phillis		x		B	I. Goodwin	
1778	--	NN			x	B	" "	Phillis' child
1778	60	Phillis	x			KP	M. Underwood	
1778	20	NN	x			B	E. Plaisted	age 9
1778	0	Bash	x			B	I. Goodwin	old
1778	--	Sambo		x		KP	B. Stevens	
1779	90	Violet	x			KE	A. Raitt	
1779	30	Susanna	x			KE	A. Raitt	old
1779	120	Pharoah		x		KE	A. Raitt	
1779	--	William		x		KP	R. Follett	

* ethnicity uncertain   ** more than one   NN no name   00 slave status unknown
UNO unknown owner

DATA COMPOSITE – EARLY KITTERY & BERWICK ENSLAVED BLACKS
With Evaluation When Known

Date	£Amt.	Name	F	M	NG	Loc.	Owner	Misc.
1781	9	NN	x			K	T. Hutching	
c1779	--	E. Tobey	x			KP	M. Pepperrell	
1781	250	Cato		x		KE	J. Frost	age 16
1782	25	Peter		x		B	W. Hight	age 8
1782	0	Dinah	x			B	W. Hight	blind
1782	25	NN	x			B	" "	age 9
1783	25	Violet	x			B	W. Hight	
1784	--	Venus	x			K	E. Rogers	
ND	--	Caesar Rogers		x		KE	C. Hammond	
ND	--	NN			x	B	M. Butler	alleged 2 +

---

* ethnicity uncertain   ** more than one   NN no name   00 slave status unknown
UNO unknown owner

Appendix Two

Slave Owners and Others Possibly Involved with Slave Owning in Early Kittery and Berwick

*Abbott, Eunice – U.S. Census 1790, OFP. (CN) (B)

Adams, John (d.1768, wife Mary) – 1768 estate inventory lists mulatto girl age 13 at £9 and mulatto boy age 7 at £7.10.0. (*MPA*, 632) (KE)

Adams, Mark (d.1820, wife Mercy) – As of Jan. 11, 1772, owned Prince. 1771 MA Tax, one slave. (*VRK*, 231; Pruitt TX) (KE)

*Allen, Ephriam – Poll Taxes 1795, 1808. U.S. Census 1810, OFP. (CN) (K)

**Barnes, Joanna (possibly Mrs. Henry) – Jan. 1711, Joanna Barnes was accused of having a bastard child by an unidentified Negro man. July 3, 1711, Joanna Barns ordered to remain in custody of Constable Wilson until next session. No further record found. (*PCRM* 4:389, 5:123) (K)

Bartlett, Capt. (Josiah or Nathan) – 1746, Cumbo, Negro woman of Capt. Bartlett, baptized. (R2PC, 77, 87) (KE)

*Bartlett, Daniel – Poll Tax 1795. (K)

*Bartlett, John – U.S. Census 1790, OFP. (CN) (K)

Billings, Mark – 1771 MA Tax, one slave. (Pruitt TX) (KP)

*Bracket, Joseph – U.S. Census 1800, 1810, OFP. (CN) (B)

Bracket, Samuel Jr. (d.1801, wife Mehitable) – 1771 MA Tax, one slave. U.S. Census 1790, OFP. (Pruitt TX) (B)

Brown, Mary, widow (Madam) – 1735 estate inventory lists three Negroes at £90. Son, Samuel Plaisted administered her estate. (*MPA*, 185; *PRPNH*, 2: 423) (B)

*Butler, Ichabod – OFP, U.S. Census, 1790, 1810. (CN) (B)

---

*Possibly connected to slave owning.   ** Blacks related.   (B) Berwick.
(CN) see Appendix Three A.   (K) Kittery   (KE) Eliot area
(KP) Kittery Point.   (OFP) Other Free Persons.   (P) See Addendum to this list.

Butler, Moses (d.1823) – "He was one of the few in Maine who owned slaves, and his kind treatment of them is evinced by the fact that two of them remained with him after emancipation as long as he lived." (George H. Butler, *Thomas Butler and His Descendants* [New York: Trow's Printing and Bookbinding Co., 1886], 14, 15) U.S. Census 1790, OFP. (CN) (B)

Cane, Nathaniel – *See* Nathaniel Kene.

*Chadbourne, Humphrey (d.1667, wife Lucy) – Sept. 1667 estate inventory lists "five servant men and mades [*sic*] at £40." (YCD 2, fol. 31) (B)

Chadbourne, Humphrey – 1771 MA Tax list, one slave. U.S. Census 1790, OFP. (Pruitt TX) (CN) (B)

Chadbourne, James (d.1768, wife Sarah) – 1768 estate inventory lists a Negro wench at £28.4.8. (YCPCR, docket 2642) (KE)

*Chandler, Samuel – U.S. Census 1810, OFP. (CN) (K)

Chapman, Isaac (d.1789, wife Mercy) – July 1,1744 "Eunice Indian serv't Isaac Chapman [and] infant baptized." (*NEGHR* 151 [1997]: 361) (KP)

Chase, Rev. Josiah (d. 1778, wife Sarah) – 1775 will gave Negro girl, Phillis, to wife as long as she remains a widow. Otherwise, Phillis goes to daughter, Sally Chase. If Sally has no children, Phillis goes to Josiah's grandson, Cotton Chase. (*MPA*, 774) (KE)

Chase, Sarah – *See* Josiah Chase. (KE)

*Chauncey, Charles – Employed, starting 1748, in Pepperrell Counting House. In 1750s was owner of vessel *Betsy* engaged in slave trade. Imported thirty-nine Negroes to Portsmouth, N.H., June 1752. (William Chauncey Fowler, *Memorials of the Chaunceys* [Boston: H.W. Dutton & Son, 1858], 70; BSRPP, group 1: 33) *See also* Raitt and Lamphere. (KP)

*Chick, Amos – U.S. Census 1810, OFP. (CN) (KE)

*Clark, Samuel – Poll Taxes 1808. (KE)

Cross, Abraham A. – Mar. 14, 1738, sells Negro woman, Mezsa, to James Fogg of Kittery for £130. (Box 9.6, John S.H. Fogg Autograph Collection [Coll. 420], MeHS) (KE)

Curtis, Joseph (d. 1751, wife Sarah) – Jan. 6, 1752, inventory lists on same line "One horse £40 – a Negro man £0. (YCPCR, docket 3811) (K)

*Cushing, John – U.S. Census 1790, OFP 1800, 1810. (CN) (B)

Cutts, Mary – *See* Robert Cutts. (K)

*Cutts, Joseph – U.S. Census 1810, OFP. (CN) (K)

Cutts, Maj. Richard (d.1790, wife Eunice) – June 21, 1752, Lidia, Negro servant of Maj. Cutts, baptized. Nov. 23, 1755, Phillis owned covenant. (*NEHGR* 151 [1997]:444; FPCR, 446) (KP)

*Cutts, Richard – U.S. Census 1810, OFP. (CN) (K)

Cutts, Robert (d.1674, wife (2) Mary) – His estate inventory July 1674 lists three Negro men, "two of them ould and decrepid"[*sic*] at £45, two Negro women at £30, two Negro women children at £20 and one Negro lad at £16. No enslaved people mentioned in his will. (*PCRM*, 2: 292, 341, 360, 364; *MW*, 34) His shipyard established ca.1648. (Stackpole, 333) (K)

Dam, Jonathan (d.1748, wife Sarah) – July 8, 1748, will gave Negro woman, Diana, to his wife, Sarah, and Negro boy, Kittery, to son, Simeon. Kittery was deeded to Simeon before his father died. Jonathan's estate inventory lists only Diana at £125. (*MW*, 596; YCPCR 27:47; *MPA*, 319) (KP)

Dam, Sarah – *See* Jonathan Dam. (KP)

Dam, Simon. Simeon – *See* Dam, Jonathan. (KP)

Dearing, Ebenezer (d.1791, wife Mary) – As of Mar. 11, 1764, he owned Bess. (*VRK*, 227) (KP)

Dearing, William (d.1787) – 1771 Mass. Tax, one slave. (Pruitt TX) (KP)

Dennett, John (d.1742, wife Mary) – On Mar. 28, 1738, will gave wife, Mary, use of Negro man, Pompey, for her lifetime. After that Pompey was to go to their son, Thomas Dennett. The gift of Pompey was the first item listed in the will.

No inventory found. (YCPCR, docket 4310) (K)

Dennett, Mary – *See* John Dennett. (K)

Ellingham, William (d. ca.1676) – Dec. 7, 1663, he purchased from father-in-law, Thomas Booth of York, "one Negro boy Mingoe and one sorrel horse for three score pounds." Ellingham had sawmill at Sturgeon

---

*Possibly connected to slave owning.   ** Blacks related.   (B) Berwick.
(CN) see Appendix Three A.   (K) Kittery   (KE) Eliot area
(KP) Kittery Point.   (OFP) Other Free Persons.   (P) See Addendum to this list.

Creek before 1651 and a public house in 1660. (YCD, 1: pt.1, fol. 159; 12: 215) (KE) Note: Randolph Stakeman, "Slavery in Maine," *MeHS Quarterly* 27, no. 2 (fall 1987), quotes a secondary source stating that Thomas Bolt of Kittery sold a Negro boy, Mingo, to a son-in-law, Francis Hooke. However, that is the wrong father-in-law for Hooke and extensive research has not revealed any such sale.

Elliot, Robert (d. ca. 1724) – 1718 will states "I give Bess child Clear [*sic*] be freedom at 20 years old and Bess her time three years after my death. I give Bess a heffer [*sic*] three years old." 1724 estate inventory lists Negro woman, Bess, at £20. Also listed a Negro girl, age 3 or 4, at £9. Robert lived at Kittery Point with his son-in-law, Timothy Gerrish, "in his last days." (*MW*, 256; *MPA*, 106) (KP)

Emery, Capt. Noah, (d.1762, wife (2) Sarah) – 1761 will cites Negro woman, Fan, "who shall serve with my son, Noah, he paying each of his brothers £50 for their shares in her." Inventory of 1762 lists "Fannie" at £40. (*MPA*, 535, 539) (KP)

Emery, Noah, Jr. – See Emery Noah, Sr. (KP)

Ferguson, Daniel (d. ca.1783, wife Abigail) – July 12, 1770, his Negro girl Selah was baptized at his house. (R2PC, 112) (KE)

**Ferguson, Elizabeth – Her 1801 will states, "To Ammey Marsh I bequeath $20 together with my homespun wearing apparel & two bushels Indian meal, to Jack Robert, so called, $20 and two bushels Indian meal." Also refers to her sheep being kept by Henry Black. (YCPR, docket 5634) (KE)

Fernald, Benjamin – 1764 he advertises for "runaway Adam, age about 17, born in New England, speaks good English." Reward Six dollars. (*New Hampshire Gazette*, June 1, 1764) (K) (*See* Adam for details.)

Fernald, Capt. Dennis (d.1805, wife Sarah) – July 27, 1756, "Ran away the 24th of this instant July, from his Master Dennis Fernald of Kittery, a mulatto boy named Pomp about age 21, five feet, eight inches high, a short thick set fellow…and at same time a white girl about age 16…four dollars both or two dollars each." As of May 3, 1774, he owned Rachel and her newborn son, Primus. "July 1776 Rachel, Negro woman belonging to Capt. Fernal [*sic*], married Ned Negro belonging to Capt. Blasdel of York." Oct. 24, 1784, an unnamed Negro woman was delivered of a male child at

Fernald's house. (*OE* 1: 144; *VRK*, 135; K3PC, 18; Daniel Pierce Record Book, 4) (K)

Fernald, James (d.1740, wife Mary) – July 1742 estate inventory lists Richard, value £150 and Harry value £100. (*MPA*, 227; YCPCR, docket 5726) (KP)

Fernald, John 3rd (d. ca.1773, wife Miriam) – 1773 estate inventory lists a Negro man at £40. 1771 Mass. Tax, one slave. (*MPA*, 701; Pruitt TX) (K)

*****Fernald, Nathaniel** – Poll Taxes 1782. (K)

Fernald, Samuel – 1770 List of Personal Estates shows "Samuel Fernald & Son" having two Negroes. 1771 Mass. Tax, two slaves. (*NEHGR* 55 [1901]: 254–55; Pruitt TX) (K)

Fernald, Samuel – 1771 Mass. Tax, one slave. (Pruitt TX) (K)

Fernald, Samuel – July 27, 1760, Dinah, Negro woman of Samuel Fernald, baptized. (R2PC, 93) (Unknown which of the three Samuel Fernalds owned Dinah.) (KE)

Fernald, Thomas – 1736 account with Timothy Gerrish for "three pair of Negro's shoes." Negro woman, Dinah, Servt. Thomas Fernald, admitted Aug. 18, 1765. Mass. Tax 1771, one slave. (fol. 1:8, Elizabeth K. Hobbs Collection, Coll. 73, MeHS; Record Book, Second Church, Eliot, vol. 22, Coll. 1189, MeHS; Pruitt TX) (KP)

Fernald, William, Sr. (d.1724, wife Elizabeth) – Estate inventory of 1728 lists a Negro woman at £20. Another inventory lists a Negro woman at £40. In 1729, "this woman removed from list as not property of [his] estate at York." (*MPA*, 131, 142; YCPCR, docket 5832) (K)

Fogg, James (d.1787, wife Elizabeth) – Mar. 14, 1738, Abraham Cross of Kittery sold James Fogg of Kittery a Negro woman, Mezsa, for £130. (box 9.6, John S.H. Fogg Autograph Collection, Coll. 420, MeHS) (KE)

Follet, Robert (d.1780, wife, Mercy) – May 24, 1779 – "…in consideration of my Negro man William serving me and my family for 2 years from this date and behaving with respect to me and my assigns, [I] grant freedom to sd Negro who calls himself William Simmonds." Follet was merchant and sail-maker. Served as Master on *Raleigh* with 'Negro'

---

*Possibly connected to slave owning.   ** Blacks related.   (B) Berwick.
(CN) see Appendix Three A.   (K) Kittery   (KE) Eliot area
(KP) Kittery Point.   (OFP) Other Free Persons.   (P) See Addendum to this list.

William Follet. (*MPA*, 800; Charles W. Tibbetts, ed., *New Hampshire Genealogical Record [Dover]* 2 [1904]: 184) (KP)

Frost, Abigail – *See* Sarah Frost. (KE)

Frost, Charles (d.1697, wife Mary) – His 1691 will gave Negro man, Tony, to son, Charles, after his mother, Mary, dies. He gave Negro boy, Esquire, to son, John (age 11) when said son comes of age and gave Negro boy, Prince, to son, Nicholas, with same proviso. Nicholas died 1699 at age 8 and quit claim records show his inherited "Negro boy" (Prince?) went to brother, Charles. (*MW*, 116–17; *YD*, 7:20–21, 67.) Note: In 1676, Charles had "three boys" in house who helped scare away attacking Indians. At that time Frost only had three very young daughters. Apr. 1695 letter from Charles Frost describes Indian boy named Hector. (Stackpole, 415; *OE* 4:89) (KE)

Frost, Charles, Jr. (d.1724, wife (2) Jane) – 1724 will of Charles, Jr., gave son, Charles III, a Negro man, Hector, and, after death of Mrs. Charles, Jr (Jane), Negro man, "Peinc" (illegible, probably Prince), goes to Charles III. This will also gave Negro man, Pompey, to son, John Frost. After death of Charles, Jr.'s wife, a Negro boy, Cesar, goes to son, Elliott Frost (d.1732). Charles' 1724 estate inventory lists three Negro men at £60 each, a Negro girl and a Negro boy at £60. (*MW*, 257, 264; *MPA*, 106) (KE) *See also* Charles Frost (d. 1697).

Frost, Charles III (d.1751, wife Sarah) – His father's will of Sept. 24, 1724, gave him Negro man, Hector. Aug.12, 1740, Charles mortgages lands, livestock, a silver tankard, and Negroes, Deborah at £60, Dinah age 5 at £35, Cyrus age 3 at £35, and one-year-old Phillis at £15 to Sir William Pepperrell for £800. This mortgage discharged July 1, 1742. On Jan. 23, 1745, Frost gave daughter, Jane, a Negro girl, Phillis, and Sept. 23, 1743, he gave son, Charles IV, a Negro boy, Peter. Frost's 1752 estate inventory lists Negro boy, Silas, at £37.6.8 and Negro girl, Bess, at £20. (*MW*, 264; YCD, 22:72, 28:5; YCPCR, docket 6300) (KE)

Frost, Charles IV (d.1788) – Apr. 18, 1762, sold Negro boy, Peter, age 18 or 19, to Nathaniel Sparhawk for £45. 1770 Tax List of Personal Estates for Charles lists a Negro man. (YCD 37: 100; *NEHGR* 55 [1901]: 254–55) (KE)

*Frost, James – U.S. Census 1790, OFP. (CN) (B)

Frost, Jane (Mrs. Charles, Jr., d.1781) – Husband's 1724 will gave for her lifetime, Prince and Cesar. In 1727, her son, Charles III, as executor states "Delivered one Negro girl and one Negro boy to Mother along with 4 oxen, 43 sheep and 12 swine." The business accounts 1733–45 of Jane Frost with Timothy Gerrish includes debits for shoes for Negroes, Prince and Kittery, and credits for several weeks work for Gerrish by Prince and Kittery. (*MW*: 257, 264; YCPCR, docket 6327; fol. 8, Elizabeth K. Hobbs Collection, Coll. 73, MeHS) (KE)

Frost, Jane (b. 1724) – Jan. 23, 1745, her father, Charles Frost, III, gave her Negro girl, Phillis. (YCD, 28:5) (KE)

Frost, Madam Jane (d. ca. 1747) – Estate inventory 1749 lists Negro boy, Cato, age 16 at £250, Negro boy, Pompey, age 10 at £250 and Negro woman, Flora, at £250. No mention of enslaved people in her will. (YCPCR 8:160; *MW*, 604) (KE)

Frost, John – *See* Charles Frost (d.1697). (KE)

Frost, John – *See* Charles Frost (d.1724). (KE)

Frost, John (d.1770, wife Sarah) – 1697 will of father, Charles, gave him Negro, Esquire. Oct. 31, 1750, John writes to brother-in-law, Timothy Gerrish, to "come help Tom drive off cattle safely." His 1768 will directs that "my Negro Tom is to be sold to pay my debts."(*MW*, 116 fol. 9; Elizabeth K. Hobbs Collection, Coll. 73, MeHS; *MPA*, 626) (KE)

Frost, John – 1771 Mass. Tax, one slave. (Pruitt TX) (KE)

Frost, Mercy (Mrs. Simon) -- Apr. 22, 1770, Phillis, Negro woman of Mercy Frost, is baptized. July 14, 1771, Pomp, son of Phillis, Negro of Mercy Frost, baptized. 1771 Mass. Tax, two slaves. Her 1790 will states "The Negro woman Phillis I expect to be supported from my children in case she should stand in need...." (R2PC, 93; Records Second Church, Coll. 1189, MeHS; Pruitt TX; *YCMWA*, 89.) (KE)

*Frost, Nicholas (d.1663) -1663 estate inventory lists a servant boy 7 and ¾ years at £14. (*PCRM*, 2: 383. An editor's footnote here says numbers refer to time yet to be served, but gives no reason for his supposition.) (KE)

---

*Possibly connected to slave owning.   ** Blacks related.   (B) Berwick.

(CN) see Appendix Three A.   (K) Kittery   (KE) Eliot area

(KP) Kittery Point.   (OFP) Other Free Persons.   (P) See Addendum to this list.

Frost, Nicholas (d.1672 in Ireland) – 1674 inventory of estate lists "a servant boy 15 years old to serve seven years, £10." (*PCRM*, 2: 297) (KE)

Frost, Sarah – June 17,1763, deed, Sarah Frost to daughter, Abigail Frost, "Celia Negro girl during her term of life reserving to myself the labour and service of said Negro when I shall stand in need…during my life." Witnesses: Simon and Mercy Frost. (YCD 40:53; "Sarah Frost, deed for a Negro–1763," Misc. Box 96, Coll. 1991, MeHS) (KE) *See also* Charles Frost (d. 1751).

Frost, Sarah (wife, Rev. Alpheus Spring) – It may be that Sarah was the holder, if not owner, of Pompey, a slave born in her father, Simon Frost's, household. Pompey (Pomp) took surname "Spring" and ca.1792 moved to Portsmouth, N.H. Two persons of color are in Rev. Spring's household in 1790. (*Black Portsmouth*, 98–105; U.S. Census 1790, OFP) (KE)

Frost, Simon (d.1766, wife Mercy) – Will of 1765 lists "all my Negroes." His 1767 inventory lists Negro man, Plato, at £50, Negro woman, Phillis, at £15, Negro boy, Scipio, age 7 at £25 and Negro boy, Pompey, one year old at £6. A 1775 estate account credits "sale of Scipio Negro lad £20 and £30." (*MPA*, 598, 610, 732; YCPCR, docket 6364) (KE)

*Gerrish, Alexander – U.S. Census 1790, OFP. (CN) (B)

*Gerrish, Isaac – U.S. Census 1790, OFP. (CN) (B)

*Gerrish, John – U.S. Census 1790, OFP. (CN) (B)

Gerrish, Joseph (d. 1812, wife Anna) – 1771 MA Tax, one slave. (Pruitt TX) (KP)

*Gerrish, Samuel – U.S. Census 1810. OFP. (CN) (K)

Gerrish, Sarah (Mrs. Timothy) – 1778 inventory of estate lists "a Negro man Cuff £100." (fol. 1.12, Elizabeth K. Hobbs Collection, Coll. 73, MeHS) (K)

Gerrish, Timothy (d.1755, wife Sarah) – Midwife, Grace Foye (Mrs. James) testified that "on 9 July 1737 I delivered A Negro woman named Libby belonging to Timothy Gerrish, Esq. of a white female child born of her body named Celinda and I have at sundry times before delivered the same Negro woman of six black children." His estate inventory of 1756 lists three Negro men at £21.6.8. Gerrish had shoemaking business in 1730s and Jane Frost's slaves, Prince and Kittery, were working for Gerrish in some unknown capacity. (Kittery Town Records, Book 2: 135–36; *MPA*, 438; fol. 8, Elizabeth K. Hobbs Collection, Coll. 73, MeHS.) (KP)

*Goodwin, Daniel** – U.S. Census 1790, OFP. (CN) (B)

Goodwin, Ichabod (d. 1777, wife Elizabeth) – Jan. 1, 1748, advertisement for Negro man, Pompey, described his clothing and that he "had one ear cut…speaks good English. Reward £4." July 24, 1749, Goodwin's ad for "Pomp" states that "it is said he has changed his clothes since he ran away." July 9, 1750, Goodwin also sought runaway enslaved Indian woman. *See* Sarah-John. July 20, 1750, he again advertised for Pompey who had been fitted with an iron slave collar. "Reward £10." 1771 Mass. Tax, one slave. His 1778 estate inventory lists "an old Negro woman called Bash…of no value, a young Negro woman called Phillis and her child at £60." His 1789 estate account mentions boarding an old Negro woman for 49 weeks. He was a blacksmith. (*Boston Post Boy*, above dates; Pruitt TX; *MPA*, 766, 946; Berwick Papers Misc.1705–1810, Coll. S-3021, MeHS) (B)

*Goodwin, James** – U.S. Census 1790, OFP. (CN) (B)

*Gould, Daniel** – Poll Taxes 1795. (B)

Gowen, James (d.1781) – Feb. 1, 1748, he purchased "a certain Negro man about twenty-one years of age named Trysell from John Perry of Kittery for £112." (John F. Sprague, ed., *Sprague's Journal of Maine History*, 12 vols. [Dover, Me.: J.F. Sprague, 1913–23], 1: 224; source not cited.) (KE)

*Green, Mr.** – Poll Taxes 1808. (KE)

Gunnison, Elihu (d. ca.1752, wife Margery) – Feb. 21, 1742, Titus, a Negro servant of Capt. Elihu Gunnison, owned the covenant. In 1752, his wife's account of estate expenses list clothing, shoes, etc. "for Negro Titus a servant maid and a servant boy." (FPCR, 357; *MPA*, 421) (KP)

Gunnison, Margery (d.ca. 1769) – Inventory of 1769 lists Negro Titus at £30. 1769 estate account includes cost of Negro's board and "crs (credits?) include fish caught by Negro and leasing Negro for a day." Later cost account includes a Negro who died Apr. 10, 1771, inventoried at £30. (*MPA*, 658, 669) (KP)

---

*Possibly connected to slave owning.   ** Blacks related.   (B) Berwick.
(CN) see Appendix Three A.   (K) Kittery   (KE) Eliot area
(KP) Kittery Point.   (OFP) Other Free Persons.   (P) See Addendum to this list.

Haggin, Edmund – U.S. Census 1790, OFP (CN) (B) *See also* Tilley Haggin.

Haggin (Higgin), John – Advertisement for runaway Negro man, Prince, "well set fellow about 25 years of age, has a scar in his forehead over his left eye, had on Kersey round tail'd jacket, woolen under jacket and moose skin breeches…four dollars reward." (*Essex Gazette*, June 16–23, 1772) U.S. Census 1790, 1800, OFP. (CN) (B) *See also* Tilly Haggin.

Haggin, Mary – *See* Tilly Haggin (B)

Haggin (Higgin), Tilly (d. ca. 1777, wife Mary) – 1771 Mass. Tax, two slaves. His 1777 will gave wife Mary "all my Negroes except those I dispose of in this will…as long as she remains a widow." He gave son, John, Negro boy Caesar "who he has with him" and to son Edmund, a Negro boy called Sandy. In Aug. 1776, Tilly advertised for runaway Negro man named Newport, described as age 34, 5 feet, 5 inches tall, speaks good English and "is scar'd in his temples which was done in Guinea. Five dollars reward." (Pruitt TX; YCPCR 13:87; *Continental Journal*, Sept.9, 1776) (B)

Haley, William – Advertisement for runaway Negro man, Cato, aged twenty-five. (*Freeman's Journal*, Sept. 14, 1776) U.S. Census 1800, OFP. (CN) (K)

***Hall, John** – Poll Taxes 1808. (KE)

Hamilton, John – 1771 Mass. Tax, one slave. (Pruitt TX) (B)

***Hamilton, Jonathan** – U.S. Census 1790, OFP. (CN) (B)

Hammond, Christopher and Thomas – Said to have jointly owned an enslaved man named Cezar Rogers; later, Christopher declined ownership. The 1784 List of Polls & Property Evaluation shows a column marked "Black Persons" and Christopher Hammond's household shows one such person. (Oddly, that column shows "zero" for all other Kittery households but other Poll Lists suggest, if not show, Black presence.). (*OE*, 3: 141; "A list of the polls and of the estates real and personal of the several proprietors and inhabitants of the town of Kittery in the county of York, 1784," Coll. 2400, MeHS) (KE)

Hanscom, Moses (d.1793) -1771 Mass. Tax, one slave. (Pruitt TX) (K)

***Hanscom, Tobias** – U.S. Census 1810, OFP. (CN) (KE)

***Heard, Joseph** – U.S. Census 1800, OFP. (KE)

Higgin – *See* Haggin.

Hight, Mary – *See* William Hight. (B)

Hight, William (d. ca. 1782, wife Mary) – 1771 Mass. Tax, one slave. His 1782 will gave son, Temple Hight, after his mother's death, Negroes Dinah, Violet, and Peter. 1783 inventory lists a Negro woman blind £0, a Negro boy, age 8 at £25, and a Negro girl aged 9 at £25. (Pruitt TX; *MPA*, 819, 831) (B)

Hill, Abigail (Mrs. Thomas Wallingford) – *See* Sarah Hill. (B)

Hill, Benjamin – 1771 Mass. Tax, one slave. (Pruitt TX) (K)

Hill, Elisha (d ca.1764, wife Mary) – 1764 estate inventory lists Negro man Peter at £40, Negro woman Dinah at £35, and Negro child at £5. (YCPCR, docket 9214) (B)

Hill, John (d. 1772, wife Sarah) – 1770 will gave wife Sarah a Negro boy Peter and, while she remains a widow, was given Negro woman Florer and Negro man Jo. Otherwise, she must give Florer and Jo to whichever children or grandchildren she chooses. John's 1772 estate inventory lists Peter at £25, Jo and his bedding at £18, and Florer and her bedding at £15. 1771 Mass. Tax, two slaves. (*MPA*, 678, 680; Pruitt TX) (B)

Hill, John, Jr. – 1771 Mass. Tax, two slaves. U.S. Census 1790, OFP. Poll Tax 1795. (Pruitt TX) (CN) (B)

Hill, Sarah (Mrs. John, Jr., d.1772) – Her 1772 will directs executors to sell Peter to pay her debts. Sarah gave Negroes Florer and Jo to her daughter Abigail, wife of Capt. Thomas Wallingford. (*MPA*, 684) (B)

*Hobbs, Nathaniel – U.S. Census 1810, OFP. (CN) (B)

*Hodsdon, Benjamin – U.S. Census 1790, OFP. (CN) (B)

*Hodsdon, "Widow" – U.S. Census 1800, OFP. (CN) (K)

Hooke (Hook), Francis (d. ca.1695, wife Mary) – Feb. 9, 1685, Francis Hooke filed a quit claim on Hannah and Tom who were part of a Barbados estate inherited by Mrs. Hooke (Mary). Dec. 16, 1685, they mortgaged their Kittery Point property, house, lands, livestock, "one Negro boy Tom or Thomas," and vessels, etc., to Henry Dearing of Boston for £150 with agreement to repay on or before Oct. 1, 1686. In April 1686, it appears that Hooke gave Tom and certain other property to Henry Dearing.

---

*Possibly connected to slave owning.   ** Blacks related.   (B) Berwick.
(CN) see Appendix Three A.   (K) Kittery   (KE) Eliot area
(KP) Kittery Point.   (OFP) Other Free Persons.   (P) See Addendum to this list.

Hooke's 1695 will gave all property "including Negros" to wife Mary. He also states "My will and desire is that my boy Samuel be brought up in the fear of God and disposed of to a religious family when my wife dies." Hooke had no children of his own. (YCD, 4:53–54; *YD* 4: fol.133–34; *MW*, 108). Note: Hooke had another enslaved or indentured person, Mary Crucy,** who was found guilty of theft in 1683. Court directs that Hooke "is empowered to dispose of her to his best Advantage." (*PCRM*, 3: 182) (KP)

Hook, Mary (Mrs. Francis) – Her 1706 probate inventory lists Negro woman Hannah at £25 and a mulatto boy about two years old at £5. (*MPA*, 50) (KP)

*Hovey, Ivory – U.S. Census 1790, O.F.P. (CN) (B)

Hubbard, Phillip (d.1713, wife Elizabeth) – 1713 estate inventory lists a Negro woman at £35. (*MPA*, 65–66) (B)

*Hubbard, Mrs. Joshua (Dorcus) – U.S. Census 1810, O.F.P. (CN) Her 1817 will gave "my black girl Violet March all my day apparel, small feather bed and bedding, one chest, a kitchen table and chairs…and decent mourning [clothes]." (*YCMWA*, 290) (KE)

Hutchings, Caleb – 1771 Mass. Tax, one slave.1781 estate inventory lists a Negro girl at £9. (Pruitt TX; *MPA*, 799; YCPCR, docket 10020) (K)

Hutchings, James – 1771 Mass. Tax, one slave. (Pruitt TX) (K)

Hutchings, Martha – *See* Thomas Hutchings. (K)

Hutchings (Hutchins), Thomas (d. ca. 1772, wife Martha) – May 1770, Ned, Negro man belonging to Thomas Hutchins, admitted to full covenant. His 1772 will gave wife a Negro man Ned while she remains a widow. Otherwise, Ned goes to daughter Hannah (Mrs. Samuel Clough of York). His 1774 estate inventory lists Negro man Ned at £30. (K3PC, 26; *MPA*, 709, 712) (K)

Johnson, Samuel – May 18, 1749, advertised for an unnamed runaway Negro man, aged 25. Describes clothing and offers "reasonable reward." June 15, 1755, his Black slave, Toney, drowned Johnson's five-year-old daughter, Mary. In his confession to the crime, Toney blamed Johnson's severe abuse of him. Toney was hanged July 29, 1756. (*See* Toney for more details.) Johnson listed as Quaker, 1737. (*Boston Weekly Post Boy*, Oct. 2, 9, 16; *Boston News Letter*, Aug. 11, 1755, July 1, 1756; Daniel Allen

Hearn, *Legal Executions in New England, 1623 to 1960* (Jefferson, N. C.: McFarland, 1999), 143–44; *MHGR* 7:20) (K)

*Junkin, Robert – U.S. Census 1790, OFP. (CN) (B)

Keating, Capt. Richard (d.1773) – 1771 Mass. Tax, one slave. (Pruitt TX) (K)

Kene (Keen, Cane), Nathaniel (d.1722, wife Sarah) – In 1694, he was brought to trial for murdering his Black slave, Rachel. After a prolonged court case, he was found guilty only "of cruel beating and hard usage" of his slave and fined £5 plus court costs of £5.10s. He may have not have actually paid the fine portion. (*PCRM*, 4: 34–35, 372; Lorenzo Johnson Greene, *The Negro in Colonial America* [New York: Columbia University Press, 1942; reprint. New York: Atheneum, 1969], 234) (K)

** Lamphear, Samuel (wife, Joanna Dearing) – Dec. 1749, Master of ship involved in disastrous slave-trading voyage in which 43 of 113 African slaves died at sea. June 1752, Master of the *Betsy*, Charles Chauncey, owner, arriving in Portsmouth from Guinea with thirty-nine Negroes. Likely same group advertised for sale by Alexander Raitt on June 15, 1752. Lamphear also Master of various other vessels arriving Portsmouth from Guinea, Africa, Barbados, etc., through 1750s. Was master, Nov.12, 1755, of the *Exeter*, John Moffatt, owner, cleared for Africa and returned to Portsmouth in 1757 from Barbados with 61 Negroes? (Sparhawk to Colman, Jan. 18, 1750, William Pepperrell Papers, MHS; BSRPP, group 1: 33; *Boston Post Boy*, June 29,1752; BSRPP, group 1: 101; Log of the *Exeter*, Moffatt-Whipple Papers, New Hampshire Historical Society, Concord; *Boston News Letter*, Aug. 3, 1758.) (KP)

Leighton, John (d.1724, wife Honor) – Estate inventory of 1725 lists Negro woman at £20. (*MPA*, 108) (KE)

Leighton, Samuel – 1771 Mass. Tax, one slave. (Pruitt TX) (KE)

Leighton, Tobias (d. 1748, wife (2) Sarah) – Feb. 1736, Quamino, a Negro belonging to Leighton is convicted of stealing leather goods from Nathan Bartlett. Will of 1748 gave "my Negro boy" to son, Tobias. Estate

---

*Possibly connected to slave owning.   ** Blacks related.   (B) Berwick.
(CN) see Appendix Three A.   (K) Kittery   (KE) Eliot area
(KP) Kittery Point.   (OFP) Other Free Persons.   (P) See Addendum to this list.

inventory lists Negro boy at £350. Estate sale advert. July 7, 1751, lists "a likely Negro man" among household goods. Estate account 1752 lists Negro boy at £40. (YCGSP, 2: 129; *MW*, 590; *MPA*, 319, 403) (KE)

Leighton, Tobias, Jr. – 1771 Mass. Tax, one slave. (*See also* Tobias Leighton, Sr.) (Pruitt TX) (KE)

Leighton, William (d.1749, wife Sarah) – Estate inventory of 1749 lists Negro girl at £65. (*MPA*, 338) (B)

*****Lewis, Mary** – U.S. Census 1790, OFP. (CN) (K)

*****Lewis, Thomas** – U.S. Census 1790, OFP. (CN) (K)

Lewis, Mrs. William (widow) – Aug. 7, 1792, Dr. Pierce dressed a leg of a Negro woman in her household. Visit paid for by two days' work by a Negro hauling wood. (Daniel Pierce Record Book, 40, 41.) (K)

Lord, Capt. Abraham (d. ca. 1779, wife Margaret) – Oct. 3, 1742, Chance [*sic*], Mr. Abraham Lord's Negro, owned covenant and baptized. 1771 Mass. Tax, one slave. His 1772 will gave wife Negro woman Dinah. To son, David he gave Negro man Chaunce. (FSCRB, 58; Pruitt TX; *MPA*, 777) (B)

Lord, David – *See* Abraham Lord. (B)

*****Lord, Ebenezer** – U.S. Census 1790, OFP. (CN) (B)

Lord, Jane (Mrs. Ebenezer) – 1782 estate lists expense, detailed care and burial of an aged Negro woman. (*MPA*, 817; YCPCR 13:254) Note: Could she be Membor? Jane first married William Plaisted, who was to inherit Membor. (B)

Lord, John (d.1761, wife Mary) – 1761 will gave a Negro man to his son, Tobias Lord. However, that man is not listed in the inventory. (YCPCR, dockets 12168, 12169) (B)

*****Lord, John** – U.S. Census 1790, 1810, OFP. (CN) (B)

Lord, Capt. John (d. ca. 1769, wife Bridget) – ca. May 1762, father, Lt. Samuel's will gave him Negro boy Enos. John's 1769 estate inventory lists Negro boy Enos at £30. The 1771 estate account lists "expense for Lucy Perkins, a lame Negro servant and expense for tending Enos a Negro boy who died." (*MPA*, 641, 670) (B)

Lord, Margaret – *See* Abraham Lord. (B)

*****Lord, Mark** – U.S. Census 1790, OFP. (CN) (B)

Lord, Martha (Mrs. Samuel, d.1776) – 1764 will, "to my maid servant Sarah three of my kitchen chairs, a pine chest, a small iron pot & kettle, also one bed and bedding…my daily wearing apparel, my old black gown & hood and apron for mourning. It is my will and pleasure that at my decease she be discharged from slavery and become a free woman to be at her own dispose if she sees fit to accept of it." To my son, Samuel Lord, "my servant boy Amos called Amos Hall till he [Amos] becomes 30 years on 4 January 1784 and it is my will & pleasure that he then become free to act for himself… forever." To [25-year-old] granddaughter Martha Marshall, [I give] my servant girl Amey (called Amey Hall) to serve her till she becomes 25 on 8 January 1785. And it is my will & pleasure that at expiration of said term she become free and be at her own dispose." (YCPCR, docket 12221) Note: Amos may have gone to another heir because Samuel and John died before Martha Lord. (B)

Lord, Nathan (d.1733, wife Martha) – 1733 estate inventory lists one Negro at £100. (*MPA*, 165) (B)

Lord, Nathan (d. 1792, wife Esther) – Nov. 29, 1741, "Peter Mr. Nathan Lord's Negro baptized." In May 1762, he is given Negro man Cato in the will of his father, Lt. Samuel Lord. (FSCRB, 54; YCPCR, docket 12272) (B)

Lord, Lt. Samuel (d.1762, wife Martha d.1776) – Bought Sara, age 4, in 1720. Nov.1, 1742, "Sarah the servant of Lt. Samuel Lord owned covenant and baptized and Amy her child baptized," Child died 1742. Apr. 18, 1761, separate codicil to his will gave Negro boy Enos to son John and gave Negro man Cato to son, Nathan. No mention of Sarah. (FSCRB, 58; Lord, "Black Sara"; YCPCR, docket 12272) (B)

Lord, Tobias – *See* John Lord (d. 1761). (B)

Marshall, Martha (Mrs. Nahum Marshall) – *See* Martha Lord.

Mendum, Sareth S. (widow of Jonathan, Jr.) – 26 May 1718, sold "one Negro man aged about 35 called Seaser" to William Pepperrell for £35. (Vol. 8, John S.H. Fogg Autograph Collection (Coll. 420), MeHS) (K)

---

*Possibly connected to slave owning.   ** Blacks related.   (B) Berwick.
(CN) see Appendix Three A.   (K) Kittery   (KE) Eliot area
(KP) Kittery Point.   (OFP) Other Free Persons.   (P) See Addendum to this list.

More (Moore), Ebenezer, Jr. (wife Temperance) – 1733 estate inventory lists a Negro woman at £60 and Negro's bed and cabin, value £1. (*MPA*, 171) (KP)

Moore, Capt. John (wife Deborah) – 1751 estate inventory lists Negro man Will at £26.13.4. Unsure if same "Will" as below. No direct connection found between these two families. (*MPA*, 364) Note: In 1737, Wm. Pepperrell's ship *Eagle*, under a Capt. John Moore, sailed for Antigua. (*NEHGR* 19 [1865]:145) (KP)

Moore, Sarah (d.1744, widow of John who d.1736) – 1748 estate inventory lists Negro named Will at £200. (*MPA*, 303). (K)

*****Morrell, Joel** – Poll Taxes 1782, 1783. (B)

Morrell, John (d. ca. 1763, wife Hannah d.1765) – 1756 will states, "If my Negro Joe outlives my wife, I give him to which ever of my sons Joe shall choose for a master. My Negro Tobey shall be free when he comes of age of 24 years, except that he shall remain my wife's servant till her decease and then be free." Was blacksmith and Quaker. (*MPA*, 559; *MHGR* 7:208) (B)

Morrell, John, Jr. (d.1780.84, wife Ruth) – 1771 Mass. Tax, one slave. Poll Taxes 1782, 1783. (Pruitt TX) (B)

Morrell, Hannah – *See* Morrell, John. (B)

Morrell, Peter (d.1801, wife Sarah) – 1771 Mass. Tax, one slave. Listed as Quaker 1745. (Pruitt TX; fol. 3 "Berwick, Maine, Papers between 1705 and 1810," Coll. S-3021, MeHS) (B)

*****Morrell, Robert** – Poll Taxes 1782. (B)

*****Muggridge, Benjamin** – 1807, one person of color in household. (Misc. Coll., Kittery Town Clerk's Office) (K)

*****Muggridge, John** – U.S. Census 1800, OFP. (CN) (K)

Neal, Andrew Sr. (d.1739, wife Katherine) – Mar. 19, 1725, unrecorded will gave "little Negroe girle Named Dillo" to wife, Katherine. Negro man Quash is given to son John Neal. 1739 will only mentions Dillo. His 1742 estate inventory lists Negro "garle" at £100. Andrew listed as Quaker in 1737. (*OE* 3: 20–21; *MW*, 408; *MPA*, 215; *MHGR* 7:208) (KE)

Neal, Andrew, Jr. (d. 1757, wife Dorcas d. 1791) – 1756 will gave son, James, a Negro boy, Cesar. However, Cesar must also serve wife Dorcas and son Andrew. He adds that if James neglects to care for his mother, then she may take Cesar away from him. Further, if his son Andrew settles in Berwick, Cesar shall serve him two years and then [be returned] "as well clothed as he was when he took him." Estate inventory of 1758 lists Negro boy Caesar at £30. (*MW*, 814; *MPA*, 483) (KE)

Neal, James – ca. 1757, Cesar (later Cezar Sankey) was transferred to James and was finally manumitted ca. 1774. (Min. Dover Mtg., ii, 39, 123; H. J. Cadbury, "Negro Membership in the Society of Friends, Part 2," *Journal of Negro History* 21 (1936): 151–213 (available online at http://www.qhpress. org/quakerpages/qwhp/hcjnh2.htm (accessed December 3, 2016) (KE)

*Neal, James – Poll Taxes 1795. (KE)

Neal, John – *See* Neal, Andrew, Sr. (KE)

Neal, Katherine – *See* Neal, Andrew, Sr. (KE)

Newmarch, Rev. John (d.1754) – Estate inventory of 1755 lists Negro man Jack at £26.13.4. (*MPA*, 433–34) (KP)

*Norton, Winthrup B. – U.S. Census 1810, OFP. (CN) (B)

*Odehorn, Daniel – U.S. Census 1790, OFP. (CN) (K)

*Parhooke, Elizabeth – U.S. Census 1790, OFP. (CN) (K)

Parker, Benjamin – 1771 Mass. Tax, one slave. (Pruitt TX) (K)

Parry, John – Deed of sale, Feb. 1, 1748.49, Parry sells Negro man about 21 years of age named Trysell to James Gowen of Kittery for £112. A twentieth-century Parry descendant wrote that before Parry came to Kittery, he was a plantation owner with slaves in Jamaica, and he escaped from a slave insurrection and brought many of his slaves to Kittery where they lived and were buried on Parry farm at Sandy Hill. 1743 deed from Jos. Smalls to John Parry, "late of Jamaica, school master," 29 acres and buildings in Kittery for £300. (*OE* 3: 125; Eliot Historical Society, *Eliot Miscellany: Bits of Forgotten History* [Eliot, Me., 1876], 1; YCD, 24:153) (KE)

*Paul, Sarah – U.S. Census 1810, OFP. (CN) (KE)

---

*Possibly connected to slave owning.   ** Blacks related.   (B) Berwick.
(CN) see Appendix Three A.   (K) Kittery   (KE) Eliot area
(KP) Kittery Point.   (OFP) Other Free Persons.   (P) See Addendum to this list.

*Pepperrell, Andrew – ca.1740 order to James Kerswell: "Please to make ye Negro Phillis one pr [size] 3 shoes and charge by acct. William Pepperrell." Signed, Andrew Pepperrell. (Folder 14, Correspondence, Pepperrell Papers, 1701–1795 [MS093], Portsmouth Athenaeum) (KP)

Pepperrell, Lady Mary (d.1789) – 1759 will of husband, Sir William Pepperrell, gave her "any four of my Negros." (*MW*, 845) Mar. 25, 1764 –"Negro servant Lady Pepperrell, Cicaro, baptized." July 7, 1764 – "Infant of Cicaro & Phillis (owned by Sparhawk) privately baptized." (FPCR: 448–49) 1771 Mass. Tax, 1771, one slave. (Pruitt TX) June 27, 1773, she is listed as owner of Zilphah who on that date married Boston, owned by Capt. John Underwood. (*VRK*, 232) Her Jan.18, 1779, will states "Whereas I have liberated all my slaves, I ratify the same, viz. Cicero, Zilpah, and Dick, and whereas Dick has since died leaving two children, I give 20 shillings to each and to Cicero and Zilpah a good cow, 2 sheep and £6 sterling each…." (*MPA*, 959) This legacy was paid Jan.1790. Cicaro also received wages of £5.8.0 and Zilpah received additional £2.0.10 "as part of [her] legacy." One of Dick's children, E. Toby, was paid her 20 shillings in 1790. (YCPCR, docket 14801) Other child named Margery. Name of their mother is unknown. (*NEHGR* 151 [1997]:456) (KP)

Pepperrell, William (d.1734, wife Margery) – 1705 advert. for "runaway Negro man, Peter, c. age 20, speaks good English, of pretty brown complexion, middle stature, had on gray coat, white jacket & breeches French fall[*sic*] shoes, colored stocks, black hat." In 1706, it was reported that a Negro man and an Indian, runaways from William Pepperrell of Kittery, were captured in South Carolina and returned to Kittery. In 1714, a Boston man advertised for runaway slave, Peter, and mentioned that he was formerly a "servant" of William Pepperrell of Kittery. (*Boston News Letter*, Dec. 10, 1705, Apr. 22, 1705, and Mar. 14, 1714; Usher Parsons, *The Life of Sir William Pepperrell, Bart.* [Boston: Little Brown, 1855], 28) On May 26, 1718, William Pepperrell purchased a Negro man, Seaser [*sic*] aged about 35, from Sareth S. Mendum of Kittery for £35. (Original bill of lading, Sir William Pepperrell Papers [Coll. 35], MeHS.) In Apr. 1719, William Pepperrell purchased a Negro woman for 50 shillings. (Vol. 8, John S.H. Fogg Autograph Collection [Coll. 420], MeHS) That same year, William received five slaves on consignment from Antigua, but four died at sea and a fifth one, a woman, died three weeks after arrival (Bryon Fairchild, *Messers. William Pepperrell: Merchants at Piscataqua* [Ithaca, N.

Y.: Cornell University Press for the American Historical Association, 1954],
119). In May 1719, slave, Molly, born in his household and then raised in
William, Jr's household. (*See* Molly Miles). The 1733 will of William, Sr.,
states that "mulatto Tobey is to be free one year after my death and Scipio
is to be freed at age 40." Further, he gave daughter, Mary Watkins, "Negro
manservant George or £100 instead as she chooses" and "if sd Negro serves
her faithfully until age 40 he is to be freed." (*MW*, 344) (KP)

Pepperrell, Sir William (d.1759) – In 1740, Charles Frost mortgages his
property, including Negroes Deborah an adult, Dinah age 5, Cyrus age
3, and Phillis age 1 to William Pepperrell for £800. Mortgage discharged
1742. (YCD, 22: 72) Nov. 29, 1741, "Rebecca black serv't of Col.
Pepperrell owned the covenant." (FPCR, 357) Pepperrell's Oct. 24, 1745,
letter to wife from Louisburg siege mentions clothing for Catto. (Burrage,
100) Oct. 4, 1751, listed as owner of Beck and George Black who marry
on that date. (*VRK*, 124) Dec. 9, 1751, Pepperrell carries out a provision in
his father's 1733 will, by giving a certificate of freedom to George. (YCD
29: 116). Pepperrell's 1759 will allows wife, Mary "to choose any four of
my Negroes." Inventory not found. (*MW*, 845) Parson's *Life of Sir William
Pepperrell* (cited above) says he owned 10 or 12 slaves. *See also* Mary
(Molly) Miles and Black Richard. (KP)

Perry *See* Parry.

Plaisted, Capt. Elisha (d.1771, wife Hannah) – Apr. 18, 1722, "Cuff,
Capt. E. Plaisteds negro" owned covenant and baptized. July 3, 1743, Cuff
joined church. Elisha Plaisted of Berwick, unpublished will 1750, gave son,
William Plaisted of Berwick, Negro Coffee (Cuff?) and "my woman Negro
Membor." (William died before his father.) Elisha also mentions Negro
Scippio and a little Negro boy apparently in connection with property in
Scarborough. (FSCRB, 57, 59; D.K. Spencer Papers, OSBHS) (B)

Plaisted, Hannah (Mrs. Elisha) – her 1778 estate inventory lists nine-year-
old Negro girl at £20. The 1779 account states "By [age] 16 the young
Negro fetched more than she was appraised at thereby adding £8." (Error re
age?) (*MPA*, 764, 775) (B)

---

*Possibly connected to slave owning.   ** Blacks related.   (B) Berwick.
(CN) see Appendix Three A.   (K) Kittery   (KE) Eliot area
(KP) Kittery Point.   (OFP) Other Free Persons.   (P) See Addendum to this list.

Plaisted, Ichabod (d.1715, wife Mary) – His 1715 will gave wife Negro man Jack. To son Samuel he gave Negro man Sambo, "if he lives till my son [Samuel] comes of age." (*PRPNH* 1: 759–63) *See also* Mary Brown. (B)

Plaisted, Mary – *See* Ichabod Plaisted. (B)

Plaisted, Samuel (d. 1731 wife Hannah) – 1715 will of father, Ichabod, gave him Negro man Sambo. (See above proviso.) 1735 estate account for Samuel lists a debt of £70 to Hugh Hall for an unnamed Negro. (*PRPNH* 1: 759–60; YCPCR 5: 28–29) (B)

Plaisted, Sarah (Mrs. James) – ca.1747, has "a Negro wench." (*MW*, 6) *See* Mary Wise. (B)

*****Pray, Joseph** – U.S. Census 1790, OFP. (CN) (B)

*****Pray, Peter** – U.S. Census 1790, OFP. (CN) (B)

Pray, Samuel (d. ca. 1762, wife Sarah) – Estate inventory 1762 lists Negro man at £47.10.0, Negro woman at £37.10.0, and Negro girl at £42.0.0. (*MPA*, 546) (K)

Raitt, Alexander (d.1776) – "Kittery, June 14, 1752 – This day arrived the BETSY, Samuel Lanphier, Commander, from the coast of Guinea, with a quantity of very likely Boys and Girls of the blackest sort: All persons who incline to be purchasers may apply to me the subscriber, where they will be dealt with on reasonable terms. [Signed] Alexander Raitt." (*Boston Post Boy*, June 29, 1752) It appears this group consisted of thirty-nine Negroes as noted for the *Betsy* at the Port of Portsmouth Naval Office. Vessel owner listed as Charles Chauncey of Kittery. (BSRPP, group 1: 33) Raitt lived in Upper Kittery, but owned property near waterfront warehouses at Kittery Point. (YCD 29: 262) List of Raitt's Personal Property 1770 shows three slaves: one man and two women. (*NEHGR* 55 [1901]: 254–55) 1771 Mass. Tax, two slaves. (Pruitt TX) His 1779 inventory lists an old Negro woman, "Susa" at £30.20.12, a young Negro woman, Violet, at £90 and a Negro boy, Pharaoh at £120. Estate accounts in 1793 state, "to three Negroes which were appraised and inventoried as slaves through a mistake as they were free by nature and the laws of our land, and all of which have since absconded from their service." (*MPA*, 776, 1059–60) See list of colored persons buried on Raitt property. (*OE*, 3:143)

*****Rice, Alexander** – U.S. Census 1810, OFP. (CN) (K)

*****Rice, Samuel** – U.S. Census 1790, OFP. (CN) (K)

Rice, William – Owned Dinah and Boston. Dinah was purchased ca.1760. (Sarah Parker Rice Goodwin, "Pleasant Memories," mss coll., Strawbery Banke Museum, Portsmouth, N.H.; *Black Portsmouth*, 105) (K)

*Ricker, Mary – U.S. Census 1790, OFP. (CN) (B)

*Ricker, Tristram – U.S. Census 1790, OFP. (CN) (B)

Ricker, John – Apr. 23, 1746, "Baptized at Mr. Rickards his negros Boston, Merea, and Candace." Apr. 20, 1748, "Prince and Phillis the servants of Mr. Ricker baptized." Aug. 23, 1773, John Riker's Negro Tony died. (FSCRB, 65, 58; *NEHGR* 74 [1920]: 186) (B)

*Ricker, Gideon – U.S. Census 1810, OFP. (CN) (B)

Ricker, Joseph, Sr. (d. 1772) – 1771 will gave wife Mary "the use of one of my Negro girls for life." To sons Tristram and Joseph Ricker "the Negroes and residue of [estate] equally divided." 1771 Mass. Tax, three slaves. (*MPA*, 689; Pruitt TX) Burial ground for Ricker slaves located on Stacy Road, north side in pasture of Fred. D. Bassetts. (Spencer, *Burials*, 49) (B)

Ricker, Joseph, Jr. – *See* Joseph Ricker, Sr. (B)

Ricker, Mary – *See* Joseph Ricker, Sr. (B)

Ricker, Noah – 1771 Mass. Tax, one slave. (Pruitt TX) (B)

Ricker, Tristram – *See* Joseph Ricker, Sr. (B)

Rogers, Elizabeth (b. 1726 – d.1811, unmarried) – In addition to enslaved Dinah, she apparently acquired Venus. Between 1784 and 1802, both Blacks were treated by Dr. Daniel Pierce. Work by Venus (possibly weaving) was used to pay for his services. (Daniel Pierce Record Book, 128–29, 136) *See also* Thomas Rogers. (K)

Rogers, John – *See* Thomas Rogers. U.S. Census 1800, OFP. (CN) (K)

Rogers, Rev. John (d. 1773, wife Susannah d. 1779) – 1769 will gave wife Negro Ceasar for life and afterward to sons Nathaniel or Daniel "at Ceasar's choice." John's 1774 estate inventory lists "old bed and bedding for Negro 20 shillings. (*MPA*, 705,709; Stackpole, 708) (KE)

*Rogers, Jonathan – U.S. Census 1790, OFP. (CN) (K)

---

*Possibly connected to slave owning. ** Blacks related. (B) Berwick.
(CN) see Appendix Three A. (K) Kittery   (KE) Eliot area
(KP) Kittery Point.   (OFP) Other Free Persons. (P) See Addendum to this list.

Rogers, Susannah – *See* Rev. John Rogers. (KE)

Rogers, Thomas (d. 1776, wife Mary) – 1763 will gave son John a Negro boy Quam and a Negro girl Dinah to his daughter Elizabeth. 1771 MA Tax, two slaves. (*MPA*; 738; Pruitt TX) (K)

Rogers, William – 1771 Mass. Tax List, one slave. (Pruitt TX) (K)

Sambo – In 1778, while he was enslaved by Rev. Benjamin Stevens, Sambo bought Phillis "and all her appurtenances" for £60 from Mrs. John Underwood (Mary). (*MPA*, vi, 727) (KP)

Shapleigh, Dorcus – 1770 List of personal property shows one Negro Woman. (*NEHGR* 55 [1901]: 254–55). *See also* John Shapleigh, Jr. (KE)

*Shapleigh, Elisha – Poll Taxes 1782. U.S. Census 1800, 1810, OFP. (CN) (KE)

Shapleigh, Capt. Elijah – About 1770, owned Hetty. U.S. Census 1810, OFP. (CN) (KE)

Shapleigh, John, Sr. (d.1706, wife Sarah) – In 1683, John inherited his uncle, Maj. Nicholas Shapleigh's, estate including four Negroes. John's 1707 estate inventory listed a Negro man, Sampson, at £35. (YD 4: 43, 88; *MPA*, 52) *See* Black Will. (KE)

Shapleigh, John, Jr. (d.1759, wife Dorcas d.1780) – 1759 will gave wife, Dorcus, young Negro, Prince, and "services of a Negro woman while she keeps John's children." His estate inventory listed Primus at £35, Celia at £30, and Prince at £40. Note: Primus not mentioned in the will. (*MW*, 858; *MPA*, 507) (KE)

Shapleigh, John, 3ʳᵈ· (d. ca.1780, wife Sybilla) – 1769 will gave his wife a Negro man, Prince. His 1780 inventory does not list Prince. (YCPCR, 15:182; *MPA*, 937, 940) (KE)

*Shapleigh, Capt. John – U.S. Census 1810, OFP. (CN) (KE)

Shapleigh, Maj. Nicholas (d. ca. 1682, wife Alice) – May 26, 1676, Edward Bushnell, merchant of Boston sells a Negro man named Coffe [*sic*] "now in the custody of John Holden at Scotland on the Island of Barbados" to Maj. Nicholas Shapleigh of Kittery "for goods and considerations." His 1682 probate inventory lists "4 Neagers [*sic*]—3 men, one woman and one little Neager value all together £90." Also, two indentured Irish boys at £10 whose service ends in two years. Nephew, John Shapleigh is primary heir. In 1683, in disbursement of his estate, his wife Alice is given Black Will during her lifetime. A 1685 division of lands refers to "land [Alice Shapleigh's] Negro lives on…reserved to his sd Negro's use being about three acres…." (*See* Black Will) In 1669, Nicholas was charged as being a Quaker and ordered to stop holding Quaker meetings at his house. (SCD.9: 336; YD 5:15–16; YD 3: 126; YD 4: 52. Frederick E. Shapleigh, *The Descendants of Alexander Shapleigh the Immigrant* [Kittery, Me.: Shapleigh Family Association, 1968], 41) (KE)

Shapleigh, Nicholas (d.1752, wife Martha) – Jan. 9, 1738, Hannah, Negro servant of Maj. Shapleigh baptized. 1752 estate inventory lists "an old Negro man Samson at 20 shillings, an old Negro woman Hannah at 20 shillings." (R2PC, 77, 84; *MPA*, 380; Coll. 1189, MeHS) (KE)

Sherbourne, Henry – Mar. 18, 1787, an unidentified Negro person was treated for throat illness at Sherburne's house by Dr. Pierce. U.S. Census 1790, OFP. (Daniel Pierce Record Book, 206) CN) (K)

Skillings, Josiah (d. before 1719, wife Elizabeth) – 1719 estate inventory lists Negro woman at £30, Negro boy aged four at £20, and Negro girl aged 1½ at £15. (YCPCR, docket 17158) (K)

Skillings, Elizabeth – *See* Josiah Skillings. (K)

Sparhawk, Nathaniel (d.1776, wife Elizabeth Pepperrell) – Dec. 1749, report of 70 out of 113 Africans died aboard a slave-trading ship belonging to the firm of Sparhawk & Colman (Nathaniel and Benjamin). Reported by ship's captain Lamphier at Barbados. (William Pepperrell Papers,1664–1782, microfilm, MHS) Nov., Dec. 1754, several letters from Sparhawk to Thomas Cutt, his business manager, re shipment of six "new" Negro girls returning to Kittery Point with instructions as to their care and confinement until sold. Also references to Juba, Scipio, and Cato in Sparhawk household. Much detail regarding sales of a number other unnamed Negro females and males (*MeHS Coll.*, 2nd series, 9: 240–45). On Apr. 18, 1762, he bought Negro boy Peter "age 18 or 19" from Charles Frost for £45. (YCD 37: 100) Jan. 8, 1764, Negro servant Phillis [of] Col. Sparhawk owned covenant. (FPCR, 448). Mar.11, 1764, listed as owner of Sambo who married Bess (*VRK*, 227). July 7, 1765, his slave, Phillis' child

---

*Possibly connected to slave owning.   ** Blacks related.   (B) Berwick.
(CN) see Appendix Three A.   (K) Kittery   (KE) Eliot area
(KP) Kittery Point.   (OFP) Other Free Persons.   (P) See Addendum to this list.

was baptized (FPCR, 449). 1771 Mass. Tax lists zero "Servants for life" for Sparhawk (Pruitt TX). Apr. 21, 1776, "daughter of Negro servant Sambo, Col. Sparhawk, baptized" (FPCR, 456) (KP).

Spring, Rev. Alpheus – U.S. Census 1790, OFP. (CN). *See also* Sarah Frost. (KE)

Stacy, Benjamin, Sr. (d.1758, wife (2) Sarah d. 1763) – 1757 will gave a Negro man to wife and afterward to son Benjamin. (YCPCR 10: 54–55) Reference to Blacks' burial ground on Stacy land. (*OE* 9: 115) (KE)

Stacy, Benjamin, Jr. – *See* Benjamin Stacy, Sr. (KE)

Stacy, Sarah – *See* Benjamin Stacy, Sr. (KE)

Stevens, Rev. Benjamin (d.1791, wife Mary) – Nov. 17, 1778, Mary Underwood (Mrs. John) sold Negro woman, Phillis "with all her appurtenances" for £60 to Sambo, a slave belonging to Rev. Benjamin Stevens. (*MPA*, vi, 727; Eliza Buckminster Lee, *Memoirs of Rev. Joseph Buckminster, D.D. and of His Son, Rev. Joseph Stevens Buckminster* (Boston: William Crosby & H. P. Nichols, 1849), 54) (KP)

*Talcott, Jonathan – U.S. Census 1790, OFP. (CN) (B)

Tetherly, John (d. 1768) – 1768 will gives his brother, William Tetherly, a Negro man valued at £13.6.8. (*MPA*, 625) (K)

Tetherly, Samuel – 1747 estate inventory lists Negro man at £200. (*MPA*, 293) (KE)

Tetherly, William – *See* John Tetherly. (K)

*Tidy, Robert – Poll Taxes 1782. (K)

*Tobey, Mary – U.S. Census 1810, OFP. (CN) (KE)

*Tobey, Samuel – Poll Taxes 1782. (K)

*Tucker, Jane – U.S. Census 1790, OFP. (CN) (B)

Underwood, John (d.1795, wife, Mary) – 1771 Mass. Tax, two slaves. June 27, 1773, John listed as owner of Boston who married Zilphah. Capt. of a privateer in 1777 and Boston served onboard. John also owned Phillis when, on Nov. 17, 1778, his wife, Mary "with permission of her husband," sells Phillis for £60 to Sambo who was enslaved by the Rev. Benj. Stevens of Kittery Point. (Pruitt TX; *VRK*, 232; YCCCP box 191:15; *MPA*, vi, 727, 1111) (KP)

Unidentified owner – 1742 neighbor of Samuel Lord owned an unnamed man who married Sarah. (Lord, "Black Sara") (B)

The following are indicated as illegible names on original manuscript of 1771 Massachusetts Tax Evaluation List (see Pruitt TX):

Unidentified owner no. 0901 – 1771 Mass. Tax, three slaves. (Pruitt TX) (K)

Unidentified owner no. 0902 – 1771 Mass. Tax, three slaves. (Pruitt TX) (K)

Unidentified owner no. 1055) – 1771 Mass. Tax, one slave. (Pruitt TX) (B)

Walker, John (d.ca. 1743, wife (2) Mary) – 1743 estate inventory lists a Negro girl at £25. (*MPA*, 237; *MW*, 463) (K)

Wallingford – *See* Hill, Sarah. (B)

Ward, Capt. Nahum (wife, Dorcas) – 1752 estate inventory lists a Negro girl at £40. (*MPA*, 364, 371) (K)

Weeks, Joseph, Jr. – 1771 Mass. Tax, one slave. (Pruitt TX) (K)

Wentworth, William – 1764 advert. for mulatto man, Cato "speaks good English but stammers sometimes, age about 30, brought up on a farm… Reward six dollars." (*See* Cato for details.) 1768 estate inventory lists "a pair of moose horns, a Negro man at £8." 1769 estate account, "for supporting a Negro of the intestate quite superannuated and useless from intestate's death till this time, named Boston." (*New Hampshire Gazette,* June 1, 1764; *MPA*, 619, 644) (KE)

Whipple, Capt. William – July 4, 1742 "Pompey [owned by] William Whipple owned Covenant." 1751 estate inventory lists Negro man Pompey and Negro man Greg, both at £60. (FPCR, 358; *MPA*, 363) Note: Convicted thief, mulatto Jonathan Black, was turned over to Whipple in Feb. 1745 for service and Whipple could "dispose of him to serve someone else for a term of three years." (YCGSP, 11: 379) (KP)

---

*Possibly connected to slave owning.   ** Blacks related.   (B) Berwick.
(CN) see Appendix Three A.   (K) Kittery   (KE) Eliot area
(KP) Kittery Point.   (OFP) Other Free Persons.   (P) See Addendum to this list.

Wills, Thomas (d. ca. 1688, wife Lucy) – 1688 estate inventory included a Negro man at £12. (YCPCR 1: 7; *MPA*, 25) Lucy was widow of Humphrey Chadbourne. (K)

Wilson, Edmund (b.1743, wife Hannah) – 1771 Mass. Tax, one slave. July 30, 1772, Negro woman Cloe belonging to Edmund Wilson married Prince belonging to Mark Adams. (Pruitt TX; K3PC, 17, 28) (K)

Wise, E. – 1771 Mass. Tax, one slave. Probably Elizabeth Wise, widow of John who was son of Rev. Jeremiah Wise. (Pruitt TX) (B)

Wise, Rev. Jeremiah (d.1756) – *See* Mary Wise. (B)

Wise, Mary (Mrs. Jeremiah, d. ca.1749) – 1747 will which she makes with her husband's permission states, "it is my will that my Negro Slave Rose shall work for my daughter, Sarah Plaisted 52 days a year until her Negro wench is able to do work for her." (*MW*, 6) (B)

**Wittam – Further research needed. Surname may be linked to slave-owning. *See* List of Blacks (chapter 10).

Appendix Three (A)

Census and Tax Data

An asterisk (*) indicates surnames not found elsewhere in this project's research.

U. S. Census 1790

Kittery white households containing "Other Free Persons" (OFP, i.e. Blacks)

John Bartlett (1), Dennis Fernald (1), Mary Fernald (2), Joshua Hubbard (1), Mary Lewis* (1), Thomas Lewis* (1), Daniel Odehorn* (1), Eliza Parhooke* (1), Benjamin Parker (1), Samuel Rice (2), Eliza Rogers (2), Jonathan Rogers (1), Henry Sherbourne* (1), Rev. Alpheus Spring (2), Jane Tucker*(1).

Total OFP persons: 19

Kittery households of "Other Free Persons" and number of occupants

Cisero (as Sessoro) (2), Jack Hanscom (5), Mary Miles (5), Jack Roberts (5), Sambo (4).

Total OFP persons: 21

Kittery households of other persons of color (census taker reported as white)

Henry Black (3), Henry Black, Jr. (3), James Black (5), Catherine Black (2), Margery Black (1), Amy Marsh (1), George Patch (2).

Total persons: 17

Berwick white households containing "Other Free Persons"

Eunice Abbott* (1), Samuel Bracket (1), Ichabod Butler (1), Humphrey Chadbourne (5), John Cushing* (2), James Frost (3), Alex Gerrish (3), Isaac Gerrish (1), John Gerrish (1), Daniel Goodwin (3), James Goodwin (1), Edmund Haggins (2), John Haggins (1), Jonathan Hamilton (1), John Hill (2), Benjamin Hodsdon* (1), Ivory Hovey*(1), Robert Junkin*(1),

Ebenezer Lord (1), John Lord (1), Mark Lord (1), Joseph Pray (2), Peter Pray (3), Mary Ricker (1), Tristram Ricker (1), Jonathan Talcott*(1).

Total: 42

U. S. Census 1800

Kittery white households containing "Other Free Persons"
Elizabeth Rice [see 1810] (2), Alex. Rice (1),Richard Cutts (1), Elisha Shapleigh (1), Samuel Gerrish (1), Widow Hodsdon (1), John Muggridge (1), Ephren Allen (3), John Rogers (2), Samuel Chandler (1).

Total: 14

Kittery households of "Other Free Persons"
Black Jack (4), Cyrus (3), Jack (5), Cisero (2).

Total persons: 14

Berwick white households containing "Other Free Persons"
William Haley (1), Joseph Heard (1), Joseph Bracket (1), John Haggins (1), John Cushing (2).

Total: 6

U.S. Census 1810

Kittery white households containing "Other Free Persons"
Joseph Cutts (1), Elizabeth Rice (2).

Total: 3

Kittery households of "Other Free Persons" and number present
Phillis Pepperrell (2), Silas Sparhawk (1). See also "List of Negroes in Kittery 1810" in Misc. mss. Coll., Kittery Town Clerk's Office.

Total: 3

Eliot white households containing "Other Free Persons"
Amos Chick (2), Dorcus Hubbard (1), Tobias Hammond (1), Sarah Paul (1), John Shapleigh (1), Elijah Shapleigh (1), Mary Tobey (1).

Total: 8

Eliot households of "Other Free Persons"
Black Susan (2), Jack Hanscom (4), Susan Patch (1), Jack Robert (5).
Total: 12

Berwick white households containing "Other Free Persons"
Joseph Brackett (1), Gideon Ricker (1), Winthrup Norton (2), Ichabod Butler (1), John Cushing (1), John Lord (1), Nathaniel Hobbs (1).
Total: 8

Berwick households of "Other Free Persons"
Mariah Ricker (1), Enoch Guptil (7), Fortune March (6), Anne Williams (4), Tobias Jones (8).
Total: 26

Summary of U.S. Census Reports
1790: 39 white households with total of 61 OFP; 14 households of OFP with total of 38 inhabitants. Total OFP: 99

1800:15 white households with total of 20 OFP; 10 households of OFP with total of 14 inhabitants. Total OFP: 34

1810: 15 white households with total of 19 OFP; 12 households of OFP with 41 inhabitants. Total OFP: 60

Massachusetts Tax Evaluation of 1771
From Bettye Hobbs Pruitt, ed., *Massachusetts Tax Evaluation of 1771* (Boston: G.K. Hall & Co. Boston, Massachusetts, 1978). Total property value, when known, given in pounds sterling and number of "Servants for Life" indicated in parentheses.

Berwick: Samuel Bracket £11 (1), Humphrey Chadbourne £? (1), Ichabod Goodwin £35 (1), John Hambleton £11 (1), Tilley Haggin £43 (2), William Hight £42 (1), John Hill £30 (2), John Hill, Jr. £0.03 (2), Abraham Lord £33 (1), John Morrell £0 (1), Peter Morrell £64 (1), Joseph Ricker, Jr. £23 (3), Noah Ricker £14 (1), Elizabeth Wise £10 (1), unidentified resident no. 1055 £20 (1).

Kittery: Mark Adams £29 (1), Mark Billings £19 (1), William Dearing £16 (1), John Fernald, 3rd £12 (1), Mark Fernald £? (1), Samuel Fernald £32 (2), Samuel Fernald (Jr.?) £2 (1), Thomas Fernald £3 (1), John Frost £19

(1), Mercy Frost £11 (2), Joseph Gerrish £17 (1), Moses Hanscom £19 (1), Benjamin Hill £13 (1), Caleb Hutchings £4 (1), Richard Keating £20 (1), Samuel Leighton £15 (1), Tobias Leighton £9 (1), Benjamin Parker £? (1), Lady Mary Pepperrell £19 (1), Alexander Raitt £17 (2), Thomas Rogers £20 (2), William Rogers £12 (1), Nathaniel Sparhawk £? (0), John Underwood £4 (2), Joseph Weeks, Jr. £3 (1), Edmund Wilson £7 (1), unidentified resident no. 0901 £40 (3), unidentified resident no. 0902 £28 (3).

Massachusetts Poll Tax Data, 1782 to 1795

Up to 1793 and some years beyond, Massachusetts assessors listed for yearly poll taxing "all males ages sixteen and older including Negroes and mulattoes *except such as are under the government of a master or mistress* that tax being paid by said master or mistress [emphasis added]." Kittery Poll Tax lists for 1782–84 and 1795 indicate "excepted" males in households. Although ethnicity is not indicated, it is likely they were Black. See "Records of Kittery, Maine, Tax Book, 1767–1795" (Coll. 1189), MeHS. No such lists were found for Berwick.

> Ephraim Allen and Servant, 1795 – 2 polls
> Daniel Bartlett, son John and Servant, 1795 – 3 polls
> Nathaniel Fernald and Servant, 1782 – 2 polls
> Samuel Fernald, son Noah and Servant, 1782 – 3 polls
> Daniel Gould, son Daniel and Servant, 1795 – 3 polls
> John Hill and Servant, 1795 – 2 polls
> Joel Morrel and Servant, 1782, 1783 – 2 polls
> Robert Morrell and Servant, 1782 – 2 polls
> James Neal and Servant, 1795 – 2 polls
> Elisha Shapleigh and Servant, 1782 – 2 polls
> Robert Tidy and Servant, 1782–85 – 2 polls

Kittery Tax List, 1807

From Miscellaneous manuscript collection, Kittery Town Clerk's Office.

> White households with one person of color:
> William Litchfield

Oliver Manson
Benjamin Mugridge
Daniel Pierce

Eliot Poll Tax, 1808 – re "Servants"

From J. L. M., Willis, ed. *Old Eliot: A Monthly Magazine of the History and Biography of the Upper Parish of Kittery, Now Eliot* (Eliot, Me.: Augustin Caldwell, 1897–[1909]), 1:139, 143. Original source not given.

Ephraim Allen and Servant.
Samuel Clark and Servant.
Mr. Green, tenant at Salt Works and Servant.
John Hall and Servant.
Col. Samuel Leighton and Servant.
John Nason and Servant.
Capt. Elisha Shapleigh and Servant.
Samuel Tobey and Servant.

Additional Findings

The Misc. Papers Relating to Kittery, Maine, in the collections of Maine State Library, contains the following assorted notations:

Colored Persons 1820: Lydia Roberts, Susanna Raitt, Henry Black, Susanna Black, Jack Hanscom, Phillis Frost, Mehitable Patch (age 70) living with Jane Shapleigh family.

Notations in "Town Records, 1837 (Eliot, Maine)" (Coll. 1287), MeHS, which includes Eliot's portion of the 1837 Maine Census for Distribution of Federal Surplus Revenue, mentions the following individuals:

Henry Black (age 79), wife, Sarah (age 83) in 4th school district; mulatto Eunice Hall (age 48, in household of Capt. John Shapleigh); and mulatto Mehitable Patch and Thales Downing, Negro (age 70).

Appendix Three (B)

Marriages and Baptisms

An asterisk (*) indicates surnames not found elsewhere in this project's research.

Marriages of Blacks in Kittery and Berwick before 1785

1723, Jan. 1, Henry Miles m. Bridgit, "a free Negro woman" (*VRK,* 71)

1736, Nov. 20, Lambo/Sambo Marsh (free) m. Amey Freeman (*VRK,* 100)

1737, Nov. 18, Caesar m. Dinah (*VRK,* 100)

1737, Oct. 31, Black Richard m. Dinah (*VRK,* 100)

1747, Sept. 17, Cugis m. Deb (*VRK,* 219)

1751, June 13, Nathaniel Freeman m. Naomi Whittam (*VRK,* 143)

1751, Oct. 4, George Black m. Beck (both W. Pepperrell) (*VRK,* 124)

1751, Feb. –, Parris m. Merear "or Combo" (*VRK,* 220)

1752, Mar. –, Jess m. Combo "or Marear" (*VRK,* 131)

1754, May 18, Nicholas Collins m. Sarah Black (*VRK,* 222)

1757, Mar. 3, Mary Miles m. Richard Black (*VRK,* 125)

1764, Mar. 11, Bess (Dearing) m. Sambo (Sparhawk) (*VRK,* 227)

1772, July 30, Cloe (Wilson) m. Prince (Adams) (K3PC, 28)

1773, June 27, Boston (J. Underwood) m. Zilphah (Pepperrell) (*VRK,* 232)

1774, Nov. 23, Cezar Sankey m. Sara Sharp (Min. Dover Mtg., 123,139)

1776, July–, Rachel (Fernald) m. Ned (Capt. Blasdel of York) (K3PC, 18)

1781, Sept. 20, Margery Black m. Andrew Wood (*VRK,* 160)

1781, Nov. 7, Jock Black of Dover m. Lydia Marsh (*VRK,* 160)

1782, Mar. 14, George Patch m. Sarah Black (*VRK,* 160)

1782, May 23, Henry Black m. Sarah Spinney (*VRK,* 163)

1784, Apr. 1, Josiah Black m. Mary Patch "Blacks" (*VRK,* 163)

1784, Oct. –, Pharo Nowell m. Molly Marsh (*VRK,* 163)

1784, Dec. –, Abraham Callile (Carlisle) m. Abigail Patch (*VRK,* 163)

Other Black couples, marriage undocumented

N. D. (before 1727), Black Will and Sara (YCPCR 3, 264)

ca.1716, Anthony Freeman (Tony) and Mary (*VRK*, 79)

1715, Black Will, Jr., and Elizabeth Turbot (white) (*PCRM*, 5, 48, 49)

ca.1719, Joshua Black and Mary (*VRK*, 84)

ca. 1742, unnamed male slave and Sara ("Black Sara") (OSBHS)

1765, July 7, Cicaro (Pepperrell) and Phillis (Sparhawk) (FPCR, 449)

Baptisms of Blacks in Kittery and Berwick before 1785

1722 – Cuff,* (Plaisted), Apr. 18 (B)

1728 – Richard Black,* Oct. 27; full communion 1734 (KP)

1737 – Caesar & wife Dinah,* Nov. 18 (KP)

1739 – Pompey, Mar. 4 (B)

1740 – Dinah Black wife of Richard Black,* May 18 (KP)

1741 – Titus,* (Gunnison), Feb. 21 (KP)

1741 – Sara* & infant Amy, (Lord), Nov. 7 (B)

1741 – Peter, (Lord), Nov. 29 (B)

1741 – Rebecca,* (Pepperrell) (KP)

1741 – Cato,* Dec. 27 (KP)

1741 – Cyrus,*(Pepperrell), Dec. 27 (KP)

1742 – George & Scipio,* (Pepperrell), Feb. 24 (KP)

1742 – Richard, son of Richard black, Mar. 13 (KP)

1742 – Lidia, (Cutts), July 4 (KP)

1742 – Phillis & Leroy,* July 4 (KP)

1742 – Pompey (Whipple) & Phillis,* (Pepperrell), July 18 (KP)

1742 – Chaunce,*(Lord), Oct. 3 (B)

1744 – Enice, Indian & infant, (Chapman), July 1 (KP)

1744 – Bilhah,* Sept. 2 (KP)

1744 – Titus, son of Richard Black, Oct. 28 (KP)

1746 – Cumbo, (Bartlett), (K)

1747 – Sylvia, dr. of Richard Black, Oct. 4 (KP)

1748 – Phillis & Prince, (Ricker), Apr. 20 (B)

1755 – Phillis, (Cutts), Nov. 23 (KP)

1756 – Cloe, (Wilson), Feb. 29 (KP)

1760 – Dinah, (Ferguson), July 27 (K)

1764 – Phillis,*(Sparhawk), Jan. 8 (KP)

1764 – Cicaro, (Pepperrell), Mar. 24 (KP)

1765 – Daughter of Cicaro & Phillis, (Pepperrells), July 7 (KP)

1770 – Selah, (Ferguson), July 12 (K)

1770 – Phillis, (Frost), Apr. 22 (K)

1771 – Pomp, (Cutts), July 14 (K)

1776 – Sambo's daughter, (Sparhawk), Apr. 21 (KP)

Other Church–related Records

1746 – Hannah, (Shapleigh?) listed as church member (K)

ca. 1760s – Sarah (Lord), Marie (?) and Candis, (Ricker) singing in North Berwick Church.

Appendix Three (C)

Kittery/Berwick Men of African Descent in the Military, 1713 to 1783

Arckle/Arcules – *see* Hercules

Black, Cato – Apr. to Dec. 1775, Militia under T. Fernald. (Remick, 59)

Black, Benjamin – Noted Oct. 3, 1747, as "a common soldier." Probably served in Pepperrell's Louisburg Expedition 1745–46. (YCD 26: 267–68; Burrage, 68)

Black, Dublin – Served in A.R. 1777–80. Continental. (*MSSWR* 2:94)

Black, George – 1745 at Louisburg in Capt. R. Cutts's Co. (Burrage, 68)

Black, Henry – Served A.R. 1782–84, Mass. Reg. service. Honorable Discharge. Born 1758, died 1839. (Remick, 59; *MSSWR* 2:95)

Black, Joab – Served in A. R. 1779. (MOCA)

Black, Joel – Born 1752, served in A. R. (MOCA)

Black, Jonathan – Noted Oct. 3, 1747, as "a common soldier." Probably served in Pepperrell's Louisburg Expedition, 1745–46. (YCD 26: 267–68)

Black, Joseph – Enlisted age 18. Drummer, Continental 1778–83. Also Lt. Raitt's Militia, Eliot. State Bounty. (Remick, 59; *MSSWR* 2: 98)

Black, Joseph – Of Berwick. Served A. R. 1777–79. Continental. Died in service. (*MSSRW* 2:98)

Black, Josiah – 1758 in James Gowen's Co. at Canada. Served A. R. 1775–79. (*OE* 2: 64; MOCA)

Black, Kittery – Enlisted for three years, Continental, 1781, for town of York. Uncertain if originally from Kittery. (Remick, 60)

Black, Jr., Richard – Went to Portsmouth to enlist. Served 1776–78, Continental, died Valley Forge. (Remick, 28, 60)

Black, Samuel – Seaman on Continental ship *Raleigh*, 1776. (Remick, 60)

Black, Thomas – French & Indian War, 1757. (*Maine Wills*, 807)

Black, William – Kittery Militia, 1713, 1725. (*Statistics*, 7)

Carlisle, Cato – Served on the *Ranger's* first cruise, 1777. (Remick revised, 66, 213)

Caswell, John – N.H. State troops 1776, various local and Continental service to 1779. (Remick, 68)

Caswell, Joshua – Boatswain's mate on the *Raleigh*, 1776. Later on privateer *Dalton*. (Remick, 68)

Charles – Notes as of Kittery in 1778 when enlisting at Lynn, Mass. (*MSSWR* 3: 338)

Cicaro – Kittery Militia, 1775, R. Follett's Co. (Remick, 72)

Farwell, Cato – 1745 at Louisburg. Listed in companies of R. Cutts and Peter Staples. Also, according to Burrage, he was "Catto," a personal servant to General Pepperrell. (Burrage, 68, 78, 100)

Follett, William – "a Creole, black complexion" on the *Raleigh*, 1776. In R. Follett's Militia as "William," 1775. Was enslaved by Follett. Also changed name to William Simmonds. (Remick, 200, 218; *MPA*, 800; *NHGR* 2:184)

Frederick, Prince – Age 42, a farmer when "entered" for service by J. Frost, 1780–83. (Remick, 101; *SSPRWM*, 272; *MSSWR* 4: 26)

Hercules, James ("Arckle") – at Louisburg 1745, R. Cutts Co. of Kittery. (Burrage, 69)

Hercules, Thomas ("Arcules") – at Louisburg 1745, R. Cutts Co. of Kittery. (Burrage, 61, 69)

Marten, Isaac – of Berwick. Served in A. R., n.d. (*FPAA*, 23)

Miles, Henry – at Louisburg 1745, R. Cutts Co. of Kittery. (Burrage, 61)

Nowell, Kittery – "Servant to cook's mate" on privateer *America*, 1780. Some uncertainty if a.k.a Pharo Nowell. Though resident of Kittery by 1784, he may have come from York. (Remick, 60, 155)

Patch, Benjamin – Town militia 1754. Served at Canada 1758–60. Capt. J. Gowen's Co. of upper Kittery. 1779–80 Militia and Continental service. (*OE* 2:64; Remick, 158)

Patch, George – 1776–88, Continental. "Discharged by Gen. Washington, entitled to honorary badge for faithful service." (Remick, 159; *SSPRWM*, 999–1000)

Patch, Robert – 1775 in S. Leighton's Co. Then Continental until desertion in 1778. (Remick, 161)

Rogers, Cato – 1776 in T. Fernald's Militia, 1777 in N.H. and Mass. troops. (Remick, 171)

Sams, Cato – Oct.- Dec. 1778, Mass. State Troops. (Remick, 172)

Sams, Edward – Leighton's Co., 1776. Various periods of state and Continental service up to 1781. (Remick, 28, 172)

Sankey, Caesar/Cezar – N.H. Militia 1776, also Continental in 1781. (Knoblock, 194)

Simmonds – *See* William Follett

Tobey, John – 1745 at Louisburg, R. Cutts Co. of Kittery. (Burrage, 61, 69)

Tobey, Peter – 1775 at Fort Sullivan. On Continental ship *Raleigh*, 1778, and *Dalton* later. "A Negro who lived at Capt. John Lawrence's at [Kittery] Point and died there about 1840." (Remick revised, 189)

Tobey, Simon – "An Indian probably" in Capt. R. Follett's Co. Militia, 1775, at Kittery Point. Also served at Fort Sullivan, Dec. 1775. (Remick revised, 189; *NHPSP* 17: 33)

Underwood, Boston –July 20, 1776, was enslaved by John Underwood of Kittery Point when listed in Col. Joshua Wingate Reg. N.H. Militia bound for Fort Ticonderoga. Also served on a privateer (name unknown) with Capt. Underwood in 1777. (*NHPSP* 14: 345; YCCCP, box 191: 15)

William, *see* William Follett

Witham, James – 1776–83, Continental. Also on privateer *Queen of France*. (Remick revised, 203)

Williams, Uriah – "to westward in 1780" (West Point and Crown Point) of Berwick. (Spencer, "Soldiers," 41; *FPAA*: 27)

Acknowledgments

I am indebted to the many historians whose research and publications over the last half-century regarding early African history in the North and in New England have led the way and laid a solid foundation for further study and research. Among them, in the past decade, are the ground-breaking research and publications on the Piscataqua region's Black history by New Hampshire historians Valerie Cunningham and Mark Sammons. Here in Maine, scholars' and historians' recent research and writing are steadily revealing the impact of African Americans' lives in this state's early history. With the publication of *Maine's Visible Black History* by H. H. Price and Gerald Talbot (Gardner, Me.: Tilbury House, 2006), public awareness has reached heights greater than ever.

Were it not for the extensive research and published works on Kittery history by the late genealogist and historian, John Eldridge Frost, this project would have been all but impossible. I am especially grateful to William David Barry and the staff of the Brown Library at the Maine Historical Society for their guidance and untiring assistance in helping me locate sources of information. Appreciation is also extended to Anthony Douing and Jeffrey Brown of the Maine State Archives; Carolyn Marvin of the Portsmouth Athenaeum, Portsmouth, New Hampshire; the reference staff of the Diamond Library at the University of New Hampshire; the staff of the York County Office of Deeds; the York County Probate Office and the Town Clerk's Offices of Kittery and Berwick. Heartfelt thanks goes to The Reverend Alan Cutter (Ret.) for his assistance in bringing Molly Miles' story to light and for his most generous donation of her table to the Portsmouth Historical Society collections.

During the long process of research and eventual development of this book, I was greatly sustained by the encouragement of my family and friends. Most especially, I am grateful to Liz Nelson Weaver for her continuing guidance in the early phases of this manuscript and to

213

William David Barry, Valerie Cunningham and Joanne Pope Melish for their advice and editorial assistance. Valerie has graciously provided the Preface as well. Much appreciation is extended to Prof. Richard Candee for bringing my manuscript to the attention of the Portsmouth Historical Society. My gratitude also goes to others who also took the time to read and comment on parts of or a complete draft of the manuscript: Rosanne Adams, Thomas Hardiman, Daniel Hinchen, Norma Keim, Carolyn Marvin, Nina Maurer, Geraldine Palmer, Ann Pierce, and Robert Sheppard. Sincere thanks goes to artist Steve Thompson for his excellent illustration of a slave collar (pot-hooks).

I am also grateful to the many sponsors, listed elsewhere, whose generous contributions have made this book possible. This project has been brought to fruition under the auspices of the Portsmouth Historical Society and the Black Heritage Trail of New Hampshire. Special thanks is extended to the many staff members of those institutions, including Kathleen Soldati, Executive Director of Portsmouth Historical Society, JerriAnne Boggis, Executive Director of the Black Heritage Trail of New Hampshire, Judy Loto, Director of Development, and Gerry Ward, Consulting Curator and Editor of the Portsmouth Marine Society imprint. I am also indebted to Grace Peirce for her elegant book design and typography.

Patricia Q. Wall

Bibliography

Primary Sources

Ames, Ellis, et al. *Acts and Resolves, Public and Private, of the Province of the Massachusetts Bay.* 21 vols. Boston: Wright & Potter, Printers to the State, 1869–1922.

Anderson II, Joseph C., ed. *Records of the First and Second Church of Berwick, Maine.* Maine Genealogical Society Special Publication no. 33. Camden, Me.: Picton Press, 1999.

Anderson II, Joseph C., and Lois Ware Thurston, eds. *Vital Records of Kittery, Maine, to the Year 1892.* Maine Genealogical Society Special Publication no. 8. Camden, Me.: Picton Press, 1991.

Anderson II, Joseph C., ed. *York County, Maine, Will Abstracts, 1801–1858.* Maine Genealogical Society Special Publication. 2 vols. Camden, Me.: Picton Press, 1997.

Batchellor, Albert Stillman, et al., eds. *Probate Records of the Province of New Hampshire.* 9 vols. State Papers, vols. 31–39. Concord, N. H.: State of New Hampshire, 1907–41.

Clark, William Bell, ed. *Naval Documents of the American Revolution.* Washington, D.C.: U.S. Government Printing Office, 1966.

Dunkle, Robert, and Valerie Ruocco. "Parish Records of the First Church and Society of Kittery, Maine, 1714 to 1791." *New England Historical and Genealogical Register* 151 (1997): 39–58, 217–40, 353–70, 443–62.

Fisher, Carleton Edward, and Sue G. Fisher. *Soldiers, Sailors, and Patriots of the Revolutionary War, Maine.* Louisville, Ken.: National Society of the Sons of the Revolution, 1982.

Frost, John E. "Eliot, Maine, Congregational Church Baptisms, 1721–1831 [and other church records]." Unpublished typescript, 1983. Portsmouth Athenaeum, Portsmouth, N.H.

Frost John E. "Kittery, Maine: Third Parish Baptisms (1750–1790) and Marriages (1750–1795)." Unpublished typescript, 1983. Portsmouth Athenaeum, Portsmouth, N. H.

Frost, John E. *Maine Probate Abstracts, 1687–1800.* 2 vols. Camden, Me.: Picton Press, 1991.

Frost, John E., and Joseph C. Anderson. *Vital Records of Berwick, South Berwick, and North Berwick, Maine, to the Year 1892.* Maine Genealogical Society Special Publication no. 12. Camden, Me.: Picton Press, 1993.

Goss, David. *Massachusetts Officers and Soldiers in the French and Indian War: 1755–1756.* Boston: Society of Colonial Wars in New England and New England Historic Genealogical Society, 1985.

Hammond, Isaac W., comp. and ed. *New Hampshire Province and State Papers.* Vols.14–15. *Rolls of the Soldiers in the Revolutionary War, 1775, to May 1777.* Manchester, N. H.: Parsons B. Cogswell, 1885–86. Vols. 16-17. *Rolls and Documents Relating to Solders in the Revolutionary War.* Manchester, N.H.: John B. Clarke, 1887–89.

Hull, John T., ed. *York Deeds.* Portland, Me.: Thurston & Co., 1887.

Knowlton, John, comp. "British Shipping Records, Portsmouth, New Hampshire, 1694–1775." Microfilm printout with indexes, 2014. Portsmouth Athenaeum, Portsmouth, N.H.

Maine Historical Society. *Proceedings and Collections of the Maine Historical Society.* Portland, Me., 1923 to date.

Maine Historical Society. *Probate and Court Records of Maine.* 6 vols. Portland: Maine Historical Society, 1928–75.

Massachusetts General Court. *Laws of the Commonwealth of Massachusetts: Passed from the Year 1780 to the End of the Year 1800.* 2 vols. Boston: Manning & Loring, Printers, 1801.

Massachusetts, Secretary of the Commonwealth. *Massachusetts Soldiers and Sailors of the War of the Revolution: A Compilation from the Archives.* 17 vols. Boston: Secretary of the Commonwealth, Wright & Potter Print Co., State Printers, 1896–1908.

"Records from the First Church in Kittery, Maine, 1715–1797." Typescript, nd. National Society, Daughters of the American Revolution.

Pruitt, Bettye H., ed. *The Massachusetts Tax Evaluation List of 1771*. Boston: G. K. Hall, 1978.

Remick, Oliver P. *A Record of the Services of the Commissioned Officers and Enlisted Men of Kittery and Eliot, Maine, Who Served Their Country on Land and Sea in the American Revolution, from 1775 to 1783*. Boston: Alfred Mudge & Son, 1901. (See also Remick's personal copy of his book with marginal notes and corrections, Rare Book 30295, Portsmouth Athenaeum, Portsmouth, N. H.)

Sargent, William M., comp. *Maine Wills, 1640–1760*. Portland, Me.: Brown Thurston & Co., 1887.

Shurtleff, Nathaniel B., ed. *Records of the Governor and Company of the Massachusetts Bay in New England*. 5 vols. in 6. Boston: William White Press, 1853–54.

Spencer, Wilbur D. *Burial Inscriptions and Other Data of Burials in Berwick, York County, Maine, to the year 1922*. Sanford, Me.: Averill Press, 1922.

Spencer, Wilbur D. "List of Revolutionary Soldiers of Berwick, Maine." Unpublished typescript NNB459, Maine Historical Society.

Spencer, Wilbur D. *Statistics of Berwick, Maine including Tax List of 1700,,Militia Lists, and List of Revolutionary War Soldiers*. Augusta,, Me.: 1943.

Stackpole, Everett S. *Old Kittery and Her Families*. Lewiston, Me.: Press of Lewistown Journal Co., 1903.

Trask, Willam Blake, et al. *Suffolk Deeds*. 14 vols. Boston, Mass.: Rockwell & Churchill Press, 1880–1906.

Watson, S. M., ed. *The Maine Historical and Genealogical Recorder*. 9 vols. Portland, Me:. Printed for the editor, 1884.

Willis, J. L. M., ed. *Old Eliot: A Monthly Magazine of the History and Biography of the Upper Parish of Kittery, Now Eliot*. Eliot, Me.: Augustin Caldwell, 1897–[1909].

Manuscript Repositories

Berwick Town Records. Town Clerk's Office, Berwick, Me.

Dover Public Library Collections, Dover, N.H.

Fogler Library, University of Maine. Paul E. Taylor Collection, 1750–1953.

Kittery Town Records, Town Clerk's Office, Kittery, Me.

Maine Historical Society, Portland, Me.

Maine State Archives, Augusta, Me.

Portsmouth Athenaeum, Portsmouth, N.H.

York County Deeds, Office of the Registrar, Alfred, Me.

York County Probate Court Records, Alfred, Me.

Secondary Sources

Allen, Neal W. "Nathaniel Kene of Spruce Creek: A Portrait from the
Court Records." *Old-Time New England* 53, no. 4 (April-June 1963):
89–101.

Benton, Josiah H. *Early Census Making in Massachusetts, 1643–1765.*
Boston: C. E. Goodspeed, 1905.

Burrage, Henry S. *Maine at Louisburg in 1745.* Augusta, Me.: Burleigh and
Flynt, 1910.

Butler, G. H. *Thomas Butler and His Descendants.* Berwick, Me.: Privately
printed, 1886.

Cadbury, H. J. "Negro Membership in the Society of Friends, Part 2."
Journal of Negro History 21 (1936): 151–213.

Candee, Richard M. "Merchant and Millwright: The Water Powered
Sawmills of the Piscataqua." *Old-Time New England* 60, no. 4 (April-
June 1970): 131–49.

Coquillette, Daniel R., Robert Brink, and Catherine Menar. *Law in
Colonial Massachusetts, 1690–1800.* Publications of the Colonial
Society of Massachusetts, vol. 62. Charlottesville, Va.: University Press
of Virginia, 1984.

Cutts, Mary Pepperrell Sparhawk Jarvis. *The Life and Times of Hon. William
Jarvis of Weathersfield, Vermont.* New York: Hurd & Houghton, 1869.

Donnan, Elizabeth. *Documents Illustrative of the History of the Slave Trade to
America.* Vol. 3, *New England and the Middle Colonies.* Washington,
D.C.: Carnegie Institute, 1932. Reprint. New York: Octagon Books,
1969.

Fairchild, Bryon. *Messrs. William Pepperrell: Merchants at Piscataqua.* Ithaca, N. Y.: Cornell University Press for the American Historical Association, 1954.

Ferrow, Anne, Joel Lang, and Jenifer Frank. *Complicity: How the North Promoted, Prolonged, and Profited from Slavery.* New York. Ballantine Books, 2005.

Glatz, Lawrence S. "Maine's Black Population in the Censuses of 1790 and 1800." Portland, Me.: L. S. Glatz, 2014. Collections of the Maine Historical Society.

Gorges, Raymond. *The Story of a Family Through Eleven Centuries.* Boston: Privately printed, 1944.

Greene, Evarts B., and Virginia D. Harrington. *American Population Before the Federal Census of 1790.* New York: Columbia University Press, 1932.

Greene, Lorenzo Johnson. *The Negro in Colonial America.* New York: Columbia University Press, 1942. Reprint. New York: Atheneum, 1969.

Hearn, Daniel Allen. *Legal Executions in New England, 1623 to 1960.* Jefferson, N. C.: McFarland, 1999.

Higginbotham, A. Leon, Jr. *In the Matter of Color: Race and the American Legal Process: The Colonial Period.* Oxford: Oxford University Press, 1978.

Horton, James Oliver, and Lois E. Horton. *Slavery and the Making of America.* New York: Oxford University Press, 2005.

Kaplan, Sidney, and Emma Nogrady Kaplan. *The Black Presence in the Era of the American Revolution.* Amherst: University of Massachusetts Press, 1989.

Kelso, Robert W. *History of Public Poor Relief in Massachusetts, 1620–1920.* Boston: Houghton Mifflin, 1922.

Knoblock, Glenn A. *"Strong and Brave Fellows": New Hampshire's Black Soldiers and Sailors of the American Revolution, 1775–1784.* Jefferson, N.C.: McFarland, 2003.

Lee, Eliza Buckminster. *Memoirs of Rev. Joseph Buckminster, D.D. and of His Son, Rev. Joseph Stevens Buckminster.* Boston: William Crosby & H. P. Nichols, 1849.

Mather, Increase. *Early History of New England.* Ed. Samuel G. Drake. Boston: Printed for the editor, 1864.

Melish, Joanne Pope. *Disowning Slavery: Gradual Emancipation and "Race" in New England, 1780–1860.* Ithaca, N.Y.: Cornell University Press, 1998.

Moody, Robert E., ed. *The Letters of Thomas Gorges, Deputy Governor of the Province of Maine, 1640–1643.* Portland: Maine Historical Society, 1978.

Moore, George Henry. *Historical Notes on the Employment of Negroes in the American Army of the Revolution.* New York: Charles T. Evans, 1862.

Moore, George Henry. *Notes on the History of Slavery in Massachusetts.* New York: D. Appleton & Co., 1866. Reprint. Whitefish, Mont.: Kessinger Publishing, 1988.

Nash, Gary B. *The Forgotten Fifth: African Americans in the Age of Revolution.* Cambridge: Harvard University Press, 2006.

Nash, Gary B. *The Unknown American Revolution.* New York: Viking Penguin Group, 2005.

Parsons, Usher, *The Life of Sir William Pepperrell, Bart.* Boston: Little Brown, 1855.

Pierson, William D. *Black Yankees: The Development of an African American Subculture in Eighteenth-Century New England.* Amherst: University of Massachusetts Press, 1988.

Price, H. H., and Gerald E. Talbot. *Maine's Visible Black History.* Gardner, Me.: Tilbury House Press, 2006.

Sammons, Mark J., and Valerie Cunningham. *Black Portsmouth: Three Centuries of African-American History.* Durham, N. H.: University of New England Press, 2004.

Sprague, John F., ed. *Sprague's Journal of Maine History.* 12 vols. Dover, Me.: J.F. Sprague, 1913–23.

Stakeman, Randolph. "Slavery in Colonial Maine." *Maine Historical Society Quarterly* 27 (Fall 1987): 58–81.

Tyerman, Rev. L. *The Life of The Reverend George Whiteman, B.A. of Pembroke College, Oxford.* New York: Anson D. F. Randolph, 1877.

Vetter, Edwin. *A Pictorial Tour of Historical Markers, Plaques and Landmarks in Eliot, Maine.* Eliot, Me.: E. Vetter, 1999.

Williams, George Washington. *History of the Negro Race in America, 1619–1880.* 1883. Reprint. New York: Arno Press, 1968.

Williamson, William D. *The History of the State of Maine: From its First Discovery, A.D. 1602, to the Separation, A.D. 1820, Inclusive.* Halliwell, Me.: Glazier, Masters & Co., 1832.

About the Author

For the past forty-eight years, Patricia Quigley Wall has been involved with New England's colonial history through professional museum work, research, teaching, and writing. More recently, after meeting Valerie Cunningham and learning of her ground-breaking research on Black history in early Portsmouth, New Hampshire, Mrs. Wall wrote an historical novel, *Child Out of Place* (Fall Rose Books, 2004, for ages 10 and up), based on a fictional, early nineteenth-century Black family in that locale. Six years later, its sequel, *Beyond Freedom* (Fall Rose Books, 2010), followed that family into Boston's 1812 Black community on Beacon Hill. Both books were based on meticulous research.

Since 2004, Mrs. Wall has visited with more than 11,000 school children throughout New England, given numerous lectures and teachers' seminars—all in an effort to awaken greater awareness of the importance of this region's early African American history.

Born in Clearfield, Pennsylvania, Mrs. Wall grew up in the Philadelphia suburb of Germantown and is a graduate of Temple University (BA '53) and Pennsylvania State University (MS '64). For sixteen years, Mrs. Wall, widow of the late Robert A. Wall, was associated with the Darien Historical Society, Darien, Connecticut, as a board member and then as executive director. After moving to Kittery Point, Maine, in 1986, she worked at Strawbery Banke Museum for several years before retiring to become a volunteer docent and board member of the Warner House Museum. For five years she also served as events coordinator for the Portsmouth Historic Sites Association, a small group of house museums and historical sites in Portsmouth. Mrs. Wall now lives in Exeter, New Hampshire.

Index